The Cambridge Companion to Blues and Gospel Music

From Robert Johnson to Aretha Franklin, Mahalia Jackson to
John Lee Hooker, blues and gospel artists figure heavily in the
mythology of twentieth-century culture. The styles in which they
sang have proved hugely influential to generations of popular
singers, from the wholesale adoptions of singers like Robert
Cray or James Brown, to the subtler vocal appropriations of
Mariah Carey. Their own music, and how it operates, is not,
however, always seen as valid in its own right.

This book offers an overview of both these genres, which
worked together to provide an expression of twentieth-century
black U.S. experience. Their histories are unfolded and
questioned; representative songs and lyrical imagery are
analyzed; perspectives are offered from the standpoint of the
voice, the guitar, the piano, and also that of the working
musician. The book concludes with a discussion of the impact
the genres have had on mainstream musical culture.

ALLAN MOORE is Head of the Department of Music at the
University of Surrey, U.K. He has written widely on popular
music and is author of *The Beatles: Sgt. Pepper's Lonely Hearts
Club Band* (Cambridge, 1997), and *Rock: The Primary Text* (1993,
2002).

Cambridge Companions to Music

Composers

The Cambridge Companion to Bach
Edited by John Butt

The Cambridge Companion to Bartók
Edited by Amanda Bayley

The Cambridge Companion to Beethoven
Edited by Glenn Stanley

The Cambridge Companion to Benjamin Britten
Edited by Mervyn Cooke

The Cambridge Companion to Berg
Edited by Anthony Pople

The Cambridge Companion to Berlioz
Edited by Peter Bloom

The Cambridge Companion to Brahms
Edited by Michael Musgrave

The Cambridge Companion to John Cage
Edited by David Nicholls

The Cambridge Companion to Chopin
Edited by Jim Samson

The Cambridge Companion to Debussy
Edited by Simon Trezise

The Cambridge Companion to Handel
Edited by Donald Burrows

The Cambridge Companion to Ravel
Edited by Deborah Mawer

The Cambridge Companion to Schubert
Edited by Christopher Gibbs

The Cambridge Companion to Stravinsky
Edited by Jonathan Cross

Instruments

The Cambridge Companion to Brass Instruments
Edited by Trevor Herbert and John Wallace

The Cambridge Companion to the Cello
Edited by Robin Stowell

The Cambridge Companion to the Clarinet
Edited by Colin Lawson

The Cambridge Companion to the Organ
Edited by Nicholas Thistlethwaite and Geoffrey Webber

The Cambridge Companion to the Piano
Edited by David Rowland

THE CAMBRIDGE COMPANION TO

BLUES AND GOSPEL MUSIC

....

EDITED BY
Allan Moore

CAMBRIDGE
UNIVERSITY PRESS

PUBLISHED BY THE PRESS SYNDICATE OF THE UNIVERSITY OF CAMBRIDGE
The Pitt Building, Trumpington Street, Cambridge, United Kingdom

CAMBRIDGE UNIVERSITY PRESS
The Edinburgh Building, Cambridge CB2 2RU, UK
40 West 20th Street, New York, NY 10011-4211, USA
477 Williamstown Road, Port Melbourne, VIC 3207, Australia
Ruiz de Alarcón 13, 28014 Madrid, Spain
Dock House, The Waterfront, Cape Town 8001, South Africa

http://www.cambridge.org

First published 2002

Printed in the United Kingdom at the University Press, Cambridge

Typeface Minion 10.75/14 pt   *System* LaTeX 2$_\varepsilon$ [TB]

A catalogue record for this book is available from the British Library

ISBN 0 521 80635 6
ISBN 0 521 00107 2

Contents

Illustrations
(between pages 88 and 89)

Contributors

Matt Backer was born in New Orleans and has lived in Mexico City, Brussels, Caracas, New York, and Leamington Spa. He studied at the Berklee College of Music and the University of Warwick, but threw it all away in order to become a freelance guitarist. Artistes he has worked with include Emmylou Harris, Joe Cocker, Steve Earle, Aimee Mann, Julian Lennon, and Alan Partridge. He also composes music for film and television and his eagerly awaited solo debut *Is That All* is available on Warmfuzz Records.

He woke up this morning and had the blues.

Born and raised in San Francisco, **Graeme M. Boone** received his A.B. in Music from the University of California at Berkeley (1976); a Premier prix in music history from the Conservatoire National Supérieur de Musique, Paris (1979); and M.A. and Ph.D. degrees in Music from Harvard University (1987). He recently co-edited a collection of analytical essays on rock music (*Understanding Rock*, Oxford University Press, 1997), and wrote a monograph on the relationship between musical and verbal rhythm in fifteenth-century song (*Patterns in Play*, University of Nebraska Press, 1999). A documentary history of jazz is in preparation (*Readings in Jazz History*, Norton).

Don Cusic is the author of twelve books, including *The Sound of Light: A History of Gospel and Christian Music.* He is currently Professor of Music Business at Belmont University in Nashville, Tennessee.

David Evans received his M.A. (1967) and Ph.D. (1976) degrees from the University of California, Los Angeles, in Folklore and Mythology. He is currently Professor of Music at the University of Memphis. Evans has been a researcher of blues music since the 1960s. His *Tommy Johnson* (1971) and *Big Road Blues: Tradition and Creativity in the Folk Blues* (1982) are based on his field research in Mississippi and other southern states. Evans has written many articles, chapters, and record album notes, and has produced many albums of field and studio recordings of blues.

Dave Headlam is Associate Professor of Music Theory at the Eastman School of Music of the University of Rochester. Headlam's book, *The Music of Alban Berg*, published by Yale University Press in 1996, received an A.S.C.A.P. Deems Taylor Award (1997). Along with colleague Mark Bocko of the Electrical and Computing Engineering Department at the University of Rochester, Headlam has received three National Science Foundation Grants for research into acoustics and the development of a Music Research Lab. Headlam has published widely on musical topics ranging from popular music to the use of computers in music research.

Barb Jungr is a singer, performer, and writer. Her CDs on Linn Records have included new translations of the works of Brel and Ferre and a forthcoming collection of the songs of Bob Dylan, *Every Grain Of Sand*. Her interests and singing styles include contemporary European cabaret, chansons, gospel, blues, r&b, traditional and soul. Born in Rochdale she received her Master of Music at Goldsmiths College, London, in 1996. She won the Perrier Award in 1987 for the show *Brown Blues*, received a Gulbenkian Award to study physical theatre techniques in the early 1990s and is currently touring, singing and leading workshops internationally.

Professor of Popular Music at the University of Surrey, **Allan F. Moore** heads the Department of Music there. He is a composer and author of *Rock: The Primary Text* (a revised edition of which was recently published by Ashgate) and a study of the Beatles' *Sgt. Pepper*, in addition to many articles on popular music and modernism. On the editorial board of *Popular Music*, he also reviews occasionally for B.B.C. Radio 4.

Jeff Todd Titon is the author of numerous articles and books on blues including *Early Downhome Blues* (2nd edition, University of North Carolina Press, 1995) and *Downhome Blues Lyrics* (2nd edition, University of Illinois Press, 1990). From 1990 to 1995 he was editor of *Ethnomusicology*, the Journal of the Society for Ethnomusicology. A guitarist, he played with the Lazy Bill Lucas Blues Band and performed at the 1970 Ann Arbor Blues Festival. In 1971 he joined the faculty of Tufts University, where he taught in the departments of English and music. Since 1986 he has been Professor of Music and Director of the Ph.D. program in ethnomusicology at Brown University.

Steven C. Tracy is Associate Professor of Afro-American Studies at the University of Massachusetts, Amherst. He is the author of *Langston Hughes and the Blues*, *Going to Cincinnati: A History of the Blues in the Queen City*, and *A Brush with the Blues*, general co-editor of *The Collected Works of Langston Hughes*, and editor of *Write Me a Few of Your Lines: A Blues Reader*. A singer and harmonica player, he has recorded with Big Joe Duskin, Pigmeat Jarrett, Albert Washington, the Cincinnati Symphony Orchestra, and his own group, Steve Tracy and the Crawling Kingsnakes.

Guido van Rijn is a teacher of English at Kennemer Lyceum in Overveen, The Netherlands. In 1970 he co-founded The Netherlands Blues and Boogie Organization, whose work culminated in the annual Utrecht Blues Estafette. He has published many articles in specialist magazines like *Blues Unlimited*, *Blues & Rhythm* and *Living Blues*, and has produced seventeen LPs and CDs for his own Agram label. His Ph.D. dissertation from Leiden University was revised as the award-winning *Roosevelt's Blues: African-American Blues and Gospel Songs on FDR* (1997). A sequel entitled *The Truman and Eisenhower Blues* will be published in 2002.

Adrian York works in music education, as a media composer and as a performer. He lectures at the University of Westminster and the Guildhall School of Music, works as syllabus director for Rockschool, the popular music examination board, and directs the Jazz FM Jazzworks school workshops. Recent T.V. commissions include theme and incidental music for broadcasters including the B.B.C., I.T.V. and Channels 4 and 5. He has worked as a performer and musical director for many of the top names in popular music and jazz and at the moment is musical director of the Jazz FM Quintet. He writes regularly for *Music Teacher* magazine, contributed to the recent national curriculum syllabus in music and has his own series of popular piano arrangements (The Style File) published by Chester.

Chronology

The 130-odd entries in the chronology which follows highlight some of the factors which, by common agreement, have fashioned the blues and gospel into what we know today. It consists of the release dates of recordings whose style or wider impact is notable, of events which have helped shape both the genres and the lives of African Americans, and of the first appearance of, particularly, key styles. For this latter reason, more recent entries are limited. The emphasis must be very much on the period 1920–70, when these genres were most active. The beginning of the period is marked by the advent of recording; its end by the genres' diminution as a vital cultural force.

1619 disembarkation of first (20) Africans on American soil

1641 slavery first made legal, in Massachusetts

1698 first edition of *Bay Psalm Book* with melodies

1739 Isaac Watts' *Hymns and Spiritual Songs* published in the U.S.A. (original English publication 1707)

1780 institution of first African American church in Savannah, Georgia

1800 establishment of the revival spiritual – sacred words to folk melodies – with the Kentucky Revival

1801 Richard Allen publishes the widely used *Collection of Spiritual Songs and Hymns*

1862 first recorded reference to "the blues" in the diary of Charlotte Forten

1867 first publication of *Slave Songs of the United States*

1871 first tour by Fisk Jubilee Singers
first of the Moody-Sankey revival meetings

1883 repeal of 1875 Civil Rights Act, enabling segregationist practices

1896 U.S. Supreme Court approves Southern States' segregation laws

1897 first published ragtime: Tom Turpin's "Harlem Rag"

1903 Victor Talking Machine Records make recordings of camp meeting shouts – first recorded black music

1908 first published sheet music using the name "blues," Antonio Maggio's "I Got the Blues"

1909 U.S. Copyright Act commodifies the popular song

1910 start of mass northward migration by African Americans
formation of the mixed-race N.A.A.C.P.

1913 foundation of the first black-owned music publishing house, that of Harry Pace & W. C. Handy

1916 Homer Rodeheaver founds gospel recording label

1917 first appearance of recorded jazz, by Original Dixieland Jazz Band
"slack key" guitar craze sweeps U.S.A. – origins of bottleneck
technique
1920 first recordings of vocal blues by a black singer, Mamie Smith's
"What is This Thing Called Love" and "Crazy Blues"
women enfranchised in the U.S.A.
1921 first U.S. radio broadcast of church service
W. C. Handy sets up Black Swan Records, first black-owned
recording company
1923 establishment of "race records" as identifying genre
earliest field recording sessions (those of Okeh Records)
Bessie Smith records Sara Martin's "Mama's Got the Blues," first in a
line of moving performances
earliest appearance of boogie piano bass line, Clay Custer's
"The Rocks"
1924 first recording of a rural blues – Ed Andrews' "Barrel House Blues"
1925 regular use made of electrical recording (using microphones)
Charles Davenport records "Cow Cow Blues"
1926 Blind Lemon Jefferson begins recording, to unprecedented success
key recordings of Arizona Dranes, defining gospel piano style
first recording of solo guitar gospel – Blind Joe Taggart
1927 talking pictures mark beginning of a decline in record industry
Meade Lux Lewis records "Honky Tonk Train Blues"
J. M. Gates' recorded sermons vastly outsell Bessie Smith recordings
Blind Willie Johnson records "Dark was the Night, Cold was the
Ground"
1928 Thomas Dorsey & Tampa Red record "Tight Like That," marking the
"hokum" craze
Pine Top Smith records "Pine Top's Boogie Woogie"
first recordings by Leroy Carr & Scrapper Blackwell
1929 first emergence of "boogie-woogie" as genre term
Charley Patton (already in his forties) has his first recording session
1932 low point of blues recordings, by nos.
Thomas Dorsey & Sallie Martin establish the Gospel Singer's
convention, Chicago
1933 repeal of Prohibition – beginning of fall in sales of gospel recordings
Leadbelly "discovered" by Alan Lomax
1935 revival of boogie-woogie piano begins, leading eventually to jump
blues
1936 key recordings of Robert Johnson
first recordings of Harlem Hamfats (origin of jump blues)
first recordings by Golden Gate Quartet

1937 Sonny Boy Williamson introduces harmonica to the blues line-up

1938 John Hammond's Carnegie Hall "Spirituals to Swing" Concerts, bringing boogie-woogie to public attention

Bill Broonzy uses electric guitar, adding drums in 1942

Big Joe Turner records "Roll 'em, Pete," moving from Basie-style big band to "shout" blues

1939 introduction to gospel of the Hammond organ/piano combination

1940 T-Bone Walker begins recording

this decade sees peak of African American migration from the South

1941 first regular broadcasting slot, of Rice Miller & Robert Lockwood Jr. on K.F.F.A., Arkansas

1942 formation of Apollo Records, largely recording black gospel artists

beginning of two-year American Federation of Musicians' ban on commercial recording

Billboard sets up "race" chart, the "Harlem Hit Parade"

1943 beginning of increase in no. of blues recordings (peaking in 1947)

1945 formation of Specialty, with a similar roster to Apollo

Cecil Gant records "I Wonder," crossing over to the white market

1946 Roy Milton records "R. M. Blues," one of the first black recordings to exceed a million sales

Louis Jordan's "Choo Choo Ch'Boogie" does likewise, attracting attention nationwide

1947 Frankie Laine records "That's my Desire," attempting to combine "black" and "white" elements

formation of Atlantic Records, key blues label aimed at mixed audiences

formation of Chess Records, vital in the development of rhythm'n'blues

1948 John Lee Hooker records "Boogie Chillun'"

Radio W.D.I.A. in Memphis begins broadcasting only black music

Muddy Waters records "I Can't Be Satisfied," defining new r&b style

1949 end of "race" as genre category

Billboard adopts term "rhythm'n'blues"

B. B. King begins recording

Big Jay McNeely's "Deacon's Hop" combines gospel with hard r&b

1950 formation of Word Records, largest gospel label

1951 Jackie Brenston & Ike Turner record "Rocket 88," frequently cited as the originary r&b record

Bill Broonzy tours U.K.

1952 Mahalia Jackson sings in London, becomes known outside gospel circles

1953 Ray Charles crosses over from gospel with "I Gotta Woman"
The Orioles record "Crying in the Chapel," combining r&b with gospel, and scoring in both the pop and r&b charts

1954 Bill Haley records "Shake, Rattle & Roll"
The Chords record "Sh-Boom," initiating the doo-wop style
beginning of major decline in no. of blues recordings (bottoming out in 1963)
segregated schooling declared illegal in U.S. by Supreme Court order

1955 popularity for the blues markedly on the wane, coincident with the growing push for African American rights
Little Richard records "Tutti Frutti," identifying "rock'n'roll" with manner of performance
Chuck Berry records "Maybellene," demonstrating importance to rock'n'roll of teenage concerns

1956 (gospel) recording debut of Aretha Franklin
Elvis Presley records "Hound Dog"
Lonnie Donegan records "Rock Island Line"
Fats Domino's "Blueberry Hill" initiates a highly successful market for r&b/rock'n'roll/country crossover

1957 Sam Cooke records "You Send Me," turning his back on gospel
Norman Mailer's essay "The White Negro" reinforces white Romantic view of African American lifestyle

1958 Chris Barber brings Muddy Waters to perform in London

1959 formation of Stax Records
formation of Tamla Motown

1960 Elvis Presley records "His Hand in Mine," helping to define contemporary white gospel genre

1961 Freddie King records "Hideaway," launching ground for the U.K. blues movement

1962 Bobby Bland records key hit "Stormy Monday"

1963 black political protest in U.S.A. marked by march on Washington
Billboard closes its r&b charts because they were duplicating the content of the pop charts

1964 Civil Rights Act bans all forms of segregation

1965 James Brown records "Papa's Got a Brand New Bag"
riots in Watts district of Los Angeles

1966 coining of "Black Power" as a political slogan

1967 birth of The Jesus Movement in San Francisco

1968 Mahalia Jackson sings at Martin Luther King's funeral
James Cleveland's first Gospel Workshop of America

National Association of Television & Radio Announcers convention explodes along racial lines over the question of crossover

B. B. King plays Fillmore West to a white, not a black, audience

1969 Edwin Hawkins Singers release "Oh Happy Day," re-popularizing gospel

Gospel-singer Roberta Martin's funeral in Chicago attracts huge crowds

1970 Washington Blues Festival produced by African Americans, for them

1971 Marvin Gaye releases *What's Going On*

1972 Aretha Franklin's *Amazing Grace* crosses over strongly to the pop charts

1973 Stevie Wonder releases *Inner Visions*

1977 CBS's integrated marketing policy marks low-point in income for the majority of African American artists

1983 formation of the London Community Gospel Choir, premier such U.K. institution

1984 Prince (*Purple Rain*) and Michael Jackson (*Thriller* – 1982) appear to question their racial characteristics in their music

1985 Stevie Ray Vaughan releases *Texas Flood*, marking a resurgence of white performer interest in "authentic" blues styling

1987 *Billboard* introduces a "Hot Crossover" chart

1989 John Lee Hooker releases *The Healer*, achieving mainstream success

1998 R. L. Burnside releases *Come On In*, bringing hip-hop scratching and electronica to a raw blues style

1999 Taj Mahal, one of the most-recorded blues singers, releases *Kulanjan* with Mali musicians, marking yet another crucial stylistic crossover

2001 by the turn of the century, as an indication of the genre's continuing popularity, there are at least twenty-eight major annual blues and blues-related festivals

Preface

Some time probably in 1971, in a run-down cinema in a tiny town on the coast of middle England, a singer/guitarist then unknown to me flew for ten minutes over the simplest harmonic structure. To someone then coming to grips with the harmonies of early modernism, this performance by Ten Years After on the film of the *Woodstock* festival was a revelation, perhaps analogous in impact to the effect of people like B. B. King on a young Eric Clapton a decade earlier. There was a crucial difference, however. Having undertaken a metaphorical journey back to discovering where such performances came from, I was interested not in trying to re-create and relive that atmosphere as the British blues movement was, but in understanding it as something I could never fully partake in. It is for this reason that, as a scholar of popular music, I have undertaken to put together this volume. The twin roles of fan and scholar of popular music are now common currency, even if the necessary tensions are irresolvable, even in theory. Those tensions are, in their way, manifested in this collection. Although all the contributors to this volume are both fans and scholars, some participate in the musical practices they describe, while others (myself, for instance) only observe. We thus form a microcosm of the involvement of our readership for, while the public taste for consuming both blues and gospel is more stabilized now that it was twenty or thirty years ago, a sizeable number of people still perform the music, and are themselves involved in critical admiration of music produced up to eighty years ago.

The scope of the Cambridge Companions is large indeed, covering genres, oeuvres, repertoires shown to have had an undeniable effect on music-making in the industrialized West. It is therefore entirely appropriate that the series should contain a volume devoted to genres of music originating with a disenfranchised slave culture in small pockets of what is now the United States of America, genres which have posed a perennial challenge to the music of established culture. That challenge must remain as a subtext. Those genres, of blues and gospel, are the subject of this volume and, because they are not always deemed worthy of the depth of attention they receive here, it is valuable, briefly, to ponder the apparent differences between these genres, their developments, and those of the European concert hall and opera house where such depth of attention goes unremarked.

For many years after its appearance in the early years of the previous century, the blues was a largely improvised music. With the exception of some moments in the eighteenth and nineteenth centuries, improvisation has never really been a defining feature of the music of the classical tradition, which now in any case depends on reproducing, with various degrees of fidelity, the instructions of a usually absent (because dead) composer. Individual blues and gospel numbers did not have distinct identities – singers modified a received model in the process of performance. Items in both the classical and popular traditions, however, depend for their commercial viability on their identity, on being able to ascertain that one is listening to *this* piece or song or performance as opposed to *that*. Gospel songs, while opportunities for the display of abilities, were used as mediation between groups of oppressed individuals and a concrete, substantial, God. Classical music, to the extent that it has a "spiritual" dimension, moves only in an abstract, unfocused realm. Finally, the blues and gospel were recognized as indispensable to the very cultural survival of their users. Both classical and popular music, except insofar as they provide the opportunity for gainful employment, seem, by comparison, luxuries. There are, of course, similarities too. All the music discussed above depends now, to a greater or lesser extent, on recordings, which reduces each to the status of a reproducible product. It all, too, contributes greatly to the imaginative lives of those who spend time with it. It is the differences, however, which dominate, differences which for some years have encouraged proponents to argue for the inherent, or at least ethical, superiority of one or other tradition. No such assumption is made in this collection, except insofar as blues and gospel are seen as legitimate means of expression in their own right, requiring no defense from the practices of other musics.

It is worth pointing out here that the content of individual chapters is not rigidly delimited: singers, songs, events, are referred to in more than one place; after all, each contributor is observing the same material, from his or her own vantage point. Certain areas of possible enquiry have had to be omitted for various reasons, not least because there is a lot of research which remains to be done. And in any case, comprehensive coverage is naturally impossible – in a volume of limited size, even more so. It is my intention, however, that this Companion provides both enough answers, and subsequent questions, to enable you to deepen whatever understanding you have of those most pervasive of twentieth-century genres, blues and gospel music.

1 Surveying the field: our knowledge of blues and gospel music

ALLAN MOORE

Blues and gospel are widely familiar as generic labels, and have extensive histories both in their own right and as genres influential on other forms of music. They emerged within oral traditions of African American culture, embodying interpretation of, and responses to, experience in two differing realms (broadly, the secular and the sacred). They were then both taken up by the music industry and disseminated particularly from the 1920s. We know them through recordings, particularly, but their surrounding circumstances we know through writings. In this introduction, I want to lay out some of that knowledge, raising a few of the key questions as to how these genres function.

Although many books devoted to them treat them as separate, if related, genres, in this book we acknowledge their deep linkage. Indeed, Samuel Floyd (1995: 6) goes so far as to insist that they originated in exactly the same impulses, and that they are therefore alternative expressions of the same need. This is such a crucial issue that it is worth focusing on it straight away. Take the music of the Rev. Gary Davis. Was he a blues singer? Was he a gospel singer? In listening to him sing "Twelve gates to the city," to which genre are we responding? His guitar playing provides both the solid sort of underpinning we might expect from a street musician, together with flashes of virtuosic brilliance and moments of call-and-response patterning (that wonderful bass scale), and extensive bent thirds. The structure and content of the lyric, however, are far from this – the "city" is celestial, not earthy. Or take an avowedly blues singer. What are we responding to when Bessie Smith sings "Moan, you moaners?" Accompanied as she is by a piano and gospel quartet, she brings with her all the technique and expression she has acquired in singing of her own troubles to a determinedly gospel lyric. And what about those gospel quartets? When the Heavenly Gospel Singers let rip on "Lead me to the rock," they demonstrate their total ease with blue notes, with the blues' driving rhythm and vocal expression given by "dirty" timbres (growls, hollers etc.) These may be relatively extreme examples, but they demonstrate audibly that there was no clear dividing line between the blues and gospel in the lives of (some of) their exponents. Add to this such frequent crossing of the sacred/secular dividing line as that made by

Thomas A. Dorsey, Sam Cooke, Ray Charles, Aretha Franklin, Little Richard Penniman and others, and we begin to observe the artificiality of any such division. Christopher Small puts it trenchantly:

> It has been said that if gospel is the present-day paradigm of Afro-American religious musicking, so blues is of secular. It would be more true to say that blues and gospel are twin modern aspects of that ritual of survival which is the musical act . . . there is a good deal of quite secular enjoyment of both spirituals and gospel music, so in blues . . . there is a strong element of what can only be called the religious.
>
> (Small 1987: 191)

It is impossible to date the origin of the blues with any precision, although its roots in the music which West African slaves would have brought with them to the Americas have always been assumed. There are accounts of calls and field hollers back into the nineteenth century. Working individually in the fields in comparative quiet, such calls had practical use (to ease the drudgery of repetitive actions, or to call instructions to animals) but they would also sometimes become communal expressions, as when one field hand picked up the call from another, and so on. These workers were politically segregated. The hopes which had arisen in the wake of the 1875 Civil Rights Act, which gave blacks equal treatment in terms of access to accommodation, places of entertainment, and public transport, were dashed on its repeal in 1883. Segregation became more rigidly enforced to the extent that in 1896 the U.S. Supreme Court validated new segregationist laws (the "Jim Crow" system) enacted in southern legislatures (and which received national government sanction in 1913). These were extreme. The economic depression of the 1880s and 1890s hit African Americans hardest, as they were increasingly barred from any form of economic competition with whites. And, as the blues became identified as a recognizable genre (singers like the stylistically eclectic Henry Thomas and Charley Patton, born in the 1870s and 1880s, are usually cited as among the first "blues" singers), someone like Patton was treated as racially "black" even though he had long, wavy hair and a comparatively light skin. The repertoire of most of these singers extended far wider than just the blues – folksongs, dances, worksongs, even minstrel songs on occasion. The term "blues," however, has attained such currency that it has come to symbolize the entire repertoire.[1]

Many of these early singers were travelers. A disproportionate number were blind or otherwise disabled (music being one of the few sources of income for such individuals), carrying their songs from community to community by railroad, by steamboats, by wagon and even by foot. As travelers, it was vital that their means of earning were portable – hence the widespread adoption of the guitar as an accompanying instrument.

(The guitar had played a role in both nascent jazz bands, for example that of Buddy Bolden in the late 1890s, and the early string bands.) Blues thus settled down in the years prior to their first recordings as an acoustic form, in which the singer accompanies him- (or less often her-) self on the guitar, particularly for various social events (dances, picnics etc.). This form has been identified by various names: country blues or rural blues (recognizing its original location) or downhome blues (a term more favored by players themselves). Geographical location is also important: there are recognizable stylistic differences between singers emanating from Texas, from Mississippi, from Alabama or from Georgia.

These differences became first consolidated, then subsequently abandoned in the steady pattern of northward migration which began in the failure of the post-war Reconstruction. It gradually increased in speed during the latter part of the nineteenth century, reaching a first peak in the years immediately before the First World War. Migrants from Mississippi, for example, tended to gravitate towards Chicago, at least in part (it must be assumed) in response to calls from militant black organizations in the North, some of whom even offered free transport. There were mixed motives at work here. Southern states clearly did not value black labor, so they were encouraged to demonstrate a responsibility to their families and their community to move northwards; the Depression made lives as southern land-workers even more difficult; the resentment felt by southerners at this desertion merely compounded matters. Leaving the South, however, created two new sets of problems and at least one opportunity. By the early part of the twentieth century, the migration had gathered such pace as to create ghettoes in northern cities, generally in the most run-down districts which were already inhabited by European immigrants, and from which new rounds of racial disharmony arose. In the North, however, a black middle class had developed into professions such as teaching and into small business ownership. Conflicts then arose between northerners' aspirations into white culture, and the more overtly distinct, black culture, being brought in from the South. In spite of these difficulties, the launch in 1910 of the National Association for the Advancement of Colored Peoples, an interracial organization, began to make strides in pushing for equality of treatment, even if that was not to have any real impact in the field of music for some time.[2]

The northward migration, however, did. In centers like Chicago and Kansas, both jazz bands and the (now-primitive) technology of the electric guitar could be found. Steel guitar strings had replaced the more traditional nylon at the turn of the century, in the desire for a louder sound, and early electric guitars were experimented with in the 1920s, but it was not until the late 1930s that an amplified open-body model was commercially viable (the solid-body instrument we all know arrived in 1952). Among the earliest blues exponents were Bill Broonzy, who did so much to popularize the blues in Europe in the 1950s, and Muddy Waters. Not only did these instruments provide a louder sound, to enable the instrument to compete on equal terms with trumpets and saxophones, but they were able to produce a harmonically richer sound, whose "dirty" timbres were seized on by players like Waters, in expressing a continuity with the rural inheritance but in updated form. Thus the "urban" blues which was to form the backbone of "rhythm'n'blues" (r&b) and subsequently "rock'n'roll," and which depended not only on the electric guitar and the (microphonically) amplified voice, but particularly the saxophone prominent in the midwestern jazz and jump bands. And indeed, the reality the urban blues dealt with also demonstrated a continuity: a new wave of migration began with the Second World War and the need for workers in the armament factories of the industrialized North, while overcrowding within the ghettoes (Harlem in particular) grew exponentially. It was only after 1950 that middle-class black aspirations began to be achieved, and as the Civil Rights movement gained momentum through the 1950s, and as accommodation to the status quo became more widely replaced by a discourse of struggle, the blues faded from black awareness, as embodying a message which was out of tune with the times.

Although this line of development of the blues appears to have some historical priority, the first recorded presence of the blues was as a very different genre. In a society as deeply divided as that of the U.S.A. at the turn of the century, to be a black woman was to suffer a double oppression, from which the world of entertainment offered one of the few avenues of escape. This opportunity may seem paradoxical until we recall, as Charles Keil (1966) observed, that while black men were seen to pose a threat to white women, black women presented a sexual appeal to white men. This presence also received support from the suffragette movement – both women's enfranchisement and the first classic blues recording date from 1920. As a genre, the sound was also very different. Rather than the itinerant soloist, we have polished performers (for whom dress was quite clearly a matter of some import) accompanied by small jazz bands, with a far more subtle individualization of expression than found among country bluesmen. Crucial to the development here was the blues which pianists played; and which developed from ragtime into barrelhouse and boogie-woogie. The piano was a far more respectable instrument than the guitar. It had already figured in the growth of ragtime, the first black style to acquire some sort of legitimacy (identified as it was by means of its composers), and featured in the first published blues, which dates to 1908. Whereas the guitar was suited to performance outdoors, in the street, the piano was both a less public instrument (indoor performance enabled control over those who would hear it) and a more public instrument (the large numbers of people invited to rent parties, for example, were there partly because of the presence of the piano player). With the Depression and the rise of talking films, live performance was hit, and the classic blues effectively died, although the combination of jazz instruments and blues vocal returned, as we have seen, in aspects of the urban blues.

Compared to the blues, gospel has both a longer and a shorter history. Longer, in that its roots can be more easily observed, because committed to paper, in the music used by the earliest European settlers. Shorter, because the term itself is of recent origin. The earliest sacred songs were a form of security, a basis for trust among those carving out a new existence in a foreign land. The continuity involved here was less with the culture they had left behind, than with the faith they had taken with them. Thus the earliest publications (such as the *Bay Psalm Book*) demonstrated subtle, but nonetheless real, differences from the development such music had undergone particularly in England. Evangelization among blacks was slow – an ideology of equality sat uneasily alongside a culture which could not operate without slave labor. Nonetheless, by the early nineteenth century, black congregations could be found, some of whom expressed their faith musically in an amalgam of both European and African practices. These were most visible in the revival movement in the South, in which spirituals as we know them arose. The communality inherent in these is, on the surface, distinct from the individuality that would subsequently come to be a feature of blues performance – rather than express the response of an individual to his or her circumstances as we find in a solo guitar blues, spirituals express a communal response, frequently using biblical texts which would have been common currency. It is better, however, to regard the same as being true of the blues – although the manner of performance may be more individual, the texts are again frequently common currency, as they migrate from performance to performance. What is notably missing from both these genres, is the striving for an originality of expression, identifying the singer as an individual distinct from the community.

Spirituals remained the means of sacred expression right into the twentieth century, even if the label sometimes changed ("gospel hymns" and "holy roller hymns" are perhaps the most notable). Authors, too, had greater visibility – maybe the clearest secular equivalent to revivalist songwriter and singer Ira Sankey would have been ragtime composer Scott Joplin, rather than any particular blues singer of a similar period. Black churches also grew, in which spirituals would form the musical fare. And, the split which existed in secular culture – between middle-class and working blacks, between North and South, between white and black – was to a certain extent played out in the sacred realm too. Prior to the Civil War, blacks and whites would often worship in the same congregation, albeit segregated within the building. Subsequently, however, the increasing racial separation forced many black congregations solely into their own communities. The Baptist and Holiness churches were only perhaps the most visible groupings. This music was, however, made available and acceptable to white audiences (as had minstrel songs before them), through traveling groups such as the Fisk Jubilee Singers. This process of making acceptable, however, entailed a simplification and standardization (and notation) of the rich (and not notatable) performance practices associated with the repertoire. Such standardization and other forms of crossover were to continue throughout the following century.

The key issue which both these genres faced as we enter the era of recordings is that of commodification. As early as 1909, it became possible to assert ownership of songs through copyright legislation, and immediately the hitherto dominant position whereby it had been the performer, and the performance, which carried identity, was challenged. Ownership in this way is a very Europeanized practice – in order to create something to be copyrighted, there is an assumption that it carries originality, that it marks out the autonomy of its creator. Assertion of ownership is necessary in order to sell the song, in order to make financial gain (or at least recompense) out of the processes needed to record it and which, until very recently, were beyond the means and the techniques of most working musicians. However, within African American culture, that is (or, at least, was) a markedly unsympathetic approach. I shall refer below to the practice which has become known as "signifyin(g)" – suffice it to say here that, singing as they have done of acknowledged shared experience, by means of shared texts, the identification of ownership of such a text is a deeply problematic concept.

So, although the term "gospel" may only have come into common usage since the 1940s, gospel scholarship has a much longer history. Before the end of the nineteenth century, gospel biographies could be found, while noted hymn-writer Ira Sankey's *My Life and the Story of the Gospel Hymns* appeared in 1906. Anthony Heilbut's *The Gospel Sound*, an early history (written as gospel was becoming subsumed within popular culture and dedicated to "all the gospel singers who didn't sell out"), finds the origins of gospel songs in the eighteenth-century hymns of writers like John Wesley and Isaac Watts, as we have seen, indeed finding in one of the latter the mood which makes it an ancestor of the blues too (Heilbut 1971: 21). It is only recently, however, that a commonsense history (of which Broughton's is only one of the more recent, if more widely read, examples) has begun to be questioned. For example, Michael Harris' recent study of Thomas A. Dorsey reconceptualized the origin of what we now know as gospel, seeing it as the interaction of old-line, protestant religion, and blues practices. Prior to Dorsey's work, gospel had been sung from notation. He inserted into such performing manners of, essentially, improvisation, which led to the rise of Mahalia Jackson, Sallie Martin and others as song-leaders. His crucial song "Take my hand, precious Lord," served to unify what were becoming disparate traditions within different sects. The continuity between the old spirituals and the new gospel is defined by Harris in terms of their both being strategies of coping within oppressive societies, a strategy which equally underpins the blues.

The first thoroughgoing histories of the blues were written by British authors. This concentration on a marginalized U.S. form by Britons is a feature not only of commentators but of players too, as this book's final chapter will observe. For many, the dominant figure in blues scholarship has been Paul Oliver. His *Story of the Blues* (1969), while historical in outlook, emphasized the importance of both lyrics and geography to an understanding of the genre, wherein different regions had their own traditions, while blues musicians were apt to wander. As I have suggested, these routes of migration remain important. The other early history, that of Giles Oakley, began life as a series of B.B.C. documentaries broadcast in 1976. Like Oliver, the approach is chronological and lyric-based, but pays less attention to geography and, in a sense, adds little new. This strand of writing remains important: Francis Davis' *History of the Blues* develops from a series of U.S.T.V. documentaries much as Oakley's had and, while new sources are used and the history is brought up to date, the format does not permit much penetration of problematic issues. Lyrics were also an early focus of study: for example, Harry Oster printed lyrics to 221 songs collected between 1959 and 1961 (with little concern for how they were sung) and arranged them according to eighteen distinct themes (cotton farming, gambling, drinking, traveling etc.). He suggested they have significance "as a reflection of folk attitudes and their functions as self-expression, catharsis of emotional disturbance, social protest, identification with society, and accompaniment to sensuous dancing..." (1969: 61), but his preference for this form (collected largely from prisoners in gaol) over what he calls "city blues" is very clear.

Oster also claimed that respondents distinguished clearly between singing blues and spirituals (1969: 4). Although he claimed they felt that one couldn't live in both worlds, this does not diminish the observation that both blues and spirituals represented strategies of coping. This claim also runs against the contemporary observation of John Storm Roberts (1972: 173–4) that the division was never clear cut. Even some of the earliest singers (Charley Patton, Son House, Skip James) provide sufficient examples of this, although singers did sometimes adopt pseudonyms, possibly to acknowledge audience unease with singers crossing such a boundary of taste. Indeed, it is with a difference of taste, rather than a difference of function, that the boundary lies.

It was with two 1960s studies, those of Charles Keil and Amiri Baraka, that our understanding of how the blues functioned socially came of age. Keil's *Urban Blues*, which originally came out in 1966, demonstrates concern not just with the forms he observed, but with the people he was writing about. A key feature of Keil's critique was his elucidation of the "moldy fig" mentality of the majority of those writing at the time (1991: 34–5).[3] Although he acknowledges that their documentation was invaluable, he laments the lack of concern they showed with current (commercialized) music. The difficulty he highlights is a perennial problem. For example, in Samuel Charters' early study of the country blues, he explores a music which fascinates him, from the position of an outsider looking in.[4] This position is always in tension with the insider's account, in the problems of potential misrepresentation it raises, but these are ultimately the same problems encountered in any reductive account. In a telling phrase, Keil downplays the importance of "originality":

> The blues artist, in telling his story, crystallizes and synthesizes not only his own experience but the experiences of his listeners. It is the intensity and conviction with which the story is spelled out, the fragments of experience pieced together, rather than the story itself which makes one bluesman better than another. (1991: 161)

We might rephrase this, in saying that it is not the "what" that counts, but the "how," noting that this represents a clear difference from most of what passes for the study of music. Keil's work was crucial for the thinking of Christopher Small, whose *Music of the Common Tongue* developed a legitimatization of black U.S. forms at the expense of the European classical tradition – the two are contrasted both musically and socially and the latter found wanting. Michael Haralambos' earlier sociological study (*Right On!*) was not guilty of the focus on "old music" which so angered Keil, but was focused on moving forward historically. Haralambos argued that, from the late 1960s onward, the acceptance by black Americans of the "accommodatory" message of the blues had been replaced by an acceptance of the message proclaimed by soul: that society should and must be changed for the better, and that they could actually be agents for such change. Albert Murray's *Stomping the Blues* also had a forward-looking focus: it was unusual at the time in that, while it made reference to country blues artists, Murray was concerned with the transformation of classic blues through aspects of jazz and the r&b represented by Joe Turner and Louis Jordan, into the basis of popular music, which explains why he is more interested in matters of performance than in, for example, lyrics. None of this, of course, is to say that the blues hasn't remained popular both in the U.S.A. and elsewhere. One of the most recent large annual European blues festivals took place in Utrecht in 1999, still drawing large crowds keen to see rare U.S. visitors – on that occasion including Johnny Jones, Tomcat Courtney, Wolfman Washington etc. Indeed, there are dozens of annual festivals worldwide, celebrating a style which has remained static for some time. Whether the recent stylistic experiments of someone like R. L. Burnside will result in a new lease of stylistic life remains to be seen.

Amiri Baraka's *Blues People* (originally published in 1963) was the first unambiguous attempt to place the blues within the cultural experience of blacks in the U.S.A. That it should have taken so long is a clear comment on its "low" status as music, on the minimal value placed on understanding the culture, and indeed on the lack of interest in understanding how music functions socially in general. Baraka saw the emergence of the blues as marking the transition from the African as transient to the African as American. He emphasizes the necessary separation of the genre while it nonetheless operates within a larger culture: "Rhythm & blues . . . was performed almost exclusively for, and had to satisfy, a [1940s] Negro audience" (1995: 169) when measured against the co-option of swing. His general thesis is clearly stated at the end of the book: he sees the

> continuous re-emergence of strong Negro influences to revitalize American popular music . . . [but] what usually happened . . . [was that] finally too much exposure to the debilitating qualities of popular expression tended to lessen the emotional validity of the Afro-American forms; then more or less violent reactions to this overexposure altered their overall shape. (1995: 220)

Nelson George's more recent epitaph is in this tradition. Defining r&b both musically and sociologically (and, for the former, seeing it as identical to rock'n'roll and as the progenitor of "soul, funk, disco, rap, and other offspring . . ." [1988: xii]), he argues that the drive for racial integration and cultural assimilation, effected largely through the intentional search for crossovers, has resulted in atrophy for the form (an atrophy partially reversed by the rise of rap and the recovery of a rootedness of the music in everyday experience in the 1980s). Blame is largely laid at the door of the major labels who moved in on the music from the late 1960s on.

This range of writings testifies to the recognition of the crucial role of the music's originators. What, though, of the music they originated? Jeff Todd Titon's *Early Downhome Blues* was the first influential study of the musical facets of the genre, although, as an ethnomusicologist, Titon treats them firmly within the context of the culture from which they arise. He notably attacked the simple concept of the "blue third" as a harmonic construct, arguing that the scale degrees are far more fluid than in other Western musics. This study also makes use of lyric analysis, finding a range of formulae (there because the blues are frequently invented on the spot) which parallel the formulaic nature of the melodies. The crucial concept here is that of "song families" whereby bits of material (lines of lyric, melodic shapes) migrate from one song to another, within family lines.[5] This forms an important point of difference between gospel and blues, for Anne Dhu Shapiro (1992) has argued that this aspect is far less important in spirituals than are particular performance practices: call and response, minimal lyrics and the free variation of short melodic phrases. Formally, gospel seems to be less regulated than the apparently ubiquitous "twelve-bar blues."

Histories of music in the U.S.A. have been around for years, but Eileen Southern's attempt to write a history of the music of African Americans was a vital move. Her history is concerned to trace all forms of music-making and, although her focus is clearly on the legitimation of the music (blues is treated as a precursor of jazz, for instance, while r&b and gospel are passed over very swiftly), an argument now clearly dated, the willingness to be comprehensive is notable. This is also the case with two other studies appearing at around the same time. Harold Courlander's *Negro Folk Music U.S.A.* places both blues, and what he declares singers term "Anthems," in the wider, explicit, context of worksongs, singing games, dances and the like. With primary concentration on texts, there is again a lack of interest in commercialized forms. The context for John Storm Roberts' *Black Music of Two Worlds* is what are now known as "African retentions" throughout the Americas, an aspect that has become of increasing importance. For Roberts, it is the general qualities of performance practice which he finds clearly originating in the West African Savannah. For Samuel Floyd, it is specific techniques of call and response.

In adopting this focus, Floyd's *The Power of Black Music* utilizes a specific theoretical model, that of "Signifyin(g),"[6] and the way it is manifested in music, through historicized adaptations of the "ring shout" realized as call-response textures:

A twelve-bar blues in which a two-measure instrumental "response" answers a two-measure vocal "call" is a classic example of Signifyin(g). Here, the instrument performs a kind of sonic mimicry that creates the illusion of speech or narrative conversation. When performers of gospel music, for example, begin a new phrase while the other musicians are only completing the first, they may be Signifyin(g) on what is occurring and on what is to come, through implication and anticipation ... it is sheer, wilful play – a dynamic interplay of music and aesthetic power, the power to control and manipulate the musical circumstance.

(Floyd 1995: 96)

This represents a more subtle example of the over-riding influence these genres have had on popular music – not only have they exerted stylistic influence, but recent interpretations suggest that the very practice of borrowing material from earlier songs and thereby commenting upon them has become internalized within popular music practice.

This Companion attempts to learn from both the strengths, and what contemporary scholarship would regard as deficiencies, in some of the positions outlined above. Following this introduction, Jeff Todd Titon takes issue with the very stylistic labels we have become used to, and which I have simply employed above, in order to show how they do not necessarily articulate the most accurate way to represent the music. In so doing, we are reminded that our understanding is always only provisional. This is followed by outline histories of each genre, viewed as sufficient in their own right: both Don Cusic and David Evans provide fairly unproblematic histories of gospel and the blues respectively, outlining the current state of knowledge of their development. This follows from the need, in any historical discussion, to be able to place periods of change and stability against each other, chronologically, and to gain a sense of both central and marginalized issues at particular times.

We then switch focus to more specific details of the blues and gospel. Graeme M. Boone takes twelve recordings, choosing as varied a range of material as possible, and provides a detailed discussion of pertinent features of each: in this, they can at least address those questions of detail which are important across the field. Six of these are blues, six gospel (including a comparison of three versions of "Take my hand, Precious Lord"). Audiences do, after all, recognize blues and gospel songs through hearing them, by noting certain sonic features. Through these discussions we are introduced to some of the key musical decisions performers make. Steve Tracy then explores the conditions under which the makers of these genres have had to operate, using their own words where possible, acknowledging that such an understanding becomes more secure the closer we can pay heed to those intimately involved.

The three subsequent chapters focus on the genres by way of the most notable instrumental forces employed: the voice, the guitar, and keyboard instruments (complete coverage of all instruments is impossible in the space available). Vital here, then, that the writers are also professional performers – a rare commodity. Both these genres being fundamentally vocal, the voice is necessarily privileged. Barb Jungr provides a detailed discussion of the ways we can focus on the "how" of singers' performances, to get closer as listeners to understanding the effect these voices have on us. Matt Backer and Adrian York then discuss the development of these genres from the perspectives of the guitar and piano, calling attention to particular details of pattern and articulation. We then return to the voice, but through discussion of the lyrics that such voices articulate. Guido van Rijn's chapter, which focuses on the lyrics employed in particular key collections, acknowledges that this is a greatly under-researched area of scholarship, and his chapter suggests some norms to inform further research. The final chapter returns to the historical stage, beginning from the view that the histories of the separate genres require contextualization within an understanding of the role the blues and gospel have played in the development of popular music generally. In its entirety, that issue is too generalized for this collection, and it is in any case addressed in readily available histories of popular music. Dave Headlam's chapter specifically focuses on the ways these genres have at various times "crossed over" from their core markets in order to reach larger audiences, asking what has been lost or gained in such transactions.

2 Labels: identifying categories of blues and gospel

JEFF TODD TITON

Entering the world of blues and gospel music literature is like entering a botanical garden: nomenclature is everywhere. Singers' nicknames intrigue: Gatemouth Brown, Big Time Sarah, Lazy Bill Lucas, Mojo Buford, Bumble Bee Slim, The Devil's Son-in-Law, Cow Cow Davenport, Blind Lemon Jefferson, Blues Boy King, Driftin' Slim, Honeyboy Edwards, Howlin' Wolf, Muddy Waters – the list goes on and on. Names of blues songs suggest real and imagined worlds: "The Gone Dead Train," "Judge Harsh Blues," "Tim Moore's Farm," "Rough Dried Woman," "Don't Lose Your Eye," "Bye Bye Bird," and "Money, Marbles and Chalk," to name but a few. Perhaps more pertinent to this book, a formidable terminology classifies blues and gospel music according to style, genre, period, and geographical location. Promising mastery and control, these labels conceal a good deal of confusion and misleading information. On the other hand, without labels it is difficult to discuss music – or anything else – in its historical, geographical, and formal aspects.

Names exert control. An anecdote concerning the provenance of gospel music will reveal the stakes involved in naming. George Nierenberg, the filmmaker who conceived, shot, and edited *Say Amen Somebody* (1983), the best-known documentary film about African American gospel music, had asked me to be a consultant, to suggest ideas for filming, and to review footage. Looking over the rough cut, an early edited version, I directed a comment toward the inevitable historical section, suggesting that he provide something about the origin and early development of the term "gospel hymn," particularly in the last few decades of the nineteenth century as a descriptor of a genre of religious music composed by white Americans such as Fanny Crosby (1820–1915), and made widely popular in mass religious revival meetings by Ira Sankey. Ultimately he determined that inserting a historically accurate definition of gospel music would, in this film context, be too confusing for the general audience. For political considerations, then, the place of gospel song in music history is problematic from the very start. No one except Charles Keil has ever seriously suggested that white Americans invented blues music but, because it is in blues where terminology really bristles, I will leave off commenting on gospel music, and from here on confine myself to blues.

Nomenclature organizes contemporary thinking about blues among listeners, record collectors, and researchers. Consider the labels in guidebooks about blues. The chapters in *The Blackwell Guide to Recorded Blues* (1991) are titled according these historical, stylistic, and geographical categories: "Songsters and Proto-Blues," "Early Deep South and Mississippi Valley Blues," "Texas and the East Coast," "'Classic' Blues and Women Singers," "Piano Blues and Boogie-Woogie," "The 1930s and Library of Congress," "Rhythm and Blues," "Postwar Chicago and the North," "Down-Home Postwar Blues," "Postwar Texas and the West Coast," "Louisiana, New Orleans, and Zydeco," and "Soul Blues and Modern Trends." A similar list of titles organizes the blues section of *The New Grove Gospel, Blues and Jazz* (1980): "Origins," "From Songsters to Blues Singers," "Publication and Recording," "Classic Blues," "Southern Folk Blues," "String, Jug, and Washboard Bands," "Piano Blues and the Northern Migration," "Southern Blues in the 1930s," "Urban Blues in the 1930s," "Postwar Blues on the West Coast," "Postwar Chicago," "Soul Blues," "Research and Rediscovery," "White Blues," "Zydeco," "Composition," "Form and Content," "Music and Techniques." The more recent books reflect increasing acceptance of diversity. *Blues for Dummies* (1998) divides "the many shades of blues" into the following styles: Classic Female Blues, Jump Blues, Country Blues, Piano Blues, British Blues, Modern Electric Blues, Modern Acoustic Blues, Rhythm & Blues, and Soul Blues. The same book also classifies the following "regional blues styles": Chicago blues, Delta blues, Memphis blues, Texas blues, West Coast blues, Louisiana blues, and New Orleans blues. The *All Music Guide to the Blues* (1999) offers the same labels, no doubt because blues writer Cub Koda had a hand in them both. But in the *All Music Guide* Koda offers a few additional style categories: Jug Bands, Piedmont Blues, Harmonica Blues, Songsters, Texas Electric Blues, Blues Slide Guitar, Jazz–Blues Crossover, Blues Rediscoveries, and Blues Rock.

Behind the geographical labels lie older anthropological notions of closed, isolated peasant communities. The idea is that because musicians living close to each other learn from one another, musical communities develop in which ideas and musical style are shared. Styles and genres in musical communities are said to take on different casts depending on the communities' degree of isolation and the inventiveness and influence of master musicians within each of them. Yet regarding blues the truth is more complex than this model suggests. Musicians were among the most mobile African Americans in the first half of the twentieth century, and many of the most influential left their mark on the musics of many communities, not just one. Some of them, like Ma Rainey and Bessie Smith, toured on the black theatre circuit. Others, like Robert Johnson and Roosevelt Sykes, traveled more informally, but just as influentially. At the same time, some outstanding blues musicians, such as Charley Patton, did stay more or less within the same geographical area, where their influence was largely confined. Population centers, such as Chicago, Memphis, and St. Louis, attracted a variety of black musicians; the music that developed in these places reflected not a single style but many, based on the diversity of the musicians who passed through. In addition, the marketing of African American blues recordings, beginning in the 1920s, via newspaper ads in the *Chicago Defender* (which circulated widely in the South), made it possible for people in one part of the nation to clip coupons and order records made by artists whom they had never seen. Youngsters like Robert Johnson, born in the early part of the twentieth century, were influenced, via recordings, by musicians, musical genres, and styles that had originated and developed well outside of their local communities. Johnson, regarded by many as the most outstanding representative of the great Mississippi Delta Blues tradition carried by Charley Patton, Son House, Willie Brown, Muddy Waters, and others, was in fact more of an innovator than a tradition-bearer. Nonetheless, as David Evans points out in his essay for this volume, certain broad regional tendencies within vocal and instrumental techniques are apparent in the history of blues, while it is also clear that particularly influential musicians, such as Muddy Waters, inspired imitators in many communities.

Besides specific geographical labels, the terms "city blues," "country blues," "urban blues," and "rural blues" will be encountered. These terms attempt to mark significant differences between pre-World War II blues (country, rural) and post-World War II blues (city, urban). The actual differences have more to do with instrumentation than geography. The Second World War was the dividing line between acoustic and electric instruments. The country bluesman was pictured as a solo performer, singing and accompanying himself on acoustic guitar; the city or urban blues singer was pictured with a band. In the pre-war period this band was the small jazz combo that accompanied women blues singers like Ma Rainey and Bessie Smith. In the 1930s and early 1940s it became the R.C.A. Bluebird house blues band accompanying singers like Big Bill Broonzy and John Lee "Sonny Boy" Williamson, and finally in the post-war era the band was understood to play electronically amplified instruments. Later, "urban" came to refer to a larger post-war band with a jazz instrumentation. The prototypical post-war city blues band could be found in Chicago, with one or two electric guitars, an electric bass, a piano, and an amplified harmonica. The prototypical urban blues band was B. B. King's or T-Bone Walker's, without the harmonica (a rural remnant) but with a saxophone or even a horn section.

These classifications do not always hold. Country blues was sung and played in cities and by people who grew up there. City blues was played in the rural areas. Lightnin' Hopkins, for example, was regarded as a country bluesman; his 1959 debut album for Folkways presented him as a folk blues singer, accompanied by his acoustic guitar. Samuel Charters, who recorded him, waxed romantic in the album notes, calling Hopkins the one of the last living exponents of country blues. Ironically, when Charters found him, Hopkins had a career singing blues and playing electric guitar in Houston, sometimes solo and sometimes with a drummer or harmonica player or bass player. Hopkins had also been prolific in the recording studio in this city blues style, with hundreds of commercial blues 78s to his credit in the dozen or so years after World War II. Today Hopkins is recognized for what he was, an outstanding composer of lyrics, an average guitarist, moody, humorous, and an important regional figure in the history of blues. Whether he was a country or city bluesman does not seem important.

A glance at the labels in the most recent blues guides reveals the increasing attention paid to modern blues, particularly blues performed outside the community of its origin: that is, performed by and for non-African Americans. The earliest writers on blues took note of the music's popularity among whites in the 1910s and 1920s, and some pointed to the few hillbilly recording artists who incorporated blues into their repertoires. These included Frank Hutchinson, Dock Boggs, Sam and Kirk McGee, the "father" of bluegrass, Bill Monroe and, importantly, the first real star of country music, Jimmie Rodgers. But most blues researchers understood that roughly until the 1950s and the era of the Civil Rights movement, blues was a music of the African American underclass: they had invented it, nurtured it, and popularized it primarily in their own communities. Given this history, combined with prevailing notions about authenticity, white blues was considered derivative and inauthentic. Indeed, for some audiences of an older folkloristic persuasion, along with a fairly strict definition of blues along formal lines, modern electric blues was suspect: it sounded too much like rock'n'roll. That feeling prompted Charters to view, and represent, Lightnin' Hopkins as a country bluesman. European audiences in the 1950s enjoyed the acoustic blues of Big Bill Broonzy, but the electric guitar, electric bass, and amplified harmonica in Muddy Waters' band was not widely appreciated. Waters, of course, preferred the powerful, electric sound, as he (and the recording company he was with, Chess Records) were hoping to score some hits on the rock'n'roll charts. By the mid-1960s, however, resistance to electric blues was disappearing in the wake of the sheer popularity of the amplified sound among a new, young adult audience; and like moths to a flame, white musicians were drawn to playing the blues, first in Britain and then in the United States. (Their efforts at singing were not as convincing.) For example, the label "British Blues" in *Blues for Dummies* and *The All Music Guide to Blues* refers to the English blues bands of the

1960s such as The Rolling Stones (who took their name from a Muddy Waters blues song and whose early albums contain cover versions of 1950s Chicago blues), John Mayall's Bluesbreakers, and Cream, the last two featuring guitarist Eric Clapton. The subsequent popularity of these British bands in the United States brought the blues into U.S. rock music, with the result that some enormously popular rock bands were essentially blues bands (e.g., Janis Joplin with Big Brother and the Holding Company; Led Zeppelin) while rock lead guitar style evolved through blues into the "heavy metal" genre so popular during the 1970s and 1980s. Thus the "blues rock" label is important in the aforementioned contemporary guides to blues, and it (and British blues) refers chiefly to white musicians such as The Allman Brothers, Bonnie Raitt, Johnny Winter, Eric Clapton, and Stevie Ray Vaughan. "Soul blues," on the other hand, is a code term that refers to African American musicians whose blues style and approach reflects the gospel-influenced soul music that arose in the 1960s with Ray Charles, James Brown, Otis Redding, Aretha Franklin, and other black singers and musicians. Purveyors of soul blues include Bobby "Blue" Bland, Junior Parker, Albert King, Z. Z. Hill, Junior Wells, Magic Sam, and Robert Cray.

The classificatory taxonomy one encounters in the botanical garden groups plants by similar characteristics; the labels thus aid in making the generalizations needed to discuss form, function, origins, and evolution in the plant world. The early blues enthusiasts who created the various genre, style, geographical, and period labels were not merely trying to organize their record collections; they hoped that this taxonomy would aid discussions of the historical development and geographical diffusion of blues, including, perhaps, a path toward discovering blues origins. The extent to which this has been successful may be seen in David Evans' essay in this volume, which is as good an overview of the origins, characteristics, and early development of blues as can be written by a historian at this point in time. But a discussion of labels in blues and gospel music needs to attend not only to the labels that collectors, journalists, critics, researchers, and scholars use in their discussions of the music, but also to how the musicians themselves label it. Here we enter a different world, one of looser definitions and more practical distinctions.

I well recall my first extensive companionship with a blues musician. Lazy Bill Lucas was born in Arkansas, sang and played blues guitar and piano professionally in Chicago in the 1940s and 1950s, and moved to Minneapolis where he continued performing and where I met him in 1965 when I first began my graduate studies. Bill had grown up in a black sharecropping family; he learned music at an early age; as a youngster he and his family migrated north along the Mississippi. Bill apprenticed himself to legendary blues musicians such as Big Joe Williams, and as a young man to Big Bill

Broonzy; he was a blues vocalist, guitarist, and pianist in Chicago during the golden years, the time of Muddy Waters and Howlin' Wolf – indeed, he got there before they did. After a modest recording career, he moved to Minneapolis and led a blues band there, one that I later joined. What was Bill's perspective on blues? What labels and categories did he use?

Interestingly, he didn't use very many labels at all. "Delta blues," "East Coast blues," "pre-war blues," "post-war blues" – these terms held no meaning to him and he did not use them. One day he and his friend, the bass player Jo Jo Williams, were sitting in Bill's apartment talking about the older blues, perhaps in response to my interest in it. Jo Jo was reminiscing about his youth in the Mississippi Delta, and how he used to go to listen to Charlie Patton and Willie Brown. He used the term "downhome blues" to refer to their music. I asked what he meant by that. Bill answered first. "Down South, on the farm," is what the term meant to Bill. Jo Jo expanded on Bill's definition: "The word downhome, it mean back to the root, which mean where it all start at, this music, the blues and the church music, and so far as I can understand, it came from the country, the fields and the shacks and the towns that weren't but wide spaces in the highway." For Bill and Jo Jo, "downhome" was a fusion of geography with history, memory, and feeling. It occurred to me then that "downhome" was a more evocative term than "country" and I determined to adopt it in my own writings (see Titon 1990 and 1995).

Geographical style marking was important to Bill Lucas as a class discriminator, also – something that blues researchers seldom dealt with. He made a stylistic distinction between blues that was from "way back in the country" and blues that he called "sophisticated." For him, these musical styles evoked different ways of life based on wealth and opportunity. Bill never had the opportunity to learn sophisticated music. "I guess I'll just have to stick with the old funky blues," he used to say.

As an entertainer he could, and did, play music that blues historians call pre-war, post-war, Chicago, jump, r&b, and soul music. He mixed it all up in his live performances. He might follow Bessie Smith's "I Had a Dream" with Fats Domino's "Blueberry Hill" (an r&b hit from the 1950s that saw much airplay on white stations) or Ray Charles' "Should I Ever Love Again." In his set selection he was always mixing categories, I thought. If he viewed them as labels, they were markers, not boundaries. The distinction is critical. Conceived as boundaries, the labels do not work; they are too porous. As markers, blues and gospel labels point to commonalities in such characteristics as form (for example, twelve-bar blues), in style (jump blues), and in combinations involving style, time period, and geography (Memphis jug bands in the 1920s).

None of this is to say that blues musicians' judgments are infallible or that they should automatically be granted authority by virtue of their experiences. Bluesmen, like scholars, can be stupefyingly wrong in their theories. One young blues singer maintained, on the basis of research among his elders, that the original name for blues was "reals" because blues told the truth. A few researchers believed this story and it has gained some currency. Apparently, though, the singer had been told the fact that musicians played "reels" (dance tunes) before blues. Not knowing the label "reels," he heard it as "reals" and made the imaginative leap. Moreover, by now the better-known blues musicians have been interviewed almost to death, they have exchanged stories and ideas about blues at countless festivals, and as a result of this exposure they have become familiar with many of the labels that record collectors, journalists, and other researchers have attached to the music. Robert Jr. Lockwood, on hearing that I would interview him at a blues festival ten years ago, challenged me by saying he didn't think I could ask him a question he hadn't been asked before. I said I wondered if he would give me an answer I hadn't heard before, and he laughed. A good conversation and some good music followed.

3 The development of the blues

DAVID EVANS

Between 1890 and 1910 new sounds – melodic, instrumental, and verbal – began to penetrate the repertoire of African American music hitherto dominated by spirituals, functional songs of work and play, narrative folk ballads, banjo tunes, and fast-paced instrumental dance music. Drawing from all these older forms, as well as the simultaneously emerging ragtime and jazz, these sounds coalesced fully by the end of this period to the point where they could be recognized as a distinct genre of music called the blues. This new music conveyed a remarkable sense of immediacy, purporting to express the thoughts, feelings, and experiences of the singer as well as the spontaneous inventions and variations of musicians at the moment of performance. Yet for all of its immediacy, blues as a whole had a power of endurance that would sustain it throughout the twentieth century and see it at the end of that century as a major form of popular music with worldwide appeal.

Contemporary reports and later recollections of blues during this early period place the music in rural areas, small towns, and cities throughout the South, especially the "Deep South" from east Texas to central Georgia and the Carolina Piedmont region, the land where cotton was king. Blues appear to have been rarer or non-existent along the Atlantic and Gulf Coasts and in older settled regions such as Virginia or areas such as the Appalachian Mountains where the population was overwhelmingly white. From the Deep South blues flowed along arteries of commerce and transportation, the Mississippi and Ohio Rivers and the various railroad lines stretching northward and westward. Early centers of blues activity were rural areas containing large plantations worked mainly by sharecroppers, such as the Mississippi Delta, lowland regions of adjacent states, the river bottoms of southeast Texas, the turpentine, railroad, mining and levee camps, and the cities of both the South and the North that were filling up with migrants from these rural areas. People were newly arrived or preparing to leave, working on temporary or seasonal jobs or in migrant occupations, moving every year or two from one plantation to another, trying their luck in the city or returning to a more predictable existence on the farm. Blues also thrived among hobos and hustlers in the underworld of gambling, moonshining, and prostitution, and among the people floating in and out of prisons. This population was essentially a mobile labor force, cut off from the certainties of the ante-bellum plantation, having little or no formal education, competing with white immigrant laborers, and desperately trying to make a living and find a safe harbor from racial harassment. Blues had less appeal for those who were able to hold onto farms that their families had established during the Reconstruction era following the Civil War (1861–65), for the religious segment of the black population who viewed the blues as sinful, or for the upwardly mobile and educated class. But for those who supported the blues, it was their music for dance and recreation, humor, philosophy, courtship, even at times approaching the status of a religious cult and a way of life. For its performers it could become their means of making a living.

The hopes of Reconstruction and its promise of integration of the freed slaves into the mainstream of American society were dashed in a late nineteenth-century backlash of disenfranchisement, Jim Crow laws, and strict segregation. Lynching reached its peak in the 1890s and remained for another three-quarters of a century the ultimate threat against any assertion of black dignity, power, or aspiration. This threat fell hardest on the children of the freed slaves, the first generation to grow up in a freedom that turned out to be not really free, cut off from their parents' experiences, resented by the southern whites who had lost the Civil War, and denied any real opportunity for advancement in American life. With its social institutions under siege, a sense of individualism grew in the black community, and this is reflected in blues and the other new musical forms that arose at this time in the form of solo performance or increased soloing within ensembles, virtuoso improvisation, and increased competition among musicians leading to "cutting contests" and "carving." Individualism, of course, was a growing factor in white society at this time, related to industrial competition, but for whites it often became a vehicle for opportunity and success. For blacks it was a matter of survival.

The blues genre

Several characteristics of early blues became the genre's identifying features. One of these was the use of seemingly ambivalent "blue notes" at certain points in the scale (see Chapter 5). Blues players and singers also tended to improvise and vary their melodic lines, instrumental parts and lyrics, and to experiment with sound quality, using growling, screaming, wailing, and falsetto singing and the muffling, snapping, sliding, and bending of notes. This spontaneous quality created the impression that the thoughts, feelings, and expressions of the moment were quite important, turning attention away from the song as product of a deliberate and often arduous process of composition, toward the performance itself and the personality and uniqueness of the performer. Blues also elevated the role of the musical instrument within popular song, making it a second voice, integral to the song itself, punctuating, commenting upon, and answering the vocal line. Early in its development blues became especially associated with the twelve-bar, three-line AAB pattern, which seemed to lend an asymmetrical quality to the blues. Finally, blues introduced to popular song a new frankness, breadth of subject matter, and assertiveness. The songs demanded to be taken seriously, thus causing their singers and the subculture they represented to be taken seriously as well. Blues were distinctly secular and worldly, unsentimental, sexually explicit, and ironic, with an undertone of deep dissatisfaction. All these characteristics were new or unusual within popular American music, often contradicting established rules of Western musical form and performance style as well as popular stereotypes and expectations of black music. Often they shocked the musical, social, and moral sensibilities of those outside the culture, yet this new music had within it a strange fascination that demanded attention and caused it to influence almost all developments in American popular music of the twentieth century as well as much of the rest of the world's music. Ultimately blues would outlast many of the genres and styles that it influenced.

Although blues emerged as distinctly new, it developed from older types of music. Much of its vocal material is derived from the "hollers" of lone workers. These songs were generally free flowing, melismatic, spontaneous expressions set to pentatonic tunes containing blue notes, commenting on the work situation itself or the singer's love life. There were also types of solo religious expression, prayers and sermons, with a similar musical structure. Most blues singers were exposed to these types of work song and religious expression early in life and were able to adapt some of the melodic character, subject matter, emotional intensity, and spiritual depth of these songs to the developing blues. But blues generally had a more rigid structure than these unaccompanied songs, for blues was a vocal and instrumental genre that often served as music for dancing. The formal mold that gave shape to this loose vocalizing came largely from folk ballads. The ballad was an old European form of narrative song well established in southern Anglo-American folk tradition, which blacks began to adapt soon after Emancipation. Increasingly blacks began performing ballads to the accompaniment of banjo, guitar, or other instruments at fast tempos for dancing. They created original songs on such characters as "John Henry" the railroad worker or "Jesse James" the outlaw. Black balladry reached its peak of popularity and creativity in the period 1890–1910 as the blues genre was developing. By this time almost all these ballads celebrated characters who acted outside the law and organized society or who were in some way bold and "bad." Many of these new ballads proved popular with white singers, who learned them from black musicians in work camps, waterfront dives, gambling dens, and bordellos, and began composing similar songs themselves. Many of these songs (such as "Stagolee," "Frankie and Albert," "The Boll Weevil," and "Railroad Bill") used a three-line form consisting of a rhymed couplet followed by a one-line refrain. The couplet lines were roughly in iambic heptameter verse. The three lines began respectively with tonic, subdominant, and dominant harmonies, by the end usually resolving to the tonic. The emerging blues genre borrowed this structure, reducing the length of all of the lines to a rough iambic pentameter to leave space at the end for an instrumental response, converting the textual pattern to AAB, often slowing the tempo in order to make the songs more suitable for the increasingly popular couple dances such as the "slow drag," and changing the thematic focus from third-person tales of "bad" men and women to first-person statements in which the singer was the protagonist. Not all early blues conformed to the twelve-bar form: two-line (eight-bar) and four-line (sixteen-bar) blues drew from other forms of ballads and social songs or represented contractions or expansions of the three-line form. Some blues lines had their length extended by repeated short melodic-rhythmic phrases or "riffs." Much older black instrumental dance music, played on fiddles, banjos, and other instruments, was structured on the riff idea, from where it entered the blues.

The blues amalgamated various elements derived ultimately from European and African musical traditions, although they are above all products of their time, place, and sociocultural conditions and contain other elements that are distinctly American and original. In general, the European elements tend to be formal, and they are usually modified or transformed through the influence of African stylistic characteristics. The iambic pentameter, for example, is familiar from Renaissance authors and may have been absorbed by blues singers through their often limited schooling. But a line like "I gót the blúes and cán't be sátisfíed" would never be sung by a blues singer in this strictly metrical manner. Instead, its accents would be displaced, giving life and strength to syllables and words that would otherwise have a weak impact on the listener. This sort of improvisational variation is typical of African singing, which rarely corresponds to set poetic metrical patterns. In most blues, in fact, this metrical structure has become unrecognizable. The harmonic sequences are also typically European, but the subdominant and dominant harmonies are often only partially expressed or merely suggested by a single note, and melody and harmony are typically drawn back to the tonic at the end of each line, reasserting the essentially African modal character of this music. Blues performers often subvert the twelve-bar pattern with its standard harmonies rather than reinforce it. The main instruments of blues music – guitar, piano, harmonica, along with violin, mandolin, string bass, trumpet, clarinet, saxophone, and the drum set – are all of Western manufacture, but blues players have found ways of creating percussive effects, bent notes, and other sounds on these instruments that were never intended for them but which spring from techniques familiar in African music. Many secondary instruments of the blues – jug, kazoo, washboard, washtub bass, and a one-stringed zither played with a slide technique – are all derived from African prototype instruments, often preserved in American tradition as children's instruments until blues put them to use. Many other basic characteristics of the blues are typically African as well, including the call and response of voice and instrument, the use of repeated riffs, flexibility of pitch, timbral variety, the mixing of tonal and percussive sound qualities, and the use of instruments as voices. Songs of social commentary, praise and derision, boasting and self-pity are also common in many African traditions, and aspects of the lifestyle of blues singers and the social position of the outsider can be observed in African minstrel and *griot* traditions.

Blues appear originally to have been the expression of one voice and one instrument – normally guitar, piano, or harmonica – all of which were relatively new to black American music at the end of the nineteenth century. Male singers usually played their own accompaniment, while female singers more often had someone else, usually male, accompanying them. There is much evidence for solo performance in the earliest reports of the blues, and it remained common among black musicians through the 1950s, taking on extended life since then through the international blues revival. Duets of two guitars, guitar and harmonica, guitar and piano, and larger combos of these and other instruments, variously known as jug, juke, washboard or skiffle bands, emerged on recordings in the 1920s but are known to have been in existence earlier. These larger combinations were especially characteristic of urban centers, where musicians would band together in order to make more money and compete with more polished and urbane ensembles. As the blues form coalesced and gained popularity in the black communities in the early years, it was also adopted by more established types of groups, such as vocal quartets and string bands featuring fiddle, banjo, or mandolin. Ragtime pianists began playing pieces in the blues form, and dance bands adopted it, in the process beginning to transform themselves into jazz bands. Traces of three-line blues strains show up in a number of published piano rags before 1910, along with what appear to be attempts to express blue notes in print. When jazz emerged on commercial recordings from 1917, the number of blues tunes in the repertoires of the earliest bands was truly remarkable. It goes without saying, of course, that much of the essential improvisational and "hot" quality of jazz springs from the blues.

The earliest blues

From its very beginning blues was a commercial music. Many early performers were paid entertainers at dances and minstrels playing for tips in public places, but the money made in the earliest years was relatively small change. No stars were especially associated with this music, and no performers had more than local fame. Furthermore, blues represented only a portion of what they performed. In later recordings of some of the oldest-known blues artists, those born in the 1870s and 1880s such as Henry Thomas, Frank Stokes, and Lead Belly, we find many songs besides blues – ballads, social dance tunes, ragtime and "coon" songs, and spirituals. These performers needed music for all tastes and occasions. The name "blues" had not yet been applied to a whole musical genre, and for many musicians and audience members this music probably consisted of a handful of tunes that constituted a small portion of a varied repertoire. Some of these tunes were novel enough at the time to become widespread over much of the South, songs such as "Poor Boy Long Way from Home," "Red River Blues," the semi-narrative "Joe Turner," and the ragtime-like "Make Me a Pallet on the Floor."

As blues began to be adopted by bands with some formal training (like W. C. Handy's) and began to appear occasionally as odd strains in ragtime tunes, the music was ready to take on a popular identity of its own. This process of consolidation into a recognizable genre occurred between 1908 and 1914 through the appearance of published tunes bearing the word "blues" in their titles and the representation of blues songs on the vaudeville stage in southern black urban communities. Milestones in this process were the 1908 New Orleans publication of Antonio Maggio's "I Got the Blues" and the 1909 "I'm Alabama Bound," subtitled "The Alabama Blues," credited to white New Orleans theatre pianist Robert Hoffman. Although not exactly in the twelve-bar format, it contains three-line verses with the lines beginning respectively with tonic, subdominant, and dominant harmonies, and typical blues subject matter in the lyrics. The song spread quickly and soon developed variants like any folksong. It would take another three years for a new wave of blues titles to be published. Meanwhile, southern black vaudeville entertainers were adopting into their repertoires this and other blues songs, some of them of their own composition, and enjoying audience success. By 1911 performers like ventriloquist Johnnie Woods, pianists Baby Seals and Kid Love, and vocalists Laura Smith and Estelle Harris were gaining reputations as blues specialists and blues could regularly be heard in theatres in the Tri-State Circuit centered in Memphis.

In 1912 four more blues tunes were published, "Dallas Blues" by white Oklahoma City musician Hart A. Wand, "Baby Seals Blues" by the professional black vaudevillian and pianist, "The Memphis Blues" by black Memphis band-leader W. C. Handy, and "The Negro Blues" by white minstrel show performer Leroy "Lasses" White of Dallas. That whites were credited as the composers of two of these, as well as the two earlier tunes published in 1908 and 1909, indicates that blues were sufficiently established to easily reach southern white ears through performances by black street musicians and bands hired to play for dances. More blues songs were published in the next two years, including Handy's "St. Louis Blues" in 1914, which became one of the greatest hit songs of the twentieth century. By this time, any vaudeville singer in America, black or white, could easily acquire a blues repertoire of several songs, even without any direct contact with the blues environment.

While several prominent white vaudevillians during the 1910s had reputations as delineators of Negro character in song, blues tunes constituted only a small portion of their repertoires. Among black performers in the South, however, the situation was different. Artists like Gertrude "Ma" Rainey, Bessie Smith, and Edna Benbow (later Hicks) increasingly specialized in blues material during this decade, and by its end there were hundreds of black blues singers working in the professional circuit. Many would become recording artists in the 1920s. Meanwhile, for those singers unable to compose their own blues or obtain them from the folk tradition, there was an increasing number of blues being published in sheet music in both piano and orchestral arrangements. Two black-owned publishing houses were particularly successful, that of Harry Pace and W. C. Handy founded in Memphis in 1913 and that of Clarence Williams and A. J. Piron founded in New Orleans in 1915. They published blues by their owners as well as by other songwriters. Many of these tunes contained vestiges of ragtime and popular song, including multiple musical strains, some of which were not in a blues form, introductions, narrative story lines, exaggerated sentimentality and pathos, and stereotyped "coon" imagery. Some were merely ragtime songs with a lot of blue notes. Nevertheless, they all managed to convey some degree of blues sensibility, both musical and lyrical. Increasingly the songs were composed for female singers, while males involved in blues in the vaudeville scene turned more and more to the roles of pianist and songwriter. This situation stood in contrast to that of the folk communities, where the blues performers were predominantly male. Guitar-playing blues singers remained conspicuously absent from this professional scene, however, although they were probably the most common type of blues performer in the small towns and rural areas of the South.

Between 1914 and 1920, for many Americans the blues appeared to be a new type of ragtime song expressing a more realistic view of black life and emotions and containing novel strains and inflections. When jazz burst onto the scene in 1917, shifting the focus of interest toward the performer's momentary improvisations, the new musical stylists featured many blues tunes. Audiences could now view blues as a type of jazz. The problem was that few Americans except for blacks and southern whites had heard authentic blues. White society bands recorded blues, as did white jazz bands following the initial 1917 success of New Orleans' Original Dixieland Jazz Band. A few black bands recorded blues in the wake of the jazz craze, including those of Handy, Wilbur Sweatman, and James Europe, but these were units of highly trained musicians whose backgrounds were in ragtime, ballroom dance music, military bands, and circus and minstrel show music. This music was for them essentially something to be exploited as a trend in popular music. Whether it was viewed as ragtime, jazz, or a separate genre mattered little.

Early blues recordings

In 1920 the first vocal blues by a black singer was released on a phonograph record. The artist was Mamie Smith, a veteran of the vaudeville and cabaret circuit, and the song was "Crazy Blues," composed by black songwriter Perry Bradford, who also led the band that backed the singer and helped to manage her career. The tune was arranged in the manner of a popular song, but it contained a blues strain. The lyrics told in a rather melodramatic way how the singer's man had left her, causing her to go crazy and in the end get high on "hop" and shoot a policeman: it sold phenomenally well. Other record companies, all of them based in or near New York, followed the lead of Mamie Smith's company, Okeh, and signed up blues talent for recording. "Crazy Blues" established something of a formula that would be used for the next few years: a female star drawn from the northern vaudeville or cabaret scene or working in a current stage show, performing a song by a male professional songwriter (who might also be her pianist, band leader, manager, or husband), accompanied by a five- to eight-piece jazz band. Many of the songs contained multiple strains, not all of them in a blues form, and most were complaints about no-good men. These singers (the most important being Mamie Smith, Lucille Hegamin, Trixie Smith, Alberta Hunter, Ethel Waters, Lizzie Miles, and Edith Wilson) were professional entertainers, some of them dancers and actresses as well, for whom blues was just part of their repertoire. Few wrote many of their own songs.

In the early 1920s most blues records by black artists were released in the regular popular series by such companies as Okeh, Columbia, Arto, Bell, Pathé, Paramount, and the black-owned Black Swan. These records were generally available to white buyers, although the majority of purchasers were black. Realizing this, and attempting to expand their major customer base, the companies by 1923 established series of "race records" of blues, gospel, and jazz music to be marketed almost exclusively in black communities and advertised in black newspapers. Most white consumers thus became cut off from records by black artists except for those by jazz figures with the broadest mass appeal like Louis Armstrong and Duke Ellington. From this point onward, however, blues records became progressively more bluesy. In 1923 a new wave of female singers from the southern vaudeville circuit began to record, and other companies like Victor, Vocalion, Brunswick, Ajax, and Gennett got into the race recording business. Some of these singers like Ma Rainey, Bessie Smith, and Ida Cox, composed a good bit of their own material, and more of their songs employed a single twelve-bar strain with variations. Most were now accompanied not by a full jazz band but by a pianist, sometimes with one or two other instruments such as trumpet, trombone, clarinet, or banjo, using leading soloists from the jazz world, although some (Smith, Rainey, Sara Martin) were occasionally accompanied on record just by one or two guitarists, a banjo player, a guitar and fiddle, or a small jug band.

Themes of these songs were more realistic, and lyrics and tunes drew more from folk sources. Paramount, Gennett, Brunswick, and Vocalion began making recordings at Chicago and other midwestern studios, drawing on the local and regional talent base that was generally closer to blues sources than that of New York. Okeh Records even made field trips to Atlanta in 1923, followed by further trips to St. Louis and New Orleans. Most of these new singers (Lucille Bogan, Clara Smith, Viola McCoy, Bertha "Chippie" Hill, Sara Martin, Sippie Wallace, Rosa Henderson, Victoria Spivey) had rougher voices than the first wave of recording artists and sounded more comfortable handling blue notes. Man / woman duos also began to record, including such veteran vaudeville acts as George Williams and Bessie Brown, Leola B. and Kid Wesley Wilson, and Butterbeans and Susie. Most of their songs were original stage routines set to bluesy ragtime tunes and dealing with the battle of the sexes. There are recordings of a few solo male performers, mostly from the vaudeville scene, such as female impersonator and yodeler Charles Anderson, New Orleans singing banjoist Papa Charlie Jackson, one-man-band Hezekiah Jenkins playing guitar and harmonica, and Louisville guitarist Sylvester Weaver who also played on some of Sara Martin's records. A few came from the juke houses and streets, such as Atlanta twelve-string guitarist Ed Andrews and one-man-band Daddy Stovepipe.

The artist who broke open the recording field for male self-accompanied solo blues singers was a guitar-playing street singer from Dallas named Blind Lemon Jefferson. Recording in Chicago around the beginning of 1926, he sang elaborate blues melodies in a vocal range that stretched to two octaves, and played extended single-note runs on the guitar, displaying a seemingly inexhaustible supply of improvisational ideas performed with amazing virtuosity. At first he relied largely on traditional blues lyrics in constructing his songs, but by 1928 he was displaying more lyric originality and a rare compositional skill. Jefferson's records sold widely, and he served as a role model of success and the standard of musical excellence for many other singer-guitarists. His playing anticipated by about fifteen years the improvisational single-note style of electric lead guitarists of the early 1940s, such as Aaron "T-Bone" Walker, who as a child used to lead Jefferson around on the streets of Dallas. Another influential singer-guitarist, whose recording career began around the same time, was Lonnie Johnson, originally from New Orleans but relocated to St. Louis. Johnson came from a more sophisticated musical world than Jefferson, being equally adept on violin and piano and comfortable performing in vaudeville theatres and with jazz musicians. As spectacular a musician as Jefferson, he served as another role model and influence to aspiring guitarists and blues singers. Both artists were known for bending strings in their playing and have been cited as influences by B. B. King and other later electric blues guitarists.

Two factors contributed to the success of Jefferson and Johnson and artists like them who recorded in subsequent years. One was the invention of the electrical recording process, which came into general use in 1925. The use of a microphone enabled records to convey a wider frequency range of sound, reducing surface noise and allowing regional accents and rough voices (as well as light voices and instruments such as guitars and pianos) to be heard better. The second was the decision by many of the companies to record away from their main studios located in northern cities. Electrical recording equipment was lighter in weight, more portable, and less sensitive to environmental variables. Record companies were facing increased competition from radio, which seemed to provide unlimited free entertainment, whereas records typically cost 75 cents for six minutes of music. The companies had to find new markets, and one of these was the audience for blues by black performers, who hardly ever appeared on radio (a situation that prevailed with only a few exceptions up to the end of the 1940s). The success of Jefferson and Johnson indicated that there was a market for southern blues straight from the barrelhouses, street corners, and house parties. Although Okeh Records had been making a few field sessions as early as 1923, the companies started this practice in earnest in 1926: Atlanta, Dallas, and Memphis were favorite locations up to 1931. Sessions lasted a few days to a couple of weeks in rented hotel rooms, auditoriums, or office buildings, and gospel music, sermons, jazz, country music, ethnic music, and more mainstream popular music were also recorded. The audience for downhome blues could be reached through advertisements in the black press and distribution networks reaching to music and furniture stores in black urban neighborhoods, even to southern plantation commissaries.

Blues with guitar or piano

Between 1926 and 1931 a large number of solo guitar playing blues singers were recorded in both the northern and the temporary southern studios by over a half dozen record companies. Besides Jefferson and Johnson, they included Henry Thomas, Furry Lewis, Charley Patton, Son House, Tommy Johnson, Ishman Bracey, Mississippi John Hurt, Skip James, Barbecue Bob, Peg Leg Howell, Blind Willie McTell and Blind Blake, almost all born in the 1890s or early 1900s. About half of them also recorded folk ballads, spirituals, minstrel and ragtime tunes, and other older material, but many concentrated almost entirely on blues: after about a quarter century of development blues music was enough to sustain the musical interests and careers of plenty of performers. This situation would prevail for the remainder of the twentieth century.

Enough singer-guitarists were recorded in this era that it is possible to categorize most in terms of three regionally differentiated approaches to blues performance style. One of these encompasses East Texas and adjacent portions of Oklahoma, Arkansas, and Louisiana. Here the melodic lines are often wide ranging and free flowing, almost like field hollers. The guitar pounds away with every beat on a single muffled note or group of notes in the bass, while free-flowing and seemingly improvised treble lines answer the voice. Sometimes, in blues apparently designed more for listening than for dancing, the guitar virtually drops out during the singing, only to come back with a string of notes as a response. Blind Lemon Jefferson epitomized this approach, which would prove to be influential on later electric guitarists who would apply it to an ensemble format where other instruments could be counted on to keep the beat and provide the harmonic background.

Another stylistic region might be called the Deep South, stretching from the Mississippi Valley eastward to Central Georgia. Its heart was the Delta region of northwest Mississippi, an area of large plantations and an overwhelmingly black rural population where blues was intensely cultivated along with the cotton crop. Blues from this region display the greatest intensity of emotional feeling and seriousness of content, perhaps reflecting the harshness of life there. The guitar playing tends to be very percussive, with the slide style heard frequently, and many tunes are constructed from repeated riffs. Melodies are often pentatonic, and harmonic development is little emphasized. Singers rely heavily on a shared body of lyric verses and phrases in constructing their songs. Altogether, it is a stark, minimalist approach to the blues, effective through its hypnotic power. It proved to be very influential post-1945, when the guitar became electrified and harnessed to the sound of a small ensemble that could reinforce the music's intensity.

The third blues region encompassed the East Coast from Florida to Maryland, stretching westward through the Piedmont, the Appalachian Mountains, and the Ohio River Valley to central Kentucky and Tennessee. Here the influence of ragtime, popular music, and Anglo-American folk music could be heard in the blues. Guitarists tended to play patterns of alternating bass notes or an alternating bass note and chord, in the manner of ragtime, with spectacular virtuoso playing in the treble range, featuring frequent harmonic changes and passing notes and chords. The rhythms were lighter, and most players adhered strictly to the twelve-bar or some other standard format. It was in many respects the opposite of the Deep South style. Some of its greatest exponents were blind or otherwise handicapped musicians, fully professional in music on account of their disabilities. This style reached its peak of development in the 1920s and 1930s and, perhaps because of its textural and harmonic density, did not translate well into a later electric and ensemble format.

During this period blues guitarists were also recorded in combinations with other instruments. There were duos of two guitarists, such as Frank Stokes and Dan Sane (the Beale Street Sheiks), or Memphis-based Memphis Minnie and Kansas Joe (McCoy), and Tommy Johnson and Charlie McCoy (Joe's brother) from Jackson, Mississippi. The Mississippi Sheiks were a stripped-down string band of just guitar and fiddle, while Peg Leg Howell's "Gang" from Atlanta consisted of two guitars and a fiddle. The Dallas String Band used a mandolin, guitar, and string bass. Larger combos of three to five musicians were especially found in the black urban communities and were variously known as washboard or jug bands (from their emblematic instruments), skiffle bands (derived from "scuffle" and suggesting their difficult musical existence), juke bands (from the juke house environment where they often performed), and spasm bands (from their irregular and impromptu pattern of performing and their use of "pick up" musicians). They played in clubs, street corners, parks, serenading in residential neighborhoods, on excursion boats and trains, at store openings and sales, and at private parties in homes and hotels, and were popular with white as well as black audiences. Jug bands were recorded in Memphis (Memphis Jug Band; Cannon's Jug Stompers), Dallas, Birmingham, Cincinnati, and Louisville, here often displaying a greater affinity for jazz and popular music sounds and instrumentation. Walter Taylor's band from Kentucky consisted of guitar, banjo, washboard, and kazoo, and there were other combinations of string, wind, and percussion instruments recorded at this time. Although these bands recorded some ragtime and popular tunes, their main repertoire was blues, and they can be viewed as the first real blues bands, containing some of the elements in prototype form that would occur in more modern ensembles.

Pianist-singer Leroy Carr and guitarist Scrapper Blackwell, based in Indianapolis, took the lead in popularizing this type of duo which, from 1928, became another foundation of modern blues ensembles. Carr's plaintive singing was set to a full, rolling, rhythmic piano, with Blackwell's single-note guitar lines cutting through like a knife. Blackwell played a steel-bodied instrument, giving him added volume to match that of the piano. It became an immensely popular and influential combination, spawning many imitators and outlasting Carr's death in 1935. A variation on this set-up, one that came to be known as "hokum" blues, was also created in 1928 by two musicians based in Chicago, pianist Thomas A. Dorsey ("Georgia Tom") and guitarist Hudson Whitaker ("Tampa Red"). The latter also played a steel-bodied guitar, often in the slide style. Hokum blues typically used the verse form of couplet and refrain, had fast tempos, and dealt humorously with sexual topics, often full of *double entendre.* Dorsey and Whitaker, sometimes with Big Bill Broonzy substituting on guitar, often recorded as the Hokum Boys or Famous Hokum Boys, but these names were also used by other musicians. The style's popularity would last through the 1930s, and sexual themes have remained part of the blues ever since. A number of the female vaudeville singers and male-female duos also recorded hokum blues in the late 1920s and early 1930s in an attempt to counter slumping record sales that came with the onset of the economic Depression.

It was not until the end of 1928 that solo piano blues emerged as a clearly defined format on records, although earlier players (Hersal Thomas, Will Ezell, "Cow Cow" Davenport) had recorded. Success was achieved that year with Chicago pianist Pine Top Smith's "Pine Top's Boogie Woogie," a dance-oriented instrumental piece with jive talking by Smith carrying on an imaginary dialogue with dancers. An eight-to-the-bar riff was heard prominently in the bass, modulating according to the twelve-bar harmonic scheme, a pattern that took the name "boogie-woogie." Smith's blues was the sound of the saloon or "barrelhouse" (another name given to this style) and the urban house party. His success opened up the recording studios to many other solo pianists (Romeo Nelson, Montana Taylor, Alex Moore, Charlie Spand, Speckled Red) from this environment in both Chicago and the South. Instrumental solos were common: many of these men had been accompanists to singers, while the piano being a loud instrument and the player in a small noisy saloon or house party having to face into it and away from the audience, made any singing hard to hear. The success of this style came as the Depression was setting in, so most of the records sold in small quantities, and few of the artists had more than one or two recording sessions.

Consolidation

The Depression brought about the bankruptcy of almost all of the companies that had been making "race records." Sales were reduced to a trickle, and in 1932 hardly any blues records were made. Another casualty was the vaudeville theatre circuit that had sustained so many, particularly female, artists. Contributing to this decline was the growing popularity (since 1927) of talking pictures, which were cheaper to run than live music and more attractive to audiences because of their novelty. A few vaudeville singers (Ida Cox, Victoria Spivey, Trixie Smith) soldiered on, but recording sessions were rare, and they had to combine the occasional theatre show with appearances in cabarets, road houses, and tent shows. Most retired or faded into obscurity, while a few like Ethel Waters and Hattie McDaniels enjoyed success in the limited roles available to them in Hollywood films. Some made comebacks in the 1940s as the jazz revival got under way. Most female blues artists of the 1930s, such as Merline Johnson, Lil Johnson, Alice Moore, and former vaudeville singer Lucille Bogan, sang in a rougher style like that of their male counterparts and used similar accompaniments of a solo pianist or a small combo of piano, guitar, and sometimes one or two other instruments. Memphis Minnie and Georgia White even played their own guitar and piano respectively. Male artists, however, would become the leading forces in the blues from the 1930s on, while most women singers, such as Lil Green and Rosetta Howard, tended to combine their blues with pop material.

1933–1942 saw a consolidation of the blues recording industry and a certain homogenization of sound in the music. Three record companies emerged to dominate blues recording during this period. American Record Company had Vocalion and several other labels, and eventually revived the Okeh label. In 1938 they became part of the Columbia Broadcasting System. RCA Victor's Bluebird label was the successor to the old Victor Records, and Decca Records was a new company started in 1934. New York and especially Chicago became the locations for most recording sessions, and two Chicago talent scouts and producers, Lester Melrose and J. Mayo Williams, controlled much of the access to recording for blues artists by the mid-1930s, while Art Satherly and a few others roamed the South to work with talent there. Although the companies visited Dallas, San Antonio, Atlanta, and Charlotte with some regularity, field sessions for blues artists were considerably less frequent. Chicago and New York were the places to be for those artists who wanted to get on records. Juke boxes and discount chain stores accounted for an increasing share of record sales, and the companies began to take an assembly line approach to blues recording. They sought artists who were multiply talented as singers, songwriters, and instrumentalists, and they often recorded them in massive sessions that yielded eight or more master recordings in a few hours. Many of these artists sustained recording careers of a decade or more and often appeared as sidemen on one another's records or helped as songwriters and talent scouts. Despite the tendency toward consolidation during this period, there was still a considerable variety of styles to be heard, with some emerging lyric commentary on political subjects.

Three artists of the 1930s with deep roots in the blues traditions of Arkansas, Mississippi, and Tennessee created styles on the piano, guitar, and harmonica that seemed to consolidate their pasts and would point them in their future direction as components in electric blues ensembles. Roosevelt Sykes (from Helena, Arkansas) recorded almost every year from 1929 to the 1970s, in formats from solo to eight-piece band. He displayed great virtuosity and independence of the hands, especially on slow blues where the left kept up an insistent beat deep in the bass while the right ranged freely over the upper and middle keyboard playing horn-like passages with plenty of flattened thirds and sevenths representing blue notes. Younger pianists from the same Mid-South region, such as Memphis Slim and Otis Spann, picked up this style and helped popularize it in ensembles during the 1940s and 1950s. For most of the 1930s, Sykes was based in St. Louis, a city famed for its piano players since the ragtime era. St. Louis was also home to Walter Davis, who specialized in rather sad lyrics and played in a simplified and idiosyncratic version of Sykes' style, and Peetie Wheatstraw who, in contrast, presented the image of the wild reveler and played in a rhythmic style closer to the older barrelhouse tradition. His vocal mannerism of leaping into the falsetto range became widely imitated. A number of southern barrelhouse pianists had a more improvisational right hand. Among the most successful were Little Brother Montgomery, based in Jackson, Mississippi, and Walter Roland from Birmingham. Texas pianists based in Houston, Dallas, San Antonio, and Shreveport, Louisiana, were the most extensively recorded, due largely to continuing field trips by the record companies to this region. Their playing used a variety of bass patterns and was improvisational in the right hand but generally with more harmonic development than that of their counterparts in the Deep South and Chicago. Pianists like Black Boy Shine, Rob Cooper, Andy Boy, Pinetop Burks, and Black Ivory King worked a regional circuit of roadhouses and urban saloons in the Southwest, a region which survived the Depression somewhat better than the rest of the country. From *c.* 1935, Meade Lux Lewis, Albert Ammons, Pete Johnson and Jimmy

Yancey led a revival of recording classic boogie-woogie piano. These were virtuoso players who rarely sang, and by 1940 boogie-woogie began to be appreciated as a form of instrumental jazz, being the first solo blues style to achieve mass acceptance with a white audience. It reached its peak of popularity during World War II, but continued thereafter to influence the piano styles heard in jump blues bands and in the fields of country music and rock'n'roll.

Robert Johnson from Robinsonville, Mississippi, was heir to the impassioned singing and harsh percussive Mississippi guitar style of Son House, Willie Brown, and Charley Patton, and this is reflected especially in Johnson's slide playing on the records he made in 1936 and 1937. But he also listened to smoother players like Lonnie Johnson and especially to pianists like Sykes, Wheatstraw and Carr. Johnson's recordings reflected all of these influences (see Chapter 5). He died in 1938, but his influence would be heard over ten years later in the electric ensemble work of fellow Mississippi and Arkansas guitarists who had migrated to Chicago, such as Muddy Waters, Elmore James, Eddie Taylor, Johnny Shines, and Robert "Junior" Lockwood. Blues rock guitarists from the 1960s on were inspired by Johnson's songs and style as well as his mysterious image, and a boxed collection of his complete recordings became a platinum record in the 1990s. Other Mississippi blues guitarists such as Bukka White and Big Joe Williams represented the rough Deep South style on recordings during the 1930s and early 1940s, while the melodically denser and more harmonic Piedmont style was successfully recorded by such artists as Joshua White from South Carolina, Buddy Moss from Georgia, and Blind Boy Fuller from North Carolina. White and Fuller's successor Brownie McGhee, along with harmonica player Sonny Terry from North Carolina and guitar evangelist Reverend Gary Davis, resettled in New York City in the 1940s, influencing the nascent folk-music revival scene there. Another set of blues guitarists in the 1930s, Kokomo Arnold, Casey Bill Weldon, Oscar Woods, and Tampa Red, incorporated the Hawaiian practice of playing long melodic lines with a slider, in contrast to the older blues practice of using the slider to play short riffs.

Solo harmonica was recorded during the 1920s by such artists as De Ford Bailey and Jaybird Coleman, but because the performer cannot play and sing at the same time, it more often was heard in a blues setting with other instruments. Alone, it was often confined to novelty pieces such as train imitations. In the late 1920s and early 1930s the harmonica began to be heard in duets with guitar and in jug bands. Learning from fellow West Tennessee harmonica players Noah Lewis, who had played in Cannon's Jug Stompers, and Hammie Nixon, who had accompanied guitarists Son Bonds and Sleepy John Estes, Sonny Boy Williamson from Jackson, Tennessee, consolidated the instrument's position in an ensemble setting. Between

1937 and his death in 1948 Williamson recorded with groups ranging from simply two guitars or guitar and piano to a five-piece band, adding bass and drums. His playing was full of bent blue notes and had a vocal quality that seemed to flow seamlessly in and out of his singing. He influenced countless other players in the 1950s and later, most notably the great Little Walter. His major rival during this period was Sonny Terry, who was an equally spectacular player, notable for his interjection of vocal whoops in his playing and his falsetto singing.

Many of the most popular blues artists during the 1930s and early 1940s had come from the Deep South to Chicago. They helped establish this city as a key destination for other artists and as a continuing center of blues recording. Besides the female artists mentioned earlier, the most popular of these stars were guitarists Big Bill (Broonzy), Bumble Bee Slim, Bill Gaither, Tampa Red, and Johnnie Temple, pianists Jimmie Gordon, Blind John Davis, Curtis Jones, Memphis Slim, and Big Maceo, harmonica players Jazz Gillum and Robert Lee McCoy, and Washboard Sam. Frankie "Half Pint" Jaxon, a vaudeville veteran, and Doctor Clayton, whose singing anticipated the melismatic quality of later soul blues stylists, were popular vocalists. To the middle of the 1930s the typical instrumentation was guitar and piano in the Carr / Blackwell style, or two guitars. Thence there was increasing supplementation by such instruments as string bass, washboard, and harmonica.

Another kind of blues ensemble began to be heard from 1936 onward, pioneered by a Chicago group calling itself the Harlem Hamfats. Led by singer and guitarist Joe McCoy, they consisted of two guitars, piano, bass, drums, trumpet, and clarinet, combining elements from Mississippi blues and New Orleans style jazz. The jazz musicians represented the many players at this time who were unwilling or unable to adapt to the more regimented big band swing style and who found refuge with blues artists trying to obtain a fuller and more sophisticated sound. The success of the Hamfats inspired the creation of similar groups in Chicago and elsewhere, including Ollie Shepard and His Kentucky Boys and Louis Jordan and His Tympany Five. Big Bill, Tampa Red, Jimmie Gordon and others experimented with bands of a similar instrumentation, while Johnnie Temple, Frankie Jaxon, and Rosetta Howard borrowed the Harlem Hamfats for some of their recordings. Groups of this sort proved to be another of the foundations for later blues bands.

Toward the end of the 1930s, the electric guitar entered the blues, adopted by some of the leading Chicago stars, including Big Bill, Tampa Red, Memphis Minnie, and Lonnie Johnson. In 1941 Arthur "Big Boy" Crudup emerged, playing electric guitar but singing with a raw country voice. He was accompanied at first only by a string bass, but by the mid-1940s he had added drums. His sound was a precursor of the harsher electric blues that would soon be recorded by other Mississippi migrants to Chicago like Muddy Waters. It also had a major influence on Elvis Presley and the beginnings of rock'n'roll in the 1950s.

Blues in transition

The 1940s were a transitional time for the blues, for the homogenizing trends were reversed and new styles emerged. The military draft for World War II broke up many blues groups and removed musicians from their communities. During the war a shellac shortage and a strike against the recording studios called by the American Federation of Musicians crippled the record industry. New independent record companies founded by entrepreneurs from varied backgrounds sprang up in cities all across America, especially after the war and the strike ended, and they drew upon local talent in many cases. Many recorded black music, including blues. The post-war years were a time of prosperity, even for blacks to some degree. Many had left the rural South during the war for military service and jobs in the North, the West Coast, and southern cities, fleeing poverty and racism, while the increasing mechanization of agriculture and the decline of the sharecropping system drove many others to the cities. By the end of the decade the first of many radio stations with an all-black on-air format was established in Memphis, broadcasting a steady diet of live and recorded blues.

Most of the established Chicago blues stars of the pre-war years continued to record in the 1940s for the three major companies and sold records in good quantities thanks to superior distribution. But by the end of the decade their sound was passé, and these companies soon got out of the blues field, leaving it entirely to the independent labels and a largely new cast of characters. The electric guitar had meanwhile become increasingly prominent: by the early 1950s it had given new life to solo country blues, making the sound of Lightnin' Hopkins and Li'l Son Jackson from Texas and John Lee Hooker from Detroit by way of Mississippi, louder and more insistent. Hopkins performed in a somewhat spare version of the style created by Blind Lemon Jefferson, while Hooker featured pentatonic tunes without many harmonic changes and boogie rhythms drawn from piano and ensemble blues. Although most of the solo guitar performers were based in cities, their country origins were quite apparent in their voices, lyrics, and sound.

At the opposite end of the spectrum were the blues shouters and crooners, who projected an air of comfortable urbanity. Some of them did not play an instrument but, like their pop music counterparts, left that chore to others. Their music suggests the post-World War II mood of confidence, progress, sophistication, and growing assertiveness in black urban America.

They remained popular into the 1950s. The shouters sang with big, husky, authoritative voices, offering lyrics on upbeat themes of partying, drinking, love-making and other good-time activities, or messages directed at the opposite sex that made it clear that the singer meant business. The preferred style of accompaniment for shouters was the five- to seven-piece jump band, evolved from older groups like the Harlem Hamfats and Louis Jordan's Tympany Five as well as scaled-down big bands. Most of the musicians were versatile jazzmen. A honking, bleating, shrieking saxophone with some bebop flavoring became the most prominent lead instrument, while drums and a boogie-woogie-styled piano were also prominent. A number of the singers, in fact, played saxophone or drums in their bands. Few were guitarists. Some of the shouters were pianists, although these musicians more often tended to be crooners preferring a smaller, softer, "after hours" format such as piano and lightly amplified jazzy guitar with string bass and/or light drums, following Nat "King" Cole and other jazz and pop singers. Shouting and crooning were two sides of the same coin, both urbane and sophisticated, and some singers were adept at both styles. Although early strongholds of these styles appear to have been Kansas City and other midwestern cities stretching down to Oklahoma and Texas, their greatest flowering was in California, where many migrants from this area had settled during and after World War II and where there were many new independent record companies. Some of the pioneer shouters had experience in the big swing bands that were popular in the 1930s and early 1940s. Louis Jordan himself had worked in Chick Webb's band. Jimmy Rushing and Joe Williams sang with Count Basie's Orchestra in Kansas City, and Jimmy Witherspoon and Walter Brown sang with Jay McShann's band there. Big Joe Turner was another Kansas City shouter, who worked with big bands and boogie-woogie pianists and managed to carry his style into rock'n'roll in the 1950s. Wynonie Harris from nearby Omaha, a highly popular shouter, had sung with Lucky Millinder's Orchestra. A big voice and commanding presence were undoubted advantages when singing with these large aggregations. Singers from Texas and Oklahoma especially wound up on the West Coast. More of them played instruments than their counterparts from further north, including drummer Roy Milton, guitarist Jimmy Liggins, and alto sax player Eddie Vinson, along with a host of crooning/shouting pianists: Charles Brown, Floyd Dixon, Joe Liggins, Little Willie Littlefield, Ivory Joe Hunter, Amos Milburn, and Percy Mayfield. But there were shouters and crooners in many other cities of the Midwest and South: New Orleans (Roy Brown, Cousin Joe), Charlotte (Nappy Brown), Atlanta (Billy Wright) and Ohio (Bull Moose Jackson, Tiny Bradshaw, and H-Bomb Ferguson). Rufus Thomas and Gatemouth Moore were from Memphis, while even Clarksdale, Mississippi, had a jump band, Ike Turner's Kings of Rhythm. Crooning pianists Cecil Gant and Johnny

Ace were from Nashville and Memphis. Veteran Lonnie Johnson enjoyed another of his periodic comebacks as a blues crooner. Some shouters worked within vocal groups (the Midnighters, the Five Royales, and the Coasters) using jump band instrumentation and specializing in blues on humorous and sexual topics, making the transition to rock'n'roll in the 1950s. There were also female shouters with backgrounds in gospel singing, and crooners influenced by jazz and pop singers, especially Billie Holiday. These singers included Dinah Washington, Ruth Brown, Little Esther, Big Maybelle, Etta James, Big Mama Thornton, and singing pianists Camille Howard, Hadda Brooks, Nellie Lutcher, and Julia Lee.

In the late 1940s and 1950s in Chicago, a small electric combo format developed, combining some characteristics of both the solo electric guitarists (the raw quality and closeness to country roots) and the jump bands (volume, power, and urban aggressiveness). Black people were streaming out of the plantations of the Deep South, often heading straight for Chicago, Gary, Detroit, Minneapolis, Milwaukee, and Cleveland. Because of its prior importance in blues and the presence of many new independent record companies, Chicago became the focal point for this new style. The bands featured typically one or two electric guitars, usually a harmonica played through an amplifier, drums, and perhaps string bass, piano, or even a saxophone. Some of the earliest groups were just harmonica and two guitars. The singing guitarists had often started out as solo performers on acoustic instruments in the South and built or joined a band after they came to Chicago. There was little obvious jazz influence: the musicians had grown up in the country, and they were loud and raw. Repeated riffs, bottleneck guitar, and wailing harmonica abounded. Muddy Waters and Howlin' Wolf, two leaders in this movement, were both from Mississippi and had been influenced by older country blues artists such as Charley Patton, Son House, and Robert Johnson. Other prominent figures were guitarists Jimmy Rogers, Elmore James, Eddie Taylor, J. B. Lenoir, and Bo Diddley, all from Mississippi, harmonica players Little Walter, Junior Wells, and Jimmy Reed, and pianists Sunnyland Slim, Willie Mabon, and Otis Spann.

Chicago was not the only place where this sound existed: artists like Baby Boy Warren and Bobo Jenkins had a similar sound in Detroit, and it could be heard in the Delta itself in Willie Love, Sonny Boy Williamson No. 2, and Woodrow Adams (Howlin' Wolf and Elmore James had recorded in this format in the South before they headed to Chicago). From the late 1950s a regional variant of this style emerged in the Baton Rouge area, with artists like Slim Harpo, Lazy Lester, Lightnin' Slim, and Lonesome Sundown combining influences from the Delta, Chicago, New Orleans, and Texas. Another late developing regional variant was found in the hills of northern Mississippi, built around a riffing electric country blues guitar and rhythms influenced by local fife and drum bands. Some of its chief exponents were Junior Kimbrough, R. L. Burnside, and Jessie Mae Hemphill. Although this style existed by the 1960s, it wasn't recorded to any extent until the 1980s, too late to make a national impact among black listeners whose tastes in blues had moved on.

Two other interesting small combo variants emanated from Louisiana. From the Creole population came *zydeco* blues, featuring the electric accordion as the lead instrument with vocals occasionally sung in French, exemplified by Clifton Chenier. This style developed among Creole migrants in urban southeast Texas, especially Houston, in the early 1950s, but it soon spread back to southwest Louisiana where it has remained entrenched. New Orleans, with its rich jazz tradition strongly grounded in the blues, developed a sound built around piano, a horn section and drums. It is closer to the blues shouter and jump band style but with the unique rhythmic sensibility and vocal phrasing of New Orleans: a number of the blues use an eight-bar rather than twelve-bar form. Pianists Professor Longhair and Fats Domino, guitarist Smiley Lewis, and vocalist Earl King were prominent here.

Modern styles and the move to rock'n'roll

Rock'n'roll during its earliest years grew largely out of elements from electric country blues, Kansas City blues shouters, and Chicago and New Orleans small combo blues. The unifying factors were a fast danceable beat and lyrics that appealed to adolescent sensibilities. Chuck Berry and Bo Diddley introduced sounds from Chicago blues, while Fats Domino, Little Richard, and Larry Williams introduced New Orleans elements. Most rock'n'roll artists from the Memphis area were whites who had absorbed the blues, both from direct contact and through radio and records. Elvis Presley, Carl Perkins, Jerry Lee Lewis, and others enjoyed initial popularity with black listeners, and these "hillbilly cats" appeared for a time to be turning blues into an integrated music, while other black artists from Memphis and Mississippi, such as Rufus Thomas and Ike Turner, were also involved. By 1960, rock'n'roll and blues had diverged, with the former becoming a predominantly white field. Black secular music became categorized as either blues, r&b, or a newly emerging "soul music."

The most enduring blues sound post-1945, and one that strongly influenced rock'n'roll, was the electric lead guitar, featuring horn-like melodic lines and extreme use of string bending. This is a sound that requires a band of some size to provide a harmonic and rhythmic background. Modern electric guitar emerged in the mixed jazz-blues musical environment of the

Southwest and Midwest. Oklahoma City jazz guitarist Charlie Christian and Dallas blues guitarist Aaron "T-Bone" Walker, who had known one another in the early 1930s, are generally regarded as pioneers of this style, although its blues roots can be traced back to the work of Blind Lemon Jefferson. Although Jefferson performed solo on an acoustic instrument, his extended improvisational lines and string-bending anticipated ideas these younger musicians would develop when the instrument became amplified. It was Walker and other Texas guitarists, mostly relocated on the West Coast, who would spread this style in the blues world of the 1940s. Among the other prominent early performers were Saunders King, Pee Wee Crayton, Clarence "Gatemouth" Brown, and Lowell Fulson. The latter, originally from Oklahoma, evolved from a country blues to a lead guitarist over the course of his early recording career in the 1940s. Later Texas guitarists such as Johnny Copeland, Albert Collins, and Johnny "Guitar" Watson carried this style forward. While Walker preferred a "jazzy" sound on an amplified hollow-bodied instrument, the younger guitarists generally strove for a more "electric" sound, often on a solid-bodied guitar.

Certainly by the early 1950s, blues guitarists outside the Texas–West Coast axis, such as Memphis-based B. B. King, were being affected by this new sound. Like Walker, King preferred to work with large bands containing a full horn section. He brought a harder edge to his playing, however, and displayed less jazz influence. King's records during the 1950s were immensely popular with black audiences, and he did much to spread the popularity of this guitar sound. By the mid-1950s it could be heard in Chicago small-group blues in recordings by Otis Rush, Buddy Guy, Magic Sam, and others. Older Chicago artists like Howlin' Wolf and Muddy Waters began employing younger players to add this sound to their bands, and by the end of the decade hundreds of blues guitarists had mastered this style.

Formerly a gospel singer, B. B. King was also a pioneer blues vocalist, introducing a gospel-influenced "soul" style in the early 1950s, demonstrating a highly emotional, often pleading quality, with extreme use of melisma and occasional leaps into the falsetto range. Otis Rush and Buddy Guy sang in this style, as did Bobby Bland, who was not an instrumentalist, while Ray Charles and James Brown took soul singing into the field of rock'n'roll and beyond. Soul blues has remained the most popular style with black audiences to the present, often in association with the sound of electric lead guitar and a horn section, as in the work of Little Milton, Albert King, and Z. Z. Hill.

From the late 1950s, following the incorporation of electric bass and keyboards into blues ensembles and the ascendancy of electric lead guitar and soul blues singing, blues experienced a slowdown in its evolutionary development within the American black community. Popular blues in 2000 sounded little different from popular blues in 1960. Innovative artists such as Jimi Hendrix had their main influence in rock or jazz, while stylistic outgrowths of blues, such as soul music and funk, were generally viewed as new and distinct genres. Blues became increasingly a music of nostalgia and a symbol of cultural heritage or "roots" for black audiences. Songs with self-conscious titles, like "Why I Sing the Blues," "I'll Play the Blues for You," "Down Home Blues," and "The Blues Is All Right" became popular hits. The 1990s witnessed the emergence of a number of sons and daughters of prominent blues artists of an earlier era as well as other younger black artists who explored older historical styles such as solo country blues. Most of these new artists have performed mainly for white American and international audiences.

This halt in stylistic evolution coincided with major political victories of the Civil Rights movement, which removed or ameliorated many of the social factors that had contributed to the rise of blues as a form of expression. The Civil Rights movement stressed collective action and used adaptations of spirituals, sung by groups, to express its goals. It had little use for the individualistic and socially marginal stance of the blues singer. This halt also coincided with the growth of white interest and involvement in the blues. This was not an entirely new phenomenon. White folklorists, collectors, record company executives, songwriters, and even a few musicians had been involved in the documentation and production of African American blues almost from the beginning. Southern white audiences, especially, had patronized artists such as Charley Patton, Blind Lemon Jefferson, and Bessie Smith, as did some of the more astute early white jazz fans. Whites even began to perform blues within the genres of country music and later rock'n'roll, sometimes creating distinct styles such as the "blue yodel" and "rockabilly," but whites working in these styles never viewed themselves primarily as "blues singers." It was the folk-music revival that began to change the role of whites in the blues. During the 1940s and 1950s Leadbelly, Josh White, Big Bill Broonzy, Brownie McGhee and Sonny Terry began to gain a white following at coffee houses, college concerts, and left-wing political events. By the early 1960s a number of veteran country blues artists, who had made great recordings in the 1920s and 1930s, were rediscovered and brought before these same audiences. Soon a few white solo performers, such as John Hammond, Jr., began to emerge as blues specialists. By the early and mid-1960s one could also witness the phenomenon of the white electric blues band both in the United States and Great Britain. From that time onward blues has grown in popularity among American whites and internationally, until by the end of the century there were undoubtedly far more non-black performers than blacks viewing themselves as blues specialists. Most of these performers have continued to work within established contemporary blues parameters or have explored and re-created historical sounds, creating new songs, sometimes developing new themes to reflect a more modern lifestyle, and maintaining a high level of instrumental virtuosity. Although its stylistic development has slowed, blues has increased and broadened its audience, until today it is more popular than ever.

4 The development of gospel music

DON CUSIC

Psalms and hymns

Although a distinctive American voice would not truly emerge until the nineteenth century, the musical roots of modern America were planted in the seventeenth and eighteenth centuries.

The settlers in the Jamestown and Plymouth colonies were not the first to come to the New World; in fact, the first Europeans to establish themselves in America were the Spanish explorers who came through Mexico and the southwestern area of what is now the United States. The first gospel songs sung in the New World have been traced to the Roman Catholic Church through the inhabitants of what is now the southern U.S.A. and Mexico. Catholic service books were published in Mexico as early as 1556 and the main effect of this Catholic influence was to introduce the Gregorian chant, sung in Latin, to America.

However, the true settling and growth of what became identified as the United States came from the European settlers who peopled the eastern seaboard and then began moving westward; the roots of U.S. American music are embedded in the European culture these settlers left behind.

The Reformation in Europe brought a new song, sung in the vernacular (not in Latin) by the entire congregation. Two basic forms emerged here: the chorale (associated with the Lutherans and Moravians), and the psalm tune, which developed among the Calvinists. Both the French and English sang psalms which were paraphrased in regular meter, to which were added paraphrases of other lyric passages from scriptures. They sang "God's word" from the Bible. The Lutherans also sang "God's word," but welcomed devotional poems written by individuals. The Puritans of New England came from the Calvinist tradition and the transition in America from scriptural to devotional poems – psalms to hymns – was a long and gradual one, hindered by the Puritans' strict adherence to the psalms. Musically, there was a major difference as the Lutherans and Moravians made use of the organ and orchestral instruments in worship while the Calvinists and English dissenters sang metrical poems in unison without musical accompaniment.

The first book published in America was *The Whole Book of Psalmes Faithfully Translated Into English Metre*, commonly known as *The Bay Psalm Book*. It appeared in 1640 in the Plymouth colony in Massachusetts and contained the first version of psalms made by Americans and used in American churches. The success of the *Bay Psalm Book* was immediate, with 1,700 copies in the first printing and 2,000 copies of a new edition in 1651. In all, there were twenty-seven editions of this book printed in New England and at least twenty in England (the last in 1754), and six in Scotland. The ninth edition, published in 1698, was the first to contain music to accompany the texts. Prior to that, only the words were printed; they were sung to a known melody with a handful of melodies fitting a large number of songs.

In the eighteenth century, some changes evolved, basically reflecting the changes occurring in England. The Methodists and their Methodism brought the Wesley hymns to New Jersey and the later comers to New England imported the hymns of Isaac Watts. Ironically, the initial resistance Watts encountered with his hymns in America was the same he had encountered in England; his "hymns of human composure" were not literal renderings of the psalms but rather came from the human heart. During this time, the psalm was still the predominant form of gospel music, sung in churches as well as homes.

During the 1600s and early 1700s, the New England congregations were noted for singing their psalm tunes at a very slow tempo, known as the "old way." As with most religious customs, its adherents defended it as the "only proper mode" for performing music in church. This was challenged in the early part of the eighteenth century by advocates of the "new way," who encouraged singing by note instead of rote, briskly in harmony rather than slowly and in unison. The state of singing had sunk to a low from years of having no formal music training for singers, and from having psalm books with texts but no melodies to read.

This problem was met by the rise of the singing school, giving instruction and training in the rudiments of music to members of a church or community, and also by the rise of the singing master in the eighteenth and early nineteenth centuries. These singing masters came into a community, gathered up a class through word of mouth and door-to-door canvassing, and taught for about a week. At the end of that week, students were able to read music and had learned some new songs.

While psalm singing dominated the seventeenth century and continued through the introduction of hymns in the eighteenth century, the nineteenth century was marked by the emergence of the denominational hymn. Although tenors had generally sung the melody in earlier times, sopranos sang the melody in the nineteenth century. In the seventeenth century, one person "set the pitch," then the entire congregation sang the psalm. However, the eighteenth century brought the emergence of the musical elite – the choir – which changed the seating pattern (and architecture) within the church. During this time, a gallery was often erected over the entrance vestibule and sometimes on three sides of the church, with the choir sitting apart from the congregation.

The development of tune books (books which contained melodies) was due primarily to enterprising individuals who developed these books for singing school classes, church choirs and, eventually, for the organist. There was an obvious convenience in having the music associated with the words, although they were generally on opposite pages. After the mid-nineteenth century, the congregation hymnal with words and music appeared. The words were generally under the tune on the same page and sometimes several texts were given for one tune.

The eighteenth century saw a secularization of sacred music occur that would not only help make that music more appealing to a wide public, but also carry it outside the church where it would stand alone outside the worship. The churches of New England adopted Calvinist practice by prohibiting musical instruments or choirs in their public worship, thus separating themselves from the professional music traditions of the Roman Catholics, the Lutherans, and the Anglicans. In the latter churches, the emphasis on the music had shifted from the congregation to a designated group of singers singing to a non-participating audience, like in a theatre. The introduction of choirs led to more elaborate songs.

Spirituals

The revivals that followed the Revolutionary War, known as "The Great Awakening," were not highly organized affairs and cannot be traced in a logical, sequential manner; rather, there were a number of religious freedom fires. As the country pushed westward, these revivals sprang up in various areas of the country for several generations, offending organized religion because revival preachers paid no heed to denominational lines, preaching wherever they could gather a crowd.

The Revolutionary War had capped the great concept of "freedom" that had been raging in the colonies. In the urban areas, the rationalism which fueled the French Revolution and provided new breakthroughs in science and philosophy caught hold. However, in the untamed parts of the country, this rationalism had little appeal; the settlers had neither the time nor the inclination to ponder intellectual enlightenment. These people needed a faith that was vibrant and alive, full of emotion and comfort, that let them relate to the lonely, danger-filled wilderness and a life steeped heavily in individualism. Thus, it was a "free" religion that took hold.

Socially, the new free religion was perfect for the common man who was poor. Sinful things were from the rich and were to be condemned;

hence the rich pursuits of gambling, drinking and such were quickly labeled as sin and railed against. The large urban areas became dens of iniquity while rural America provided the most fertile soil for folk religion. Here, it grew and spread, watered with an emotional spirituality that provided a comfort to the lonely settlers while fanning the flames of hell. While this folk religion came under no organizational guidelines, one basic tenet ran through it – all institutional mediacy between an individual's soul and the Redeemer must be rejected – all, no matter what their station in life, had access to God.

As the settlers moved westward, they moved beyond the influence of established churches and were served by a new kind of preacher, born on the frontier, or at least familiar with frontier life. Although such preachers generally had little formal education, they did have the ability to move audiences and would preach wherever people could be assembled. The "camp meeting" was born from the lack of a central church in the vast rural regions and because the settlers lived so far apart. These camp meetings brought people together for several days from large surrounding areas with families bringing food and living in their wagons, the women sleeping inside and the men on the ground underneath or in improvised shelters.

The Baptists were a particularly free group with dissensions breaking out within their sect about predestination, grace and a number of other theological issues. Within neither Britain nor America did they accept a central church authority; in music this meant they were devoted to "free" singing rather than singing songs prescribed to them by others. The spirit of the folk Baptists dominated this time of revivals after the Revolutionary War and the songs they chose to sing differed greatly from the psalms of the Puritans with their long texts. The revival spirituals, born from these mass meetings, emphasized choruses, refrains, and repeated lines.

In the period from 1780 to 1830, a great body of folk texts appeared in the gospel tradition. Great Britain and the young United States were full of folk tunes at the time and religious folk often put religious verses to popular secular tunes. The wedding of religious lyrics and folk tunes probably began around 1770 and continued strongly through this period. The composed tunes of the pre-Revolutionary War period in America remained unknown to the rural Americans who had moved westward, so they used tunes from the folk tradition for their worship. The source for these American folk tunes was primarily British – from England, Scotland, and Ireland mainly – with only a handful from other sources.

The Kentucky Revival of 1800 established the revival spiritual in America. The Kentucky Revival was not the first and was similar to a number of other revivals that preceded it; however, the flames here seemed to burn higher and brighter because of a number of favorable conditions. One was the ethnic background of the population: primarily Gaels (Irish, Scots-Irish,

Scottish, Welsh) who were known as highly emotional people. Another factor was climatic-geographic. The Kentucky farmers had a period of leisure during the summer from the time their crops were planted until harvesting time (as opposed to their New England counterparts who had a short summer) and the dry roads and trails invited long trips to big gatherings. Also, the dry, hot summers lent themselves to meeting outdoors, thereby accommodating large numbers of people. The final factor was the lack of organized, established religion in that area, which meant no religious or civil authorities had to be battled for these revivals to occur.

The crowds at these gatherings had to sing from memory or learn songs that were easily repetitive and took little effort to learn, because there were no song books. Here, the revival songs were in the hands of the people as the real exhortational activity – praying, mourning and other physical exercises – was by and for the crowd. The singers controlled the songs but the crowds would join in the chorus, on a short-phrase refrain or on a couplet which struck their fancy. This led to the development of revival songs with repetitive passages.

The verse-with-chorus idea spread quickly with some choruses proving so popular they were interjected into other songs with different verses. There developed two types of revival songs at this time: the repetitive chorus and the call and response where a line was sung by the singer and the crowd sang the responding line, which always remained the same.

This was the time when the folk tradition of song – an oral tradition that had begun in Britain and other parts of Europe – took over in religious music. The settlers moving west had little if any music training and neither song books nor established churches. When the revivals caught hold, music was returned to the people who responded with a congregational type of singing reminiscent of the earliest Puritans, albeit much more emotional and active. They had to depend upon tunes they already knew, much as the first Puritans did with their songs. But the nature of the revivals caused a major change. The melodies had to be altered to accommodate choruses that everyone could learn quickly. Thus the song leader would know the verses but everyone could know the chorus and would join the song on these choruses or on lines that repeated themselves. This was democracy in action; everyone could feel a part of this religion and singing. Moreover, the choruses spoke the feelings of the settlers.

As the first half of the nineteenth century ended, the old-time religion faded as the cultural environment gave way to the Industrial Revolution and the Civil War. After the Civil War, the second half of the nineteenth century witnessed a new religious trend appear as the wild, emotion-packed camp meeting style of religion gave way to a more solemn, sober movement, centered in the urban areas with the music of the gospel hymns.

The folk hymns and spirituals were the last gospel songs to be perpetuated solely in the oral tradition, although they survive now because they were collected in print and because folklorists collected them on tape. Although some were written anew by individuals, many of the hymns come from the broadside ballad tradition and the folksongs brought to the U.S.A. from Europe. The Negro Spirituals are often black adaptations of white songs, influenced heavily by the African origins of black Americans but reflecting the culture of a people united and suppressed in America.

The songs of this period reflect the oral tradition as well as the revival spirit of singing "spontaneously," without books, led by a singer with the congregation joining on key lines, phrases, or the chorus. These are songs easily learned and easily remembered. They are also easily changed and adapted from singer to singer, congregation to congregation, with the chorus or key lines remaining and the verse lyrics subject to individual changes. They are timeless songs because of the repetitiveness but also because of their emotional appeal. They are songs that can inspire joy or comfort in sorrow, a verbalizing of people's feelings and thoughts. Within these songs are the roots of blues, country, modern gospel and rock'n'roll. Musically and lyrically simple, their power rests in their emotional impact and their ability to be learned and sung easily: some examples include "Remember, Sinful Youth," "The Hebrew Children," "Didn't My Lord Deliver Daniel" and "Were You There? (When They Crucified My Lord)."

Differential practices in South and North

The history of gospel music in the South differs from that of the North, primarily because of the agricultural economy of the South, and the use of slavery to work the large plantations.

The first slaves were brought to Virginia by Dutch traders in 1629. Soon, a whole economy and way of life was based on slavery, particularly in the South where large plantations grew acres of cotton and needed slave labor to keep them going. Slavery grew quickly in North America and soon there was a bustling slave trade spawned by Europeans between Africa and America. From 1720 to the 1760s over 150,000 new African slaves arrived in America. Many Christian whites perpetuated the myth that blacks were descendants of the biblical Ham, wicked son of Noah, and that their bondage was a mark of sin from God.

There was, however, some early concern among white colonial Christians about the salvation of blacks. Cotton Mather, the venerable New England preacher, argued that blacks had souls; however, many whites refused to baptize blacks because this act inferred certain liberties on black individuals that whites were reluctant to bestow. Mather solved the problem somewhat by offering the alternative of huge indentures imposed by masters on Negroes which would ensure slavery after baptism. The belief that African blacks were slaves because God had ordained it was a concept many American whites openly embraced and promulgated. There was an obligation connected to this – the "White Man's Burden" – that required whites to convert African Americans to Christianity in order to save their souls.

The conversion of blacks was guided by the same principles as those of whites: each individual was expected to confront God and make his decision for Jesus, be "born-again" or "get religion." Many white settlers carried their black slaves with them during the early camp meetings at the beginning of the 1800s and the blacks heard psalms and camp meetings songs. Traveling preachers preached to both white and black audiences on southern farms because small congregations were often not segregated. The slaves made a number of conscious attempts to reproduce the songs they heard but often sang these songs in a different manner, affecting rhythms which were different from the original and, because of an insufficient vocabulary or inability to recall the words correctly, different lyrics or lyrics which have been reproduced as Negro dialect, markedly different from white speech. Musically, then, the spirituals, because born from slavery, became separate from the southern folksongs primarily because of the differences in the black and white cultures and the particular aptitude of African Americans for rhythms.

While the early white settlers placed a heavy emphasis on the words with the music being incidental – a handful of tunes were used, often interchangeable with different sets of lyrics – the black American felt a need to emphasize music over the words. But it was more than just a different melody; it was a whole new rhythm, an entirely new "feel" to the songs which became defined as black gospel. So, even though the blacks and whites often sang the same words, learned from the same sources, the results were two entirely different songs, with the black gospel songs rhythmical in a way the white songs never were.

The spirituals were created by a people bound in slavery and were an integral part of the culture in the early nineteenth century. However, it was not until after the Civil War that the spiritual was first recorded in print. The first major book containing words and music of spirituals was *Slave Songs of the United States* in 1867, but the first real awareness of the spirituals came with the Fisk Jubilee Singers' *Jubilee Songs* and their tour of northern cities in order to raise money to help their financially strapped institution in the post-Civil War years when the black education movement was struggling to survive and thrive. Still, the blacks' gospel music was virtually ignored by white Christians and it was not until the twentieth century that denominational hymnals included spirituals.

Musicologist and folk-music collector George Pullen Jackson noted in the early part of the twentieth century that many of the black spirituals had white origins and could be traced back to the British folksong tradition and early American camp meetings. Many later called his conclusions racist for denying African origins for these songs. Jackson was correct in tracing these songs to their source; however, he ignored the musical rhythms that defined black gospel, tracing only words and melodies. In addition, he overlooked the development of the "holiness" movement in the latter part of the nineteenth century which was a source of an essential difference between black and white gospel music.

"Holiness" songs

The roots of the holiness church go back to the 1890s and the "Latter Rain Movement" which sought to "irrigate the dry bones" in churches. Pentecostal congregations, characterized by this intense emotionalism in the worship service, developed all over the country, especially among the poor and depressed. The term "holy rollers" comes from this movement because people are liable to scream, shout, dance, jump or roll on the floor for Jesus. These churches place a heavy emphasis on being "saved, sanctified, and filled with the Holy Spirit" which means a possession by the Spirit so the person is not chained to this world but free to act or say whatever God wants done or said, using the individual's voice and body.

The black holiness churches feature a great amount of singing and dancing in their services, with half of the service usually comprised of music. These churches were the first to use musical instruments in the service, instruments that churches had long considered "of the devil." Conservatism has long been a staple of American Christianity and the mainstream African American churches, while usually more emotional than white churches, generally rejected the intense emotional involvement and extreme physical activities the holiness churches introduced as a regular part of their services.

There are foot-stomping and hand-clapping up-tempo songs in holiness churches, songs replete with complex rhythms, but the archetypal holiness song is a slow chant, often begun as church starts or later, during a prolonged series of shouts and outbursts. The ministers, with their strong personal charisma and elaborate showmanship, are the key factor in the holiness churches and they are required to lead the church to a spiritual high during the service that will enable the congregation to face six hard, troublesome weekdays. The faith is composed of mystery, divinely inspired intuition and visions that cannot be explained in this world. Holiness church is the antithesis of rationalism.

Both the spiritual jubilee tradition and the jubilee singers tradition come from the songs developed amongst the African American population at the beginning of the nineteenth century. While these songs were established before the Civil War, the Moody-Sankey hymns came along after the Civil War, which serves as a convenient dividing place for these two kinds of black gospel songs. The Fisk Jubilee Singers sang a variety of songs (including "Amazing Grace") in a very "formal" and (classical) "European" presentation, while the "spiritual jubilee tradition" generally refers to songs such as "Go Down, Moses" and "Roll, Jordan, Roll" that were sung before the Civil War within a much more informal presentational format. However, the black gospel music tradition that has evolved really began to take form at the beginning of the twentieth century, when African Americans began to publish their own music.

Early gospel: Dorsey

The key figure in black gospel songwriting and publishing is Thomas Dorsey, who became known as a great personality, composer, publisher, performer, teacher, choir director and organizer as well as minister of music for the Pilgrim Baptist Church in Chicago. More than any other individual, Dorsey defined contemporary black gospel music, even though he was not the first African American to have his songs published. That honor belongs to C. Albert Tindley, who wrote during the early 1900s and was a great influence on the young Dorsey, particularly with his great classics "I'll Overcome" (later altered to become "We Shall Overcome") and "Stand By Me." But it was Dorsey and his songs that unified the movement which became black gospel, giving a definition to the music that has survived through the twentieth century.

Dorsey, of course, was a gigantic figure in gospel music outside his publishing. He trained and accompanied countless singers and fought for recognition against ministries and church musicians who were opposed to their using his songs in churches. Finally, the National Baptist Convention (Negro), which convened in Chicago in 1930, allowed the performance of two Dorsey songs and the reaction from delegates charted the direction for black gospel.

Dorsey had first made a name for himself in secular music, under the name "Georgia Tom," writing "The Stormy Sea Blues" for Ma Rainey and "Tight Like That" for Tampa Red. But with gospel, he found his calling and his true genius took root and flourished. As director of the gospel choir at Pilgrim Baptist Church in Chicago, Dorsey helped a number of singers and had a forum for writing and experimenting with new songs he composed. This material ushered in a new era for black gospel and other new songs emerged as the great singers – most of whom came out of choirs (often Dorsey's) as soloists – developed. As black gospel was recorded and released, these singers could establish national reputations and influence others who would never have seen or heard them otherwise. This served to unify black gospel and increasingly bring it to the attention of white churches and singers, who were influenced by the style and rhythms, and often copied some of the songs and bought some of the records.

The 1930s were Dorsey's most prolific time as the Depression created a need for his optimistic, uplifting songs. He used the blues form in his melodies and his decidedly gospel lyrics were aimed at the poor and outcast. Part of genius is subconscious and Dorsey's use of blues and jazz musical forms seems often not to have been deliberate.

As the music became more accepted in the churches, Dorsey's stature as a songwriter grew until he was, in the words of Mahalia Jackson, "our Irving Berlin." The churches at this time – the early twentieth century – had suffered from a musical lapse and did not supply the emotional support or physical outlet to allow the sermons to be effective. Dorsey, along with singers like Sallie Martin, ushered in the golden era for gospel, *c.* 1945–1960. The era was carried by Dorsey's Gospel Singers' convention, established by him and Sallie Martin in 1932 at the Pilgrim Baptist Church in Chicago. This convention attracted a number of fine singers and became an institution dedicated to advancing gospel as both an art form and a way of life.

Although Dorsey's songs were written first for the black congregations, they also struck a responsive chord with whites. Two top publishers for white churches, Stamps-Baxter and R. E. Winsett, began anthologizing Dorsey tunes in the late 1930s and his two biggest songs, "Peace in the Valley" and "Precious Lord, Take My Hand," were major hits in the white market, becoming million sellers for Red Foley and Elvis Presley, respectively.

Unlike many other forms of gospel music, black gospel has a distinctive, identifiable sound making much use of jazz-derived rhythms and blues singing. This "feeling" in music, which is uniquely black, comes from a deep-felt emotionalism anchored in the African American experience and a certain hopelessness in their earthly life that is balanced with a shining hopefulness in their life to come. The inspiration of trouble, sorrow, thanksgiving and joy in addition to the highly individualistic style of the singers distinguishes black gospel from white. The same song is rarely ever sung the same way twice, with an emphasis on improvisation within the song causing each performance to be a wholly different experience for both singer and audience. This inventiveness on the part of black singers renders it nearly impossible to transcribe this music in sheet form. Although it is put on sheet music, it is rarely sung by African Americans exactly as it is written because the song essentially remains in the oral tradition, learned by rote with the sheet music serving as a source of lyrics for the singers and a guide for basic chords by piano players. While a white chorus will buy a number of copies of sheet music to learn a song – each member using a copy to sing from – the black choir will generally learn the song by ear and the only members with sheet music will be the director and piano player. For that reason, the sheet music for African Americans will usually only include the lead melody line and piano accompaniment while sheet music for whites will have all the parts – soprano, alto, tenor, bass – written out.

The holiness church has also encouraged and inspired blacks to express their own culture, rather than simply to be black versions of white churches. This has meant that black churches' evolution to a mainstream denomination has greatly differed from that of their white counterparts. With churches so segregated, this has served to divide Christianity and gospel music into two distinctive camps, black and white. While each may borrow songs and musical influences from the other, and the performers watch each other to incorporate ideas into their own performances, the congregations remain separate, often unaware of the music of their racial counterparts.

There was some black gospel recorded during the earliest part of the twentieth century (the Fisk Jubilee Singers recorded before World War I) and more recorded after "blues" or "race" became a source of recording material beginning in 1920. During the period 1926–29 when record labels were making field recordings, a large amount of gospel material was recorded. These songs were recorded at the same time that early country and blues were recorded by many of the same people. However, the Great Depression curtailed recording during the 1930s, especially among black performers, because there were few who could afford the records. Also, beginning in 1933, when Prohibition was repealed, there was less recording of gospel – both black and white – because the jukeboxes became the major buyer of records and tavern owners did not like gospel music on their jukeboxes. (It hurt the sales of booze and tended to dampen the "atmosphere" of the juke joints.)

After World War II, gospel music and secular music generally went their separate ways, with gospel recorded on recording labels dedicated to gospel, while secular music was recorded on secular labels.

Jackson, Cooke and Cleveland

Two movements within the church have proven instrumental in both gospel music as well as secular music. The "Holiness movement" in the black church and the "Pentecostal movement" in white churches nurtured a number of early rock'n'roll pioneers, including Little Richard, Elvis Presley, Jerry Lee Lewis, Sam Cooke and others who came out of these churches. This first generation of rock'n'rollers captured the spirit and frenzy of the Holiness or Pentecostal movements in their secular music. This is the essential link between gospel music and early rock'n'roll. However, later generations of rock artists, especially those from Great Britain, did not have this connection with gospel music. Gospel music's influence on secular music tends, therefore, to be through individual performers, not on the music as a whole. (The only exceptions to this are the African American groups such as the Four Tops and Temptations, who were direct descendants of the black gospel quartets.)

In the 1950s and into the early 1960s the most important artists in black gospel music were Mahalia Jackson and Sam Cooke. Both appealed first to the black church audience, then crossed over to the white audience – Mahalia in the gospel field while Sam Cooke made his greatest impact on the white audience in the pop music world.

Mahalia Jackson was clearly gospel music's greatest superstar of this period. Daughter of devout Baptist parents, she idolized Bessie Smith and the blues influence carried over to her own style, although she never left the gospel field. Initially, her repertoire was the Baptist hymns and it was the hymn that held her heart at the end; here, she could pour out her soul, using elements of the blues delivery to make each song a personal statement. During her career, Mahalia was often tempted by others to use her rich and powerful vocal talents to sing music other than gospel. However, the church was embedded in her too deeply and, wracked by guilt, she returned to gospel, where she was clearly most comfortable musically, spiritually, and emotionally.

Mrs. Bess Berman signed Mahalia to Apollo Records, a small firm based in New York, in 1946. Although the relationship with Berman was at times volatile and argumentative, Mahalia produced a string of recordings over the next eight years which were both brilliant and definitive. Her concerts during this time were equally memorial and sometimes she would spend almost half an hour on "Move On Up" or some hymn. Jackson became famous to white American audiences and began to embody the quintessential gospel singer – a black Kate Smith who was saintly, stately, and who sang with incredible power. She had her own radio and television programs beginning in 1954, the same year Columbia Records signed her and instigated a tremendous national publicity campaign on her behalf. A special feature in *Life* followed as commercial success on Columbia catapulted her fame forward even further. In the 1960s she championed the cause of Civil Rights with Martin Luther King Jr., whom she had befriended, and sang at John Kennedy's inauguration in 1961. When King was assassinated, she sang "Precious Lord" at his funeral. The final years were stormy times for Mahalia and her image was tarnished after her marriage and divorce from musician Sigmund Galloway. Still, she continued to record and tour – both internationally and in the United States – until her death at the beginning of 1972. By this time, her name had become synonymous with Gospel Music and she was an international celebrity.

The story of Sam Cooke is one that bears telling because Cooke was the first gospel artist to cross over into the pop world. Marred by a tragic ending, it is nevertheless a lesson in the appeal of gospel music to a young audience and, ultimately, to the secular world. Born in Mississippi in 1931, Sam Cook (no 'e') grew up in Chicago, where his father was a Church of Christ Holiness minister. He joined his two sisters and brother in a group called "The Singing Children" when he was nine and became a member of the Highway QC's a few years later. This latter group was an offshoot of the Soul Stirrers, perhaps the most popular black gospel quartet of the day, who wanted to form a group of young singers as a sort of "farm club" for the parent organization. Here, Cooke was coached by Soul Stirrer member R. B. Robinson, who brought him into the Soul Stirrers when lead singer R. H. Harris left in late 1950.

When Sam Cooke joined the Soul Stirrers they were already the biggest name in black gospel quartet circles. Their sex appeal was also known but it was Sam Cooke who brought the young people in droves to gospel concerts and who became the first "sex symbol" in the music, which he used as a launching pad into pop stardom. Along the way, he created a distinguishable style characterized by his semi-yodel, developed into a first rate songwriter in both the gospel and pop fields, and created the pattern of success which so many others – from David Ruffin to Jerry Butler to Lou Rawls to Johnny Taylor – sought to emulate. Cooke had just passed his twentieth birthday when he sang on his first recordings with the Soul Stirrers in 1951 and the first session yielded the Cooke penned hit, "Jesus Gave Me Water." His singing style, which touched on imitations of Harris and some attempts at "shouting" like other popular lead singers of the day, was quickly settling into his own trademark of sophisticated sanctification, effortless emotions which somehow still touched the depths of passion. Soon, he became the rage of the gospel world as young girls lined up outside venues to wait for him. Cooke, with his movie-star good looks, was the perfect male symbol – young and pretty – with a voice that could send chills up any spine.

Cooke had flirted with the idea of crossing over to pop a number of years
before he actually did so. He wanted to appeal to the white audience – there
was more money, prestige, and fame there – and he knew he could do it best
through pop music. Still, he was reluctant to take the step because of the
usual inhibitions gospel singers feel when singing for "the world." It would
not be until 1957 when he did take that step, and even then he tried to step
back into the gospel world and have his feet in both worlds. But it could not
work that way. Cooke was certainly not the first singer to leave gospel for pop
music. Dinah Washington had done it years before and Ray Charles, only a
year older than Cooke but more a veteran in the recording studio (he had
begun recording in 1948 when he was eighteen), had shown the powerful
appeal inherent in gospel music when he took a traditional gospel song,
put some secular lyrics to it, and delivered it with the gusto and delivery
of a sanctified holiness preacher resulting in the hit, "I Gotta Woman" in
1954. This heralded the r&b explosion when a number of white teenagers
discovered black music and modified it into the rock'n'roll revolution that
began in 1956 with Bill Haley and the Comets' "Rock Around the Clock"
and culminated with Sam Phillip's answer to his quest for a white man who
could sing like a black, Elvis Presley.

Other precedents for African American success in the white market were
the quartets like the Mills Brothers, Ink Spots and Orioles, who presented
a supper-club-type harmony on songs like "Crying in the Chapel." The key
year here is 1954. This is when Elvis made his first recordings in Memphis
for Sun Records, Roy Hamilton had a pop hit with the gospel song, "You'll
Never Walk Alone," and Ray Charles had a pop hit with a gospel-influenced
performance of the bawdy "I Got A Woman." Then in 1955 and 1956, a
succession of African Americans – beginning with Little Richard, Chuck
Berry, Fats Domino, the Coasters, and the Platters – opened up the musical
world for black artists to appeal to white audiences. It was a world ripe for
Sam Cooke.

The Soul Stirrers had been recording for the Specialty label, an independent Los Angeles-based firm, established in 1949 and owned by Art Rupe.
Producer Bumps Blackwell was producing the group and decided to cut
Cooke on some pop songs, although Rupe was against the move since he
had been having success with gospel and did not want that jeopardized.
The first pop single from Cooke, entitled 'Loveable' and released under the
name Dale Cook in 1957, sold about 25,000 copies but raised Rupe's ire to
the point that it ended Cooke's and Blackwell's career with the label. Since
Rupe owed Blackwell money, there was a deal settled where the producer
would get the unreleased tapes from the pop session he had cut with Cooke.
He took these over to another small label, Keen Records, which put out "You
Send Me" in the fall of 1957. It quickly went to the number one position

on both the r&b and pop charts. That began Sam Cooke's pop career and songs like "Wonderful World," "Only Sixteen" and "Everybody Loves to Cha Cha Cha," which he either wrote or co-wrote, followed before he went with R.C.A. There, his career continued to thrive with the release of his third single, "Chain Gang" and culminating with perhaps his finest song, "A Change Is Gonna Come," written after he had heard "Blowin' in the Wind" for the first time. This became a hit after his death in 1964.

Sam Cooke showed that a performer with gospel roots could have a major effect on the pop world, that the talent of gospel performers was first rate and the church – via musicians and singers who received their early training and experience there – would be a major influence on pop music in the rock'n'roll revolution from the mid-fifties through the sixties. Since the rise of soul music paralleled the rise of the Civil Rights movement this places the career of Sam Cooke in the strategic center where gospel, soul, and social activism all fused to bring about a major social revolution.

In the 1970s, James Cleveland became arguably the most important individual in traditional black gospel, because of his influence on other singers, for his help and support of other acts, as an artist whose records had an impact in gospel, and as the founder and president of the Gospel Music Workshop of America. During a period in the late 1960s and early 1970s, when African Americans struggled for self-respect as well as respect from society, Cleveland helped to provide that respect for those who were involved as singers in churches and who attended his convention. With the slogan "Where Everybody is Somebody" and the underlying theology that everyone is someone important in the eyes of God, Cleveland's convention not only helped singers and musicians with their music, it also lifted their hearts, minds, and spirits.

Thomas Dorsey had been the first to gather black choir members together for a convention in 1932. Cleveland's first convention was held in Detroit in 1968 and attracted over 3,000 registrants. The next year almost 5,000 attended the convention in Philadelphia and in 1970 over 5,000 came to St. Louis for the gathering. From there, they held conventions in Dallas, Chicago, Los Angeles, Washington, Kansas City, and New York. At each of the conventions, more classes and seminars were added to help choir members and musicians as well as radio announcers and choir directors. Each night choirs from numerous churches performed and Cleveland often dropped in to perform with a choir or sometimes solo with just a keyboard player (often Billy Preston). He was clearly the center of attention and the magnet that pulled all the disparate forces together. Cleveland's convention managed to speak to the black experience and gratified a desire for significance in a world that often treated blacks as second-class citizens. It made Cleveland more than just another gospel singer.

He had originally made his mark as a piano player, developing a hard, driving style when he played behind Roberta Martin. As a singer, he was influenced by Myrtle Scott of the Roberta Martin Singers and Eugene Smith, also of that group. The flamboyance of Smith was combined with the influences of ballad singer Robert Anderson, jazzman Louis Armstrong and blues singer Dinah Washington, once the lead singer for Sallie Martin. From Washington in particular, Cleveland discovered how to weave gospel and blues into a single style.

James Cleveland was energetic, bright and ambitious. He would go anywhere and ask anyone for a chance to sing and play. In the mid-fifties, Cleveland's arrangements caught the ears of the gospel world as he fused some secular blues and jazz influences into black gospel. He was a member of Albertina Walker's legendary Caravans and worked with such greats as Dorothy Norwood, Inez Andrews, Imogene Green and Norsalus McKissick. He was the architect of the strong, pushing gospel sound, a sound that drove a song. His gruff vocal style came after his voice changed from soprano and, as he drove himself to sing more and more, this fractured his once-beautiful voice into a deep growl. He was not a pretty singer, by anyone's standards, but was one of the most effective in putting across a gospel song and pulling emotions out of a crowd.

After recording for several labels with various groups, Cleveland signed with Savoy Records and released records with the Cleveland All-Stars (featuring Billy Preston on keyboards) and the Gospel Chimes (which featured Jessy Dixon). Finally, Fred Mendelsohn, head of Savoy, teamed Cleveland with the Angelic Choir of Nutley, New Jersey, and that's where he found his niche. Working with this choir, as well as a number of others across the country, Cleveland put out records that featured the choirs as a background and on the choruses while he worked with the verses, molding them to his own style. The 1980s saw him fall out of vogue with some of the younger black gospel performers and fans. While they moved into the slick, smooth sound influenced by r&b and disco, Cleveland remained with his raw, gutsy, blues-based soul sound. The result was a split in black gospel which resulted in two overlapping factions usually referred to as contemporary and traditional.

Conclusion

There have been large changes and progress in black gospel and this has brought it closer to mainstream music and allowed many gospel groups to sound more like the polished performers heard on the radio. The economic panacea of selling black music to white buyers has long been a part of the music industry and now permeates black gospel, letting black gospel have a larger audience, but watering it down from a raw sound to one more palatable for commercial tastes.

Indeed, in many ways they have run into one another; black gospel has influenced white gospel musically while the white gospel field has influenced black gospel from a marketing perspective. White gospel has developed three distinct "genres" in the late twentieth century. First was Southern Gospel, an extension of the singing schools in the South, which evolved into quartets and family groups who, musically, are akin to country music while their harmonies are reminiscent of barbershop quartets. Second is Contemporary Christian Music, which tends to mirror pop music in its sound. This evolved from the Jesus Revolution in the late 1960s, a counter to the counter-culture where young people with long hair and blue jeans sang about Jesus to rock music. Finally, there is "church" or "praise" music, which is music sung in churches by choirs and congregations. These songs blend the old-time hymns (some of which are still used) with contemporary songs written by songwriters steeped in pop music. Contemporary Christian Music dominates radio airplay on "Christian" stations and sales in Christian bookstores.

Black gospel does not have the network or organization for its music like white gospel. While contemporary Christian music has the network of Christian bookstores to carry their product and a number of gospel radio stations, as well as TV programs and print media to showcase the music, black gospel is generally sold in independently owned record stores (called Mom and Pop stores) in the African American sections of town and heard on black radio stations as a one-hour program. Christian bookstores have been reluctant to stock black gospel, perhaps not trusting black American Christianity as well as not finding a great demand for the distinctive black gospel record. There are, however, a number of blacks who have become increasingly acceptable to this white market; unfortunately, the gospel performer almost has to choose his own audience and those black performers who have whites buying their albums can often find they have lost their black audience.

5 Twelve key recordings

GRAEME M. BOONE

A crucial factor in recognizing blues and gospel songs as what they are, is the way they sound. Through close focus on twelve recorded performances, this chapter illuminates characteristic details of form, style, genre, and historical period. These recordings should not necessarily be understood as the "best" of their type, but as examples which typify the features under discussion.

"Fred McDowell's Blues"

Fred McDowell, voice and guitar; Miles Pratcher, guitar; Fanny Davis, comb.
Recorded September 21, 1959 in Como, Mississippi.

Recorded in early stereo during a field trip by Alan Lomax, "Fred McDowell's Blues" is suggestive of a very old style of folk blues; the generic title reflects its non-commercial origin. The two guitars provide a steady foundation, with Pratcher setting down a regular "boom-chick" beat in a swing rhythm and McDowell adding a simple repeating melodic pattern or other more prominent lines. The guitars offer a riveting support, and foil, to McDowell's voice. Their pace is upbeat, and speeds up during the song; this is characteristic of older folk blues, as is the single "drone" chord to which they remain anchored throughout. McDowell's guitar reinforces Pratcher's rhythm, but he plays other lines too, often doubled by the kazoo-like sound of Davis' comb. He tends to play a simple, repetitive riff, and when he sings, his guitar loosely follows his vocal melody. He also takes two brief instrumental solos in the middle of the song, similar to the lines he plays while singing. In the solos you can hear especially clearly his use of a slide, making a fluid and sharp-edged sound similar to that of the comb.

McDowell's voice is fairly rough and tense, and its vibrato is irregular; his articulation is loose, his words not always easy to understand. His singing is unhurried and rhythmically free, floating over the pulse of beats and bars (see Ex. 5.1). The vocal lines tend to begin around the second beat of the bar, and accented syllables commonly fall in syncopated fashion on weak beats; but each line is different, and placed somewhat unpredictably in relation to the great open spaces of the accompaniment. The song has a loose but recognizable tune, organized into three phrases that correspond

	1	2	3	4	1	2	3	4	1	2	3	4	1	2	3	4
BEATS	1	2	3	4	1	2	3	4	1	2	3	4	1	2	3	4
LYRICS		Lord	I'm			goin	down	south		ba	by					
BEATS	1	2	3	4	1	2	3	4								
LYRICS	I	believe	I	will		carry	my	girl								
BEATS	1	2	3	4	1	2	3	4	1	2	3	4	1	2	3	4
LYRICS																
BEATS	1	2	3	4	1	2	3	4	1	2	3	4	1	2	3	4
LYRICS																
BEATS	1	2	3	4	1	2	3	4	1	2	3	4				
LYRICS		Lord	I'm			goin	down	so-	uth							
BEATS	1	2	3	4	1	2	3	4	1	2	3	4				
LYRICS		I	believe	I	will					carry	my	girl				
BEATS	1	2	3	4	1	2	3	4	1	2	3	4	1	2	3	4
LYRICS																
BEATS	1	2	3	4	1	2	3	4	1	2	3	4	1	2	3	4
LYRICS																
BEATS	1	2	3	4	1	2	3	4	1	2	3	4	1	2	3	4
LYRICS		Lord	they	[tell	not	to		bry		you]*						
BEATS	1	2	3	4	1	2	3	4								
LYRICS		ba-	by	dey's		out	dis	world.								
BEATS	1	2	3	4	1	2	3	4	1	2	3	4	1	2	3	4
LYRICS																
BEATS	1	2	3	4	1	2	3	4	1	2	3	4	1	2	3	4
LYRICS																
BEATS	1	2	3	4	1	2	3	4	1	2	3	4	1	2	3	4
LYRICS																

*The words are difficult to decipher here. Lomax transcribes this line as "Lord, they say them doctors."

5.1. Lyrics and rhythm in the first stanza of "Fred McDowell's Blues."

to the three textual lines of each stanza. In the second stanza, for example, the first half of the first line is almost entirely pinned to a high melodic note (the octave: "Lord *I'm goin' down to Louisiana* . . . "); the second half-line moves gradually downward, to conclude an octave lower (on the root or tonic: ". . . I'm gonna buy me a mojo *hand*"). The second line is functionally identical to the first, differing only in slight details ("Lord I'm goin' *down* to *Louisiana*, I'm gonna buy me a mojo *hand*"). The third line, by contrast, begins on the bottom note, then rises and falls back to the same note twice, making a double-arch shape ("*I'm* gonna fix my baby *so she won't* have no other *man*"). The distinction between a higher first pair of lines and a lower concluding line is common in blues melody. Also typical are the two basic phrase shapes (descending line; arch-shaped line) and the division of each line into two halves. But McDowell's singing is flexible. In the first stanza, for example, his third line starts high like the first two lines, rather than low; in the final stanza, the third line in drawn out to twice its expected length by repetition of its first half. Such unpredictable elements illustrate the deeply improvisatory quality of blues singing, and of McDowell's style in particular. The open-ended, shouted qualities of his style are also characteristic of the field holler, or outdoor worksong sung by African Americans in the days of slavery and sharecropping. This is another feature suggestive of early folk blues.

The wailing quality of McDowell's voice and guitar has much to do with his use of blue notes. These are flexible melodic pitches (or pitch "spaces"), opposable to the fixed pitches (or pitch "points") that form the basis for most melody, and many musical instruments, in the Western traditions. Blue notes are commonly situated around the third, fifth, and seventh degrees of the scale. The effect of these notes is striking; it includes moaning, crying, and other expressive vocal sounds that cannot be captured within a common fixed-pitch melody, but that have musical value in the blues. Blue notes also have a harmonic dimension, since their fluid intonation (most famously, the blue third) creates dissonance against the fixed note that underpins them in supportive chords (such as the major third in Pratcher's tonic chord). McDowell's singing, like his guitar playing, is full of blue notes; in his first line, for example, there are several – "Lord I'm goin' down south baby, I^7 be*lieve*^{7} I *will*^{5} *carry*^{5} *my*^{3} girl" – although no simple labeling can capture the richness of his intonations. Significantly, he never sings on the second or sixth degree of the scale. His melodic language is pentatonic, touching on only five scale degrees, of which three involve blue notes (1, *3*, 4, *5*, *7*).

The lyrics of the song are in simple blues form. Each stanza comprises three lines: the first two are identical, the third rhyming (line structure: **a a b**; rhyme scheme: a a a). Poetically as well as musically, the repetition of the **a** line allows the performer to reaffirm an idea or feeling. That build-up leads to the release of the concluding **b** line, with its rhyming word and its own consequential idea or feeling. The repetition of the **a** line serves another purpose also: it gives the performer time to think about a **b** line, and is therefore useful when stanzas are improvised or modified on the spot, as often happens. In this recording the third stanza consists of three identical **a** lines, without any contrasting **b** line. This seems to have been a feature of early blues, in which the antecedent/consequent format of **a a b** was not so firmly entrenched. Here again, "Fred McDowell's Blues" is suggestive of an old style.

Do the lyrics, taken together, tell a coherent story? It depends upon your point of view. Some stanzas appear in many blues songs, and their inclusion could have been simply improvised. Then again, we can infer a progression of ideas centering on the singer's mate. First he wants to take her with him (first stanza); then it becomes clear that he wants to control her (second). But that leads to thoughts of sadness (third) and suicide (fourth), implying the futility of his efforts with her, or more broadly, in life. The reality may reconcile both views. Blues lyrics that circulate and recombine in countless songs tend to center on elemental issues of personal suffering and survival, sex, and love; individual songs will draw on this poetic resource, arriving at an individual presentation that paints its own picture, but also relates to other songs and to universal blues themes. The simplicity and open-endedness of images such as McDowell's only makes them more evocative; in this manner, good blues singing can take on an existential dimension, communicating the deepest emotions with an incisive, uncluttered directness.

"Cross Road Blues" (take 1)
Robert Johnson, voice and guitar.
Recorded November 27, 1936 in San Antonio, Texas.

Due to its remarkable expression and subject matter, "Cross Road Blues" is one of Robert Johnson's best-known songs. Its style is rooted in the folk blues tradition, but reflects the virtuosity and self-consciously distinct style of a professional musician. Johnson's rhythm is similar to McDowell's in its intensity, its regular, swinging beat, and its gradually quickening tempo; but Johnson is playing alone, and his guitar has to satisfy the roles of rhythm, chords, and melodic highlights all at once. His pace is also slower, with a plodding, insistent quality that recalls boogie-woogie piano style. The effect of the song is no less energetic, though, thanks to his rapid ornaments and stream of musical ideas.

Johnson's bars and phrases are stretched or compressed at whim. Here or there the four-beat bar literally skips a beat, especially just before the beginning of stanzas; and pauses between phrases are drawn out to make room for the spinning out of an idea on guitar (see Ex. 5.2). There is some similarity to McDowell's approach, but Johnson leaves much less open space, and his volatile solo guitar style gives his music a dramatic edge. From time to time he strums the beat on the low strings alone; more commonly he strums other strings too, beating out rich chordal riffs that alternate between the mid- and high range of the guitar, a diversified technique that leaves much of the texture implied. Like McDowell, Johnson plays high riffs with a slide, giving them an especially liquid, wailing quality. Occasionally, he also strikes just one note and lets it ring in the air for a moment. This occurs as a response to words in the middle of the third line of each stanza, e.g., "I believe to my soul now – [*twang*] – old Bobby's sinkin' down" (riff **d** in Ex. 5.2). Johnson seems to be having fun with the guitar, at the same time demonstrating mastery of its possibilities and confidence that the listener will be able to hang on for the ride.

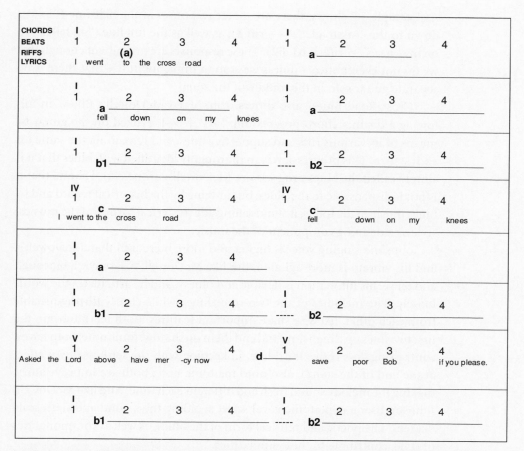

5.2. Lyrics, guitar riffs, rhythm, and chord progression in the first stanza of "Cross Road Blues" by Robert Johnson.

        The restless energy of Johnson's guitar makes for a fascinating relationship with his voice. McDowell, too, played high-pitched guitar riffs while singing, but Johnson's riffs are distinct musical ideas (numbered **a** through **d** in Ex. 5.2), following their own path through the stanza. They anchor the rhythm by beginning at the same place in each bar, namely, the first offbeat, whereas his vocal phrases move around quite a bit. As a result his voice and guitar compete, in a high-powered musical dialogue. An essential factor here, as in McDowell's singing, is the pause after each line, and shorter pause after each half-line: these breaks allow the meaning of the words to sink in, a new breath to be drawn, expectation to rise concerning the next phrase, and the instrument(s) to respond to the voice. McDowell's guitar retreated to a supportive role during his pauses, but in "Cross Road Blues" the pauses between vocal lines are filled by the attention-grabbing guitar riffs.

As Example 5.2 shows, there are guitar responses at the half-line ("I went down to the crossroad..." → riff **a**), as well as the full line ("... fell down on my knees" → riffs **a, b1, b2**). These responses are prominent enough that we do not even notice – unless we stop to think about it – that there is no separate guitar solo in the middle of the song.

"Cross Road Blues" also differs from "Fred McDowell's Blues" in following a distinct chord progression: I–IV–I–V–I, evoked on the guitar by means of its various riffs and supportive lines, and remaining the same for each stanza. This progression is so thoroughly identified with blues that it is simply called the blues progression. McDowell's drone chord shows that it is not indispensable to the blues, but judging by the historical record and by blues music made today, it stands alongside the lyrical form and the musical style as a defining component of the music.

Johnson's singing voice is higher and more mercurial than McDowell's, and his vibrato is more agitated. But like McDowell, his tone is a bit rough and tense, his intonation is flexible and bluesy, and he articulates the words loosely. The melodies of the two recordings, while clearly distinguishable from each other, likewise share important features. Both tend to begin the first two lines on a high note and end them on the low, tonic note; both have a contrasting, less active third line, in keeping with the settling-down effect at the end of the stanza, also onto the tonic note; both are improvisatory, making the melody sound fresh and different each time. And like McDowell, Johnson uses a pentatonic vocal scale, avoiding the second and sixth scale degrees. The poetic and musical form of the blues, as well as commonalities of style, contribute to these similarities.

The words to "Cross Road Blues" give a highly individual twist to this song. In the rural South, the crossroad, leading to and from many places, was itself an important place for travel and commerce, and therefore also a place of possibilities and danger. Johnson plunges us into a mood of anxiety and even desperation, without telling us exactly why. In the first stanza, the crossroad seems like a point of fateful, perhaps spiritual, encounter; this recalls the folk theme of a crossroad as the scene of a Faustian meeting with the Devil. He then proclaims his loneliness and isolation (stanza 2), and the inevitable, transitory passage of day and of his own life, with reference to fellow bluesman Willie Brown (3 and 4). The final stanza, making reference to a "sweet woman," suggests that even love and sex, those staples of blues and of life, cannot protect Johnson from his fate. Approaching the momentous crossroad, he does not know which way to go and finds himself utterly alone. Johnson delivers these lines simply, and with a sense of humor matched by his playful guitar style; it is when we stop to think about them that their dark meanings begin to emerge and coalesce.

CHORDS	I		I⁷		IV		V	
BEATS	1	2	3	4	1	2	3	4
CORNET								
LYRICS	I hate	to	see			the	evening sun	go
CHORDS	I				I⁷			
BEATS	1	2	3	4	1	2	3	4
LYRICS	down.							
CHORDS	IV				ᵇVI⁷		V	
BEATS	1	2	3	4	1	2	3	4
LYRICS	I hate	to	see			the	evening sun	go
CHORDS	I				I			
BEATS	1	2	3	4	1	2	3	4
LYRICS	down.							
CHORDS	V				II⁷		V	
BEATS	1	2	3	4	1	2	3	4
LYRICS	It makes me		think I'm			on my last		go
CHORDS	I	I⁷	dim.	IVm	I	dim.	V	
BEATS	1	2	3	4	1	2	3	4
LYRICS	round.							

5.3. Lyrics, cornet interjections, rhythm, and chord progression in the first stanza of "St. Louis Blues" as recorded by Bessie Smith.

"St. Louis Blues"

Bessie Smith, voice; Louis Armstrong, cornet; Fred Longshaw, organ.
Recorded January 14, 1925 in New York City.
Composer: William Christopher Handy.

Historically speaking, the "St. Louis Blues" is probably the most famous of all blues. It started out as a written composition – a musical blueprint, as it were, scored for voice and piano only, and lacking in blue notes and other details that can't be written down in common notation. Poetically, the composition is mostly in **a-a-b** blues form; its chords are based on the standard I–IV–I–V–I blues progression, but show interpolations as well (affecting bars 1, 2, 6, and 10–12; see Ex. 5.3), reflecting a more sophisticated harmonic vocabulary typical of urbane popular music. The melodic language is similarly sophisticated, using all degrees of the scale plus several chromatic inflections. The rhythm is arranged in a neat twelve-bar pattern, divided into three equal segments corresponding to the three poetic lines. Each four-bar segment is divided into two halves, each of about two bars' length, the first half containing one sung poetic line and the second half providing space for a response from the instrumental accompaniment. Further, each poetic line

	1	2	3	4	1	2	3	4
CHORDS	Im				Im			
BEATS	1	2	3	4	1	2	3	4
CORNET								
LYRICS	Saint Louis		wo- man			wears	a	dia-mond
CHORDS	V				V			
BEATS	1	2	3	4	1	2	3	4
LYRICS	ring							pulls the
CHORDS	V				V			
BEATS	1	2	3	4	1	2	3	4
LYRICS	man		a- round			by	her	a- pron
CHORDS	Im				Im			
BEATS	1	2	3	4	1	2	3	4
LYRICS	strings.							
CHORDS	Im				Im			
BEATS	1	2	3	4	1	2	3	4
LYRICS		Wasn't for	powder			and this	store-bought	hair
CHORDS	V				V			
BEATS	1	2	3	4	1	2	3	4
LYRICS								-
CHORDS	V				V			
BEATS	1	2	3	4	1	2	3	4
LYRICS	-	the man	I love			wouldn't go	no-	where
CHORDS	Im		II		V⁷			
BEATS	1	2	3	4	1	2	3	4
LYRICS			no-		where.		[I	got them...]

(CHORDS bottom row: Im (beat 1), II (beat 3), V^7 (beat 1 of second half))

5.4. Lyrics, cornet interjections, rhythm, and chord progression in stanza 3 of "St. Louis Blues," as recorded by Bessie Smith.

is itself divided into two halves, lasting about one bar each, with a break in the middle ("I hate to see" – *pause* – "the evening sun go down"). In sum, Handy's rhythmic format is identical to Johnson's, except that it has been ironed out into perfect regularity.

Handy's melody follows blues form, with the second phrase a variant of the first. Each phrase also falls into two halves, like the poetic lines. Instead of starting high and falling low, its **a** phrases adopt a more demure shape, rising and then falling onto the tonic note in a double arch. This style is common in blues melody; we heard something like it in McDowell's **b** line. Used as an **a** line, however, it suggests less of a shouting and more of a moaning style. In the absence of true blue notes, which cannot be written down in traditional sheet-music notation, Handy cleverly switches back and forth between major and minor thirds (e.g., "*I* hate *to* see . . ." = major third, plus brief minor-third grace note; "the morning *sun* go down" = minor third).

There is more to the composition than a blues scheme: its third stanza is sixteen bars long rather than twelve, has a I–V–V–I progression rather than I–IV–I–V–I, is in **a-a-b-b** poetic form rather than **a a b**, and switches to a minor key (see Ex. 5.4). The explanation for this difference is to be found

in the **A-A-B-A** form of popular song at that time: after two repetitions
of an initial section (**A**), a contrasting section was sung (**B**), and the initial
section then returned to round off the song. "St. Louis Blues" follows just
this pattern: its **A** (blues) sections are stanzas 1, 2, and 4 and its contrasting
B section is stanza 3. Ingeniously, then, the song is simultaneously cast in
blues and popular-song form.

The rhythmic and formal regularity of "St. Louis Blues" is due to popular musical conventions and notation, which by their very nature encourage
a predictable consistency suitable for dancing and for a variety of performing groups and contexts. Handy's syncopation is similarly controlled; he
even adds a familiar Latin touch by including a tango rhythm in the piano
introduction (which, incidentally, was not included in our recording). With
"St. Louis Blues," then, we pass from the relative idiosyncrasy of unwritten
folk-derived styles, preserved in recordings, to high commodification, mass
audiences, and urban environment of popular song disseminated in published scores. "St. Louis Blues" is a good example of what has been labeled
"city blues," as opposed to the preceding "country blues" styles.

The most famous city-blues singers were women, and the most famous
among them was Bessie Smith. Our recording of "St. Louis Blues" was made
at the height of her popularity, in 1925, and it also features the young cornet
star, Louis Armstrong, whose stunning improvisational abilities were setting
the new world of jazz on its ear at just this time. The third performer on
this recording, Fred Longshaw, was a popular and capable accompanist for
recordings of the period. The use of harmonium outside of church may
seem strange to modern ears, but it was common in homes and theatres
around the country.

The recording generally follows the form, harmonies, and melody of
the sheet music, but the musicians add significant elements too, beginning
with Armstrong's superb cornet. Because, as we have seen, blues form includes a call-and-response element, and because Armstrong's role in the
song is to respond to Smith's vocal lines, his sinuous improvisations feel
completely appropriate even though they do not figure in the sheet music at
all. Meanwhile, Longshaw successfully adapts Handy's piano part to suit the
softer and slower attack of the organ, while Smith's singing brings Handy's
tune to life in a powerful, unforgettable way. Like other city-blues singers,
she tended to take her blues at a slow pace, which allowed her to dig into blue
notes and draw out the pathos of the subject matter. She follows the broad
outlines of Handy's written melody but constantly transforms it, in true
blues fashion, to bring out the individuality of each moment. Her voice is
extraordinarily powerful, and bends the tune in a subtle way that, of course,
cannot be notated. "*Feeling to*morrow like I *feel* today": this line is a good
example of how she presses into the microtonal spaces inside a blue note,
making a sinuous melody that almost hurts in the strength of its bluesy

dissonance. The recording only begins to evoke the impact of her performances, which, according to eyewitnesses, could make listeners weep with emotion.

The lyrics of the song express a suffering that could be linked either to a specific situation or to a general, existential one. The first stanza expresses a morbid sadness; the second a desire to leave town. The third stanza explains this situation, comparing a woman from St. Louis, who has fine things and control over her man, to the speaker, who has neither. The final stanza gets to the heart of the matter: the singer has the "St. Louis blues," bemoaning the coldness and distance of her lover. To go with this summation, Handy introduces a new melody that is the most catchy, "riffy" one of all, a true hook that draws listeners and musicians back to the song over and over again. It has a repetitive rhythmic bite, and it leans particularly hard on the blue third, alternating with the tonic note: "*I've got the* St. *Louis* blues *just as* blue *as I* can be." In this fashion, Handy "signifies" the blues in a heightened way, one that in almost any setting will be understood as bluesy. It is a masterful touch, one that has surely contributed to the legendary stature of the song.

"Rock the Joint"
Jimmy Preston and His Prestonians: including Jimmy Preston, lead voice, alto saxophone; Danny Turner, tenor saxophone.
Recorded May 1949, in Philadelphia.
Composers: Harry Crafton, Wendell Keane, Harry Bagby.

During the swing era a variety of African American styles emerged that combined elements of jazz, blues, popular song, and earthy dance music. Jimmy Preston's "Rock the Joint" exemplifies the transition from smooth thirties swing, via r&b, toward the hard edge that would characterize rock'n'roll in the 1950s. It includes lead and backup singers, accompanied by alto and tenor saxophones, piano, bass, and drums. The tempo is fast, and rendered in a shuffle (swing) rhythm with a very strong backbeat (on snare and piano), bound to a rollicking boogie line (on piano and bass, doubled at first by unison horns). The harmonies follow a straightforward blues progression, with few of the interpolations typical of more sophisticated jazz. The effect is intense, celebratory, and highly danceable; the title and lyrics evoke dancing and never use the word "blues."

The lyric form is that of *refrain* blues, a common alternative to the simpler verse-blues form of the preceding examples. It retains the basic sectional pattern of **a a b**, but reorganized to set "verse" lyrics to the **a** section and "refrain" lyrics to the **-a-b** sections. Here, the refrain involves a repeated riff,

CHORDS		I				I			
BEATS	4	1	(2)	(3)	(4)	1	(2)	(3)	
LYRICS	We're gon-na	DRINK and	rock	both	young		and old		
CHORDS		I				I7			
BEATS	4	1	(2)	(3)	(4)	(1)	2	3	
LYRICS		We're	gon-na	do	the	jel- ly	roll.		
CHORDS		IV				IV			
BEATS	4	1	2	3	4	1	2	3	
LYRICS	We're gon-na	ROCK			rock	this	joint,		
CHORDS		I				I			
BEATS	4	1	2	3	4	1	2	3	
LYRICS	We're gon-na	ROCK			rock	this	joint,		
CHORDS		ii				V			
BEATS	4	1	2	3	4	1	2	3	
LYRICS	We're gon-na	ROCK			rock	this	joint,		
CHORDS		ii	V			I		V7	
BEATS	4	1	2	3	4	1	2	3	(4)
LYRICS	We're gon-na	ROCK	THIS	JOINT	TO-night.				

5.5. Lyrics, rhythm, and chord progression in "Rock the Joint."

one so catchy that a whole separate chorus is made out of it, as well as a tag ending: "We're gonna rock this joint tonight." The tune fills up the stanza space, leaving only a little room for call and response between voices and instruments, but its riffs and interplay between solo (for the verse lines) and backup singers (for the rest) more than make up for that. The verse melody leans on the seventh degree of the scale ("We're gonna *drink* and *rock* both *young* and *old*, *we're* gonna do ... "), then rises to the octave for climactic effect (... "the *jel*lyroll") before falling to the tonic below. This leads straight into the refrain, whose bluesy riff falls from the fifth degree to the third and, ultimately, the tonic. The high first line (verse) and lower concluding lines (refrain) recall the melodies of McDowell and Johnson; and Preston also uses an extroverted, shouting vocal style. His melodic language is based on the same pentatonic vocabulary as theirs, too, except that the sixth degree is sung once in the tune (in the second line: "We're gonna *do*") and used again for effect as the last note of the song.

The boogie accompaniment intensifies the rhythm of the words, which reflect their subject perfectly as they alternate between onbeat and offbeat placement, suggesting both the strength and the swing of rocking (and contrasting, in this respect, with the subtle, unpredictable vocal rhythm of the first two songs). This alternation is shown in Example 5.5, with strong onbeat syllables shown in small capitals and strong offbeat syllables shown in italics. The basic riff, "we're gonna ROCK ...," ends on the downbeat of the bar, followed after a pause by "... *rock this joint*," sung entirely on offbeats by the backing chorus, as if by rocking the beat so strongly they could shake the pillars of your body and soul, if not the dance hall. In the last line of the stanza, the two halves are finally merged into one: "we're gonna ROCK THIS JOINT . . . ," the last three words falling square onto the beats of the penultimate bar – a masterful shift onto the beat that brings everything together, followed by the clinching word ". . . TO*night*" with its final syncopated bite. Needless to say, the endless repetition of these words drives the point of the song home with perfect intensity: this is music not to draw you into the singer's troubles, fears, or hopes, but to get you right out onto the dance floor.

Solid basis in the blues, predominance of riffing, upbeat tempo, boogie influence, hard rhythmic drive, and dance-oriented lyrics in a jazz-derived band: these were classic elements of dance-oriented r&b in this era. The saxophone solos include similar heightened elements, by honking (i.e., overblowing), buzzing (i.e., singing into the horn while playing), and shrieking high notes. Perhaps most remarkable of all, though, is the influence of gospel church style, building on the strong rhythm with intense and spontaneous interjections from the group, especially in the instrumental episodes, to suggest a community of shared ecstasy in which everyone has a voice.

"(I'm Your) Hoochie Coochie Man"
Muddy Waters, vocal and electric guitar; Little Walter, harmonica; Jimmy Rogers, electric guitar; Otis Spann, piano; Willie Dixon, electric bass; Fred Below, drums.
Recorded January 7, 1954 in Chicago.
Composer: Willie Dixon.

No blues style has been more influential since 1950 than the "Chicago" style, forged by transplanted southern African Americans who adapted their downhome approach to the world of urban Chicago and the new possibilities of electric amplification. If there is a primary figure in this group, it would have to be Muddy Waters. "Hoochie Coochie Man," composed by fellow bluesman Willie Dixon, offers a fine example of Waters' mature style, having the full complement of his fifties band with two guitars, piano, harmonica, and prominent drums. The band's signature timbre, featuring distorted amplification and strong reverb, supports the powerful wail of Waters' unforgettable voice and gives powerful reinforcement to the lyrics.

At the beginning one is almost startled by the alternation of a loud riff, played in heavy, unhurried counterpoint by all the instruments together, and an echoing silence. Leading the riff is the bluesy, liquid-molten wail of Little Walters' harmonica. The riff, and the silence, are repeated nine times

CHORDS		I				I		
BEATS	4	1	(2)	(3)	4	1	(2)	(3)
BAND								
LYRICS		The gypsy woman told my mother,				before I was born		

CHORDS		I				I		
BEATS	4	1	(2)	(3)	4	1	(2)	(3)
BAND								
LYRICS		I got a boy	child's comin,			he's gonna be a son of a gun		

CHORDS		I				I		
BEATS	4	1	(2)	(3)	4	1	(2)	(3)
BAND								
LYRICS		He's gonna make pretty womens				jump	and	shout

CHORDS		I				I		
BEATS	4	1	(2)	(3)	4	1	2	3
BAND								
LYRICS		Then the world want to know				what's	this all a-bout	-

CHORDS		IV				IV		
BEATS		4	1	2	3	4	1	2	3
BAND	-								
LYRICS	But you know	I'm he-re,					e-		verybody	-

CHORDS		I				I		
BEATS		4	1	2	3	4	1	2	3
BAND	-								
LYRICS	knows I'm here,								-

CHORDS		V				IV		
BEATS		4	1	2	3	4	1	2	3
BAND									
LYRICS	Well you know I'm the	hoo-chie	coo-chie man,				e-		verybody	-
verybody									

CHORDS		I				I		
BEATS		4	1	2	3	4	1	2	3
BAND	-								
LYRICS	knows I'm here.								-

5.6. Lyrics, instrumental/vocal alternation, rhythm, and chord progression in "Hoochie Coochie Man."

in all. After two iterations Waters begins singing in the spaces between riffs, setting his fateful lyrics to hover in the silence like a call, answered by the affirmations of his band. Eventually the stop/start style gives way to a continuous playing as Waters shifts from the gypsy woman's old predictions to the present moment: the hoochie coochie man is here now, and everyone knows it.

The later stanzas continue to expound on Waters' dark, supernatural power over women, and they follow the same format, that of refrain blues: each stanza begins with four lines (eight half-lines) of verse lyrics, set to the initial I chord, and ends with two lines of refrain lyrics, set to the remaining chords. As Example 5.6 shows, the length of the verse section is eight bars as opposed to the normal four, making a total of sixteen bars for the form as a whole. The extra four bars of verse allow Waters to amplify his hoochie coochie narrative, as well as the dramatic interplay of silence and sound leading up to the refrain. The lyrics are so prominent, and their expressive message so compelling, that (as in "Cross Road Blues") the lack of a separate instrumental solo is not missed.

A closer look at the first stanza, shown in Example 5.6, illuminates some of what is so dramatic about its performance. With his strong, rough voice, Waters sings the verse lines entirely off the downbeat, in that space left between the instrumental riffs, immediately creating tension between the downbeat, as fundamental rhythmic anchor, and his own authority. The two finally collide on "*what's* this all about," preparing the very different lyric rhythm of the chorus: now Waters' phrases, rather than hovering in the middle of the bars (beats 2–3), lean hard on the downbeat, once directly ("I'm the *hoo*chie coochie man") and otherwise indirectly through intense syncopation around the fourth beat ("I'm here"). These rhythms convey both intentness of meaning and a potent sense of swing. As for the melody, Waters' chanted delivery of the verse lines makes it different from any of those we've discussed so far: they are mostly recited on the tonic degree and accented by the blue third. During the chorus Waters finally lets out his giant shouting voice, which abruptly rips up to the seventh degree ("*every*body knows I'm here"), returns to it for the naming that defines the song ("I'm the *hoochie coo*chie man"), and caps that with a unique rise to the octave in the final phrase (amplifying "*every*body") before falling back down to settle on the tonic. Earlier, we noted Jimmy Preston's use of a climactic high note late in the stanza; Waters uses the same idea, along with the same pentatonic language, occasionally touching on the sixth degree ("I'm the hoochie coochie *man*"). Here, the effect is one of virile power, first intently brooding and then, at just the right moment, roaring.

"The Thrill Is Gone"
B. B. King, vocal and lead electric guitar; Hugh McCracken, backup guitar; Paul Harris, electric piano; Gerald Jemmott, electric bass; Herbie Lovelle, drums; string orchestra arranged by Bert DeCoteaux.
Recorded June 24 or 25, 1969 in New York City.
Composers: Roy Hawkins, Rick Darnell.

If Muddy Waters led the way in developing the saltiest-sounding blues, his contemporary B. B. King, from Memphis Tennessee, did the same for the sweetest. King favored the rich, relatively clean bell-like tone of a hollow-body Gibson for much of his career (model ES-335, contrasting with Muddy Waters' hardbody Fender telecaster), and he tried, as he noted more than once, to "make it sing like the human voice" – in particular his own voice, which is celebrated for its warm timbre, fine vibrato, and sincere depth of expression. He also favored toned-down themes for his lyrics, emphasizing love, desire, and loss, but steering clear of misogyny, violence, and other darker themes. No B. B. King song is better known than "The Thrill Is Gone," a popular hit recorded at the time of his comeback in the late 1960s. The song combines the solid foundation of King's signature style with the influence of contemporary rock and soul music, including a tremolo-laden electric piano, booming electric bass, orchestral string section, and straight (rather than swing) rhythm. The form is twelve-bar verse blues, with a twist: it is in a minor key, which lends an element of pathos to the song (as it did also in the third stanza of "St. Louis Blues"), matching the lyrics, which express almost unrelieved sadness and loss. King uses his voice and his guitar with equal skill to delve into this mood.

The vocal melody is pentatonic, and based on a classic motive, falling from the blue fifth through the blue third to the tonic; there has been a variant of it in every song I've analyzed, with or without an arch shape, and it is basic to his style:

(Th') thrill^5 is^4 gone^3, the$^{(1)}$thrill^5 is^4 gone$^{4-3}$ a^{1}way^1

As we might expect, he repeats the melody for the second line. For the third, he rises up to a climax on the blue seventh ("you know you *done* me wrong") before returning to a variant of the falling-fifth motive as a conclusion. Each stanza repeats this melody, but he renders each stanza, and indeed each line, in a different way.

King's lyrics do not tell a linear story so much as circle around a simple theme, namely the singer's mournfully telling his lover that the relationship, and its magic, are over. His delivery almost never falls where one would expect, but instead hinges on offbeats, the offbeats of offbeats, or in the mysterious, ambiguous crevices between rhythmic pulses. The first phrase of the first stanza, for example, if speaking were a guide, would be rendered as "The *thrill* is *gone*," with emphases on the italicized words. King does sing the phrase that way; but he counterbalances that emphasis, too, by beginning the phrase after rather than on the downbeat, and then placing "is" on the beat while the stronger syllables "thrill" and "gone" fall in the cracks on either side (see Ex. 5.7). This placement is so subtle that we don't even notice it unless we listen closely. It is typical of King's deep sense of swing; but it also serves to bring out the special meaningfulness of each word at this specific moment in the song. The same treatment is applied to all the words of the stanza, which avoid emphasis on beats and never fall on downbeats. Only at the very end, on "day," is there an unequivocal arrival of a strong word squarely on a strong beat (although here, too, it is not the downbeat, but the weaker third beat of the bar).

CHORDS	Im				Im			
BEATS	1	2	3	4	1	2	3	4
LYRICS	The thrill	is gone,					the thrill	is gone

CHORDS	Im				Im			
BEATS	1	2	3	4	1	2	3	4
LYRICS	a- way.							

CHORDS	IVm				IVm			
BEATS	1	2	3	4	1	2	3	4
LYRICS	The thrill	is gone	ba-	by,			the thrill	is gone

CHORDS	Im				Im			
BEATS	1	2	3	4	1	2	3	4
LYRICS	a-way.							

CHORDS	bVI				V			
BEATS	1	2	3	4	1	2	3	4
LYRICS	You know you	done me	wrong	ba-	by,			and you'll be

CHORDS	Im				Im			
BEATS	1	2	3	4	1	2	3	4
LYRICS	sor-	ry some	day.					

5.7. Lyrics, rhythm, and chord progression in the first stanza of "The Thrill Is Gone."

King's guitar style in this song is also as remarkable for what it does not do as for what it does. It engages, for example, in almost no call and response with his voice (that is left, to some extent, to the backup guitar and piano). Instead, he uses unhurried solos to frame the sung stanzas. These solos are in his signature single-note style, making frequent use of bent notes and relying extensively on the tonic, as well as the blue third and fifth above it (akin to his vocal lines). They include a couple of recurring phrases, but he does not build to any strong climax, nor does he emphasize some other form of expressive development through the song. Like his singing, his guitar solos help establish a mood, and then dwell in it. In the middle of his concluding solo he rises to repeated notes on the high octave for a moment, after which the solo very gradually melts away.

A string orchestra is added to the recording, in a popular style typical of the era. It enters with the second stanza, in slow notes, then becomes more active behind the following guitar solo with a slow violin melody. During the third stanza the strings play low in their range; during the fourth, the cellos become active and the violins rise to a higher level. The long concluding guitar solo section is particularly atmospheric. The violins return to the slow melody of the first solo for one chorus, then settle on a single chord that is held for the rest of the solo while the cellos return to the melody they played in the fourth stanza. There are no more chord changes from this point on: the music simply floats forward to its fade-out ending.

BEATS	1	2	3	4	1	2	3	4
RHYTHM	X	x	X	x	X	x	X	X
LYRICS	Oh,				high	on	de moun-	tain
BEATS	1	2	3	4	1	2	3	4
RHYTHM	X	x	X	x	X	x	X	X
LYRICS	Well,				high	on	de moun-	tain
BEATS	1	2	3	4	1	2	3	4
RHYTHM	X	x	X	x	X	x	X	X
LYRICS	Well,				high	on	de moun-	tain
BEATS	1	2	3	4	1	2	3	4
RHYTHM	X	x	X	x	X	x	X	X
LYRICS	Jes- us	gon- na	make	up	my	dy-	in	bed.

5.8. Lyrics and rhythm in the first stanza of "Jesus goin' make up my dyin' bed."

"Jesus Goin' Make Up My Dyin' Bed"
Dock Reed, Vera Hall, and Jesse Allison, voice and body percussion.
Recorded May 26, 1939 in Livingston, Alabama.

This traditional spiritual was recorded during a field trip by John Lomax. The singers are not professional and the context is not church or stage, but rather a private home. The only accompaniment is a regular percussive beat that reinforces the consistent duple meter: though somewhat obscured by the poor recording quality, it appears louder on 1 and 3, weaker on 2 and 4 (see Ex. 5.8). This suggests a "down," march-like bodily rhythm, opposite to the "up," back-beat rhythm so basic to later gospel styles, but it is based on the same swinging movement from side to side. The rhythm is straight, not swung.

The three voices sing a straightforward and repetitive tune that, in each line, begins on the beat but ends with a syncopated twist. Its four phrases are cast in an **a-b-a-c** pattern common in old popular and folk music. The **a** phrase here begins on the tonic and forms an arch shape, rising to the fifth degree; the **b** phrase intensifies the same shape, beginning on the fifth and rising to the octave before it too falls back down to the tonic. After the return of **a**, phrase **c** makes a satisfying conclusion. It begins on the third, rises to the fifth, and falls to the tonic – thus echoing the preceding arch shapes – but then falls further, down to the low fifth, before resolving home. This four-square stanza, divisible into two paired phrases or four individual phrases, is very different from the threefold blues structure; and yet the song has similar arch-shaped phrases and blue inflections. The melodic style is pentatonic, too (although, as performed here, often quite high in the inflections of its third, fourth, and seventh degrees). These qualities are common to a great many spirituals, reflecting a tradition of improvisation and adaptation in African American sacred song that is every bit as rich and elemental as that of the blues, and intimately related to it. The somewhat tense timbre also recalls that of blues singers, although the sustained vibrato adds a particular sweetness that sometimes distinguishes sacred singing.

A contrasting tune, appearing at two points in the song, plays the role of a verse in relation to the above refrain tune. Its melody is also in four phrases, but is literally more "suspenseful" as all of them begin on and emphasize the higher fifth degree; three of the four end on it as well, only the last one coming to rest on the tonic. It thus expands on the upward intensification that was already noted in the refrain stanza's **b** phrase.

The words are the expressive focus of this music, and their patterning interlocks with that of the tune. The lyric form of the main stanza is **a a a B**: the first three lines are identical within each stanza, while the fourth line, identical among the stanzas, caps them with the song's focal theme. This creates a kind of verse-refrain structure within the stanza, for example:

> Oh, high on de mountain
> Well, high on de mountain
> Well, high on de mountain
> *Jesus gonna make up my dyin' bed.*
>
> Jesus, I been in de valley
> Jesus, I been in de valley
> Jesus, I been in de valley
> *Jesus gonna make up my dyin' bed.*

Powerful in this form is the threefold intensification of the **a** line, which is given particular emphasis by the reinforce-and-return melody noted earlier. The **b** line appears as a release from this pattern, as well as a refrain. Again, we note a similarity to blues form; but the difference between three- and fourfold structure is fundamental.

The words of the other, "verse" melody follow a pattern of **a b c d**, showing no repetition of lines and no later recurrence. But a sense of poetic resonance is gained through rhyme between the second and fourth lines, for example:

> When you see me dyin'
> I don't want you to cry
> All I want you to do for me
> Is to close my dyin' eyes.

The song's message is characteristic of many antebellum spirituals, juxtaposing in simple but evocative terms the terrible inevitability of death to the saving grace of Jesus. There is no narrative unfolding to the progression of ideas; instead, they suggest a simple but potent meditation on Christ's world- and life-embracing power, invoking mountains and valley, kneeling in humility, and sleeping, all in relation to death. The almost constant repetition and recurrence of lyrics is ideal for driving their meaning home; and it also invites participation on any level, ranging from casual or improvisatory to intensive and highly planned.

Our three performers give some idea of that participatory range. Dock Reed leads the group, closely followed by Vera Hall and Jesse Allison. Often the latter two do not come in on the first word(s) of a phrase or stanza. This lends a call-and-response element to their interaction with Reed, and suggests that they may be spontaneously picking up on some of the verses he chooses to intone. All three sing the same melody, but with varying approaches to rhythm, melody, and intonation; the effect is heterophonic and at times even fleetingly polyphonic. Such variable interplay between their voices, immediately striking to the listener, has an inspired and beautiful effect. As in much African American music it conveys the sense of a shared musical community, in which each singer finds value in adding a distinct and heartfelt voice to the group.

"Golden Gate Gospel Train"
The Golden Gate Jubilee Quartet: Henry Owens, first tenor;
William Langford, second tenor; Willie Johnson, baritone;
Arlandus Wilson, bass.
Recorded August 4, 1937 in Charlotte, North Carolina.

In essential ways "Golden Gate Gospel Train" is the opposite of the preceding recording. Made by a group of young urban musicians well known from their performances on radio, it is their own composition, recorded in order to be sold, and closely reflects contemporary trends in popular music and culture. Both songs are about redemption, but where the slower, meditative spiritual projected solitude, submission, and stasis in the face of death, the upbeat, extroverted "Gospel Train" projects opportunity, celebration, and movement toward heaven, never mentioning the word "death" at all. This quality exemplifies the jubilee, the leading form of African American popular sacred song during the 1920s and 1930s. "Gospel Train" also conveys the hip urbanity of other popular vocal music of the time, using jazzy sound effects and a light, somewhat nonchalant tone. Its central metaphors emphasize loud machinery and people going places, unlike those of "Jesus gonna make me," which evoked quietude and timeless, immutable nature.

From its very first note "Gospel Train" throws the listener into movement. The first words and keening whistle seem already in the middle of something, and offbeat phrasing in the fragmentary opening stanza makes it impossible at first even to be sure where the downbeat is. But soon we

									I		I		V+		V+	
CHORDS									I		I		V+		V+	
BEATS	[1	x	2	x	3	x	4]	x	1	x	2	x	3	x	4	x
LYRICS	Gos	pel			train		is	com ca	in'							You'd
RHYTHM--FILLER	Wa-		a-		a-		aw		baw	goo	doo	goo	doo	goo-doo	goo-doo	goo-doo
RHYTHM--BASS	Wa-		a-		a-		aw		baw		baw		baw		baw	ba-baw

CHORDS	I		I		V+		V+		I		I		V+		V+	
BEATS	1	x	2	x	3	x	4	x	1	x	2	x	3	x	4	x
LYRICS	bet	ter	get	your	bus'	-ness			right.							You'd
RHYTHM--FILLER	doo	goo	doo	goo	doo	goo-doo	goo-doo		doo	goo	doo	goo	doo	goo-doo	goo-doo	goo-doo
RHYTHM--BASS	baw		baw		baw		baw	ba-baw	baw		baw		baw		baw	ba-baw

CHORDS	I		I		V+		V+		I		I		V+		V+	
BEATS	1	x	2	x	3	x	4	x	1	x	2	x	3	x	4	x
LYRICS	bet-	ter	set	your	house	in or	-der		friends				You		know	the
RHYTHM--FILLER	doo	goo	doo	goo	doo	goo-doo	goo-doo		doo	goo	doo	goo	doo	goo-doo		the
RHYTHM--BASS	baw		baw		baw		baw	ba-baw	baw		baw		baw		baw	ba-baw

CHORDS	I		I		V+		V+		I		I		V+		V+	
BEATS	1	x	2	x	3	x	4	x	1	x	2	x	3	x	4	x
LYRICS	train's		gon	na	be	here	to-	night.					[Don't	you		hear ...]
INTERJECTION									Ah,				Lord!			
RHYTHM--FILLER	train's		gon-	na	be	here	to-	night						goo		doo
RHYTHM--BASS	baw		baw		baw		baw	ba-baw	baw		baw		baw		baw	ba-baw

5.9. Vocal rhythm, lyrics, and chord progression in the first full stanza of "Golden Gate Gospel Train"

orient ourselves in a steady duple meter with straight rhythm. As in other earlier twentieth-century popular music, you can hear both a slower beat (marked by the numbers in Ex. 5.9) and a faster one (whose additional beats are marked by an x); a stimulating "backbeat" element is added by rhythmic patterns and arrivals emphasizing the in-between beats. In keeping with the strong train rhythm, Owens' lead tenor voice sticks close to the beat, but he still spices it up with occasional syncopations: in Example 5.9 a softer instance is shown on "bus'ness" and "be here," and a more hard-swinging one on "order friends."

The formal outlines of the song conform to jazz-influenced popular music of the time, with a series of four-line stanzas punctuated by improvisatory solos. There is no separate refrain stanza but, as in the preceding spiritual, a refrain line occurs at the end of every stanza. Telling of the momentous arrival of the gospel train, the words exhort the listener to get ready for it, while the singers evoke train sounds – bell, whistle, wheels turning – all with their voices alone. Owens asks the listener: "Don't you hear the whistle blowin', Hear the bells a-tolling, Don't you hear the engine exhaustin' friend?" pointing to its different sounds even though we clearly hear them already; in this manner he underlines their doubly metaphorical nature. The real gospel train is metaphysical too, but a leap of faith will be necessary to hear or see it, and to climb on board. According to the refrain, "The train's gonna be here tonight"; the song's train is a harbinger of the true gospel train.

The tonality of the song blends bluesy intonation (especially the wailing third) seamlessly together with the fixed-note approach commonly used in harmonic progressions. Such exquisite blending is possible because the voices in this *a cappella* performance adjust microtonally at all moments to optimize either a wailing or fixed note, depending on what is needed. It is also possible because the song is based on just one chord, the tonic (home) major chord. As shown in Example 5.9, this chord does alternate with another chord during the stanzas, but that other chord is an unstable passing chord (augmented dominant, minus its third) that serves as a foil to the tonic, to which it inevitably returns. Using a single "drone" chord as harmonic anchor helps the song to focus on the train's rhythmic drive and on the exhortation of its gospel message.

In addition to all this, there are four "instrumental" solos in the latter part of the song – a nice touch, using voices to imitate mechanical sounds and then, on top of that, imitating another "machine" that is actually a musical instrument, whose plaintive sound imitates the human voice. That muted-trumpet sound, together with the bluesy falling line it intones over and over, recalls a tradition in jazz going back to Duke Ellington's jungle music, which itself harked back to an imagined primal earthiness of African American folk expression. Ellington's music was both playful and serious, depending on what you heard in it; the quartet's can be too.

The instrumental-style solos are emphatically based on blues style, and use its falling-fifth and arch shapes. The sung melody of the stanzas consists of variations on a basic idea, beginning on the high octave (or sometimes on the fifth), falling through blue seventh, fifth, and third, and coming to rest either on the third (in the stanza's third line) or the tonic (in the first, second, and fourth lines). This shape is similar to blues phrasing and is based on the same pentatonic framework, but the effect is distinctive due to the crisp articulation of notes, syllables, and rhythm as well as the four-square stanzaic form.

"Take My Hand, Precious Lord"
Comparison of three different versions, plus the original written composition.

Within African American gospel traditions there is arguably no more famous song than "Precious Lord," whose language, melody, and harmonies evoke strength and profundity, as well as a simplicity that is adaptable to many different styles. Recorded by solo singers in the "Watts style" of slow, free rhythm as well as in medium and upbeat arrangements, it is a good candidate for comparing different interpretations. We shall begin with a close look at the "blueprint" of the written composition, and then consider three recordings.

"Precious Lord" was created by Thomas Dorsey in 1932, essentially by adapting the poetry of a hymn by the earlier nineteenth-century composer

George N. Allen to the melody from another hymn by that same composer. The lyrics proceed in a stream of mostly self-contained anapests and occasional iambs, with emphasis on the last syllable in each cell (e.g., "Precious *Lord* | take my *hand* | Lead me *on* | let me *stand*" or "When my *way* | grows *drear*"). These create a gentle, undulating rhythm, organized into three stanzas on the following model:

	number of syllables	rhyme
Precious Lord, take my hand	six (or five)	a
Lead me on, let me stand	six (or five)	a
I am tired, I am weak, I am worn.	nine (or seven)	b
Through the storm, through the night	six	c
Lead me on, to the light	six	c
Take my hand, precious Lord, lead me home.	nine	B

While the majority of lines have a binary structure ("Precious Lord | take my hand"), every third one has a ternary structure ("I am tired | I am weak | I am worn"). This extension places additional weight on the line ending, suggesting not only an important arrival but an emphatic pause that would fill out the binary rhythm of the preceding lines ("I am tired, I am weak | I am *worn.* – – —"). This arrival is doubly heightened at the stanza endings, since the last line is identical in all three stanzas, serving as a refrain: "Take my hand, Precious Lord, lead me *home.*" The word-reversal of this refrain line in relation to the poem's opening line ("Precious Lord, take my hand") creates a lovely sense of recall and earnestness, as do further recurrences of "precious Lord" in later stanzas. The words address God directly, asking for support and guidance amid the hardships and fears of life. The simplicity of language (river, storm, night; hand, day, light) allows for a maximum of emotive resonance. "Home" at the end of each stanza signifies heaven, and also God's grace in the here and now; it is the culminating idea of the poem, and a central topic of gospel lyrics.

The melody enhances the poem's formal and expressive qualities. Its rhythm is set in a gently lilting $\frac{3}{4}$. Like the poetry, it follows a consistent pattern (eighth note, eighth note, half note), moving quickly through the weaker syllables to linger on the strong, and the pause on the end of the longer lines is doubled in length. The tune falls into two closely related halves, each containing three lines of poetry. The shorter (**a**) poetic lines that begin each half are paired together to make a broader, gently arching melody spanning four bars; the longer (**b**) lines that conclude each half are extended in their musical endings so that they too last for four bars. In this way, the stanza's music is multiply articulated, being divisible into two halves, four equal phrases, six phrases corresponding to individual poetic lines, or fourteen sub-phrases corresponding to individual poetic cells. The tune is in a folk-like style, and remains the same for all stanzas; but it contains a subtly dramatic element, for it begins quite low (on the third degree, six steps below the tonic) and reaches a climax, in the fourth of its six phrases, nine steps higher (on the fifth above the tonic). The melodic language is mostly pentatonic, but it is in a major mode, and conforms to Protestant hymn style and related folk traditions by preferring the second and sixth degrees to the fourth and seventh. For the sake of discussion, we will call the resulting framework (based on 1, 2, 3, 5, 6) a "major" pentatonic framework; it contrasts sharply with the minor or "blues" framework (based on 1, 3, 4, 5, 7) that has characterized almost all of the preceding songs in this chapter. The harmonies of the setting are straightforward and strongly grounded; most phrases begin on the tonic chord, and the underlying progression is simple and almost entirely in the diatonic major (using I, IV, and V chords). Overall, the song recalls numerous older melodies (e.g., "Amazing Grace"), a kind of family relationship that we also noted among blues melodies. But individual touches, some of which have been mentioned above, give the song its own personality. Most of them stem from Allen himself; but important ones stem from Dorsey, too, notably the inspired combination of melody and poetry, and a brief second rise to a high fifth degree near the end. As one might expect, there is no hint of blues intonation in the written composition; the only ornaments are occasional appoggiatura-like leaping notes, occurring at the end of lines 1 and 3, and in the middle of line 4. Mostly stemming from Allen, these do not imply any use of blue notes.

Five Soul Stirrers of Houston: Rebert H. Harris, first tenor; Ernest R. Rundless, second tenor; Senior Roy Crain, utility vocal; Mozel Franklin, baritone; and Jesse Farley, bass.
Recorded *c.* 1939 in Chicago or Los Angeles.

This was one of the very first recordings of the Soul Stirrers, who went onto become a leading gospel quintet in the next two decades. Despite its poor technical quality and surface noise we can already hear the classic sound of this group, showing a soulful, hard edge and bluesy roughness that sharply contrasts with the smooth, light touch of the Golden Gate Quartet and announces a new, more r&b-influenced era in gospel style. Using common gospel technique, their arrangement begins with a slow, dramatic introduction. R. H. Harris intones the tune in stop/start rhythm, pausing at the end of each three-syllable cell. The rhythm here is free, though it roughly approximates a very slow $\frac{4}{4}$ time, with each three-syllable cell filling a bar (two eighth notes followed by one dotted half-note). His strong voice is supported by block chords from the other singers, and the feeling is already urgent: the faster syllables move quickly, the supporting harmonies are close and their rhythms sharp, and all voices are sustained with intensity. Harris' melody is fairly straightforward, but still brimming with blue twists and turns, leaning especially on the tonic and the blue third. This quality increases when, after this introduction, the tempo shifts to a medium-upbeat pace in $\frac{4}{4}$ time and the supporting voices slip into a highly repetitive vamping style, using a "clanka-lank"-type rhythm to spice up the chord progression; their words are not easily discernible, but seem mostly based on "lead-a-me." Over that support Harris improvises an utterly bluesy interpretation of the song, beginning again with the first stanza, proceeding through the three stanzas, and then concluding with a reprise of stanza 1. Like Dock Reed's singers but with more urgency, Harris juxtaposes onbeat and offbeat rhythms, often ending his phrases with a syncopated twist; Dorsey's melody, though discernible, is swallowed up in his sustained outburst of musical testimony. Excepting the half-cadence arrival on the second degree midway through each stanza, his singing is marked by insistence on the tonic degree, to which almost every melodic idea (short or long) returns. Around that note of conviction he spins out a passionate string of formulas that adapt the tune to the blues-type pentatonic framework, with the addition of the second scale degree as needed to fill out the melody. Most commonly he rises to the blue third; often, expending more energy, he rises to the blue fifth. He rarely goes higher than that until the last chorus, where, in a subtle climax, he fleetingly hits a high seventh three times, opening up a maximum of vocal range. A more aggressive climax occurs earlier, however, in preparation for the third stanza: here he simply lets go with a passionate "well" on the fifth that seems to go on forever (it lasts for about six seconds).

Clara Ward, voice; with Herbert Francis, organ.
Recorded *c.* 1952, possibly in Philadelphia.

Clara Ward was admired for her musical and expressive style in slow songs, and this recording of "Precious Lord" provides a classic example. Unlike the Soul Stirrers' arrangement, hers is in a non-metrical style reminiscent of old-time hymn singing. The pace of the music is very slow; in her two-and-a-half-minute performance, she includes only the first stanza and the second half of the last one. Having no beat or meter, its rhythms are governed by her majestic sense of flow, which gives a distinct shape to each separate phrase. An electric, church-style organ alone provides accompaniment: it follows her closely, supporting her performance with swells and occasional interpolated harmonies. Ward's strong voice builds on the tune, but differently from Harris: the basic three-syllable rhythmic cell is her primary phrasing unit, and she renders it in a constantly shifting way. Often both the first and last syllable are extended, in a broad oratorical gesture (long–short–longest: "*Pre*cious *Lord, take* my *hand*"). It is chiefly on the longer syllables that she adds embellishments or "curlicues," with turns, rises, and elaborate falling motives that display a more agile voice than Harris'; some recur over and over, giving a unique signature to her style. Her ornaments draw mostly on the major-type pentatonic framework of Dorsey's song, but they also color it with an unabashedly blue-inflected approach. Particularly striking is her frequent descent to the sixth degree of the scale, below the tonic, as the lowest or ending note of her rapid formulas (e.g., "Lead me *on*"), a note she tends to intone a bit sharp. Above all, Ward shows keen sense of drama in the song, enhancing the rise and fall of its melody with various kinds of intensification, pause, and development. Like Harris, she uses higher notes for increased passion, and she reaches a culminating high octave at two different moments, both times around the climactic point of Dorsey's melody (e.g., "through the *storm*"). The second time, she prolongs the high moment a great deal by interjecting extra words on that note ("Hear my cry, *God! Ah*, hear my call, *Yes*, hold my hand"), before gradually settling down to conclude; such heartfelt improvisation gives her performance the effect of beauty, deep emotion, and the conviction of truth. Curiously, blue sevenths occur in these high climax phrases, in both stanzas; and in the second stanza, the outburst of falling ornaments at this point actually triggers a shift over to the blues-type pentatonic language for a few seconds, which returns to the major-type only for the final phrase of the song.

Mahalia Jackson, voice; with Mildred Falls, piano; Ralph Jones, organ. Recorded March 27, 1956 in New York City.

Mahalia Jackson, often called the queen of gospel singers, worked with Dorsey in the 1930s and 1940s when she was known for a passionate singing style; but she made this recording during her Columbia recording years, when her singing style was toned down and "polished" for a broad listening public. She is accompanied by the remarkable Mildred Falls on piano, as well as Ralph Jones on a muted organ part: the organ lays down a sustained but quiet harmonic foundation, while the piano embellishes Jackson's performance with arpeggios and other harmonic commentary that is just quiet and smooth enough not to get in the way of her voice. The technical quality of the engineering is high on the recording, especially by comparison with the preceding ones: it captures the full sound of the instruments, while foregrounding the richness and depth of Jackson's voice. Her basic approach, like Ward's, is slow and a-metric, and she uses the same rhythmic technique based on the three-syllable cell, drawing out and ornamenting the longer syllables at will; but her performance is more contained and introspective, and even slower in pace. The sheer power, beauty, and range of her vocal sound is breathtaking. It is marked by a distinct grainy quality, not unlike that of a blues singer, but also tempered here by a vibrato and intonation not far from classical music. At some moments her head voice dominates, light and sweet, at others it's her chest voice, belted and growling like a blues shouter; sometimes she sings with a piercing nasal projection and sometimes from the throat, with a covered, rounded sound.

She adopts the underlying major-type pentatonic framework of Dorsey's melody, as Ward did, but adds far fewer ornamental and bluesy touches. Not once does she strike a blue fifth (although once she does hit a fifth a bit low, on "pre*cious Lord*" at the end of the first stanza); and she hits blue sevenths at just two points in the song, in identical descending ornaments following the climactic "through the storm" phrases of the second half of each stanza – the same place Ward did, though without going so far as to shift to blues-type pentatonicism. Jackson's major thirds, sometimes approached by upward scoops, follow the written melody; they resonate richly with the supporting harmonies, and enhance upward melodic motion, often (though not always) occurring in rising phrases (e.g., stanza 1: "*Precious Lord*," "*I* am worn," "*Through* the storm"). Her blue thirds, commonly intoned with scooping or wavering, tend to intensify the expression and the forward, downward melodic motion; they are usually found in descending lines (e.g., stanza 1: "*Lead me on*," "*I* am tired," "Lead *me on*"). We hear something of this distinction in Ward's style, but Jackson makes much more out of it, combining a hotter blues approach and a sweeter, "straight" style of singing without sacrificing either. She arrives at a kind of hybrid – a classical gospel style, one might say – in which both idioms find their place. With her extraordinary voice, background, and musical sensibility, Jackson could make such an accommodation sound natural and deeply meaningful.

"Oh Happy Day"
The Edwin Hawkins Singers.
Recorded 1968 in Berkeley, California.

As far as the general public is concerned, there may be no more familiar recording in gospel music history than "Oh Happy Day." Featuring the commanding solo voice of Dorothy Morrison, the power and excitement of a full gospel choir, and the rich styling of soul music, it sold over seven million records and helped to launch the "contemporary" sound that has dominated gospel music since that time. Expressing the joy of being saved by Jesus, its lyrics are highly repetitive: the refrain stanza, itself containing seven statements of the title line "Oh happy day" and six of the line "When Jesus washed," is sung four times through, and the single-verse stanza, in which each line is repeated, is sung twice. This repetition actually works to the song's advantage, thanks to the glorious sound of the choir and soloist, the reassuring, uplifting message, and the soulful style, itself built on repetition.

The music begins with an instrumental introduction featuring the backup band of piano, bass, drums, and conga, intoning the chords of the second half of the main stanza. With their Latin-tinged syncopated rhythms, vamp-like pattern, and relaxed tempo, the instruments are already steeped in a soul idiom; their harmonic language is straightforward, and almost always proceeds in simple repeated pairs of chords. Over this support the soloist and choir alternate in call-and-response fashion throughout the song, with the call usually falling on one chord and the response on another, forming two layered melodies. These are diatonic, with no chromatic inflection and, in the choral parts, relatively little blue intonation either. The refrain stanza has an **a-b-a** form, with two "Oh happy day" sections (on I and IV chords) framing a "When Jesus washed my sins away" section (on IIm and V). Morrison's solo melody follows a broad but low arch form in the refrain, its first line rising from the low tonic to the third degree ("Oh happy day"), its second line falling from third back to tonic, with a flourish ("when He washed"), and its third line settling more firmly on the tonic ("He washed my sins away"). The choral responses, meanwhile, interweave their own simple pattern of chords whose melody (i.e., soprano) line is always higher than Morrison's, alternating first between the fifth and sixth degrees, then between the sixth and seventh – never making it as far as the octave – and finally returning to fifth and sixth. Overall, the pattern in this refrain is one of relaxed motion back and forth, with some intensification in the middle section. That motion blends with the bodily rhythm of the gospel chorus as it swings from side to side.

The verse stanza shows a marked increase in excitement: both chorus and solo are louder and more passionate, and their melodies begin and stay in a higher register, rising well above the octave; the chorus finishes some phrases with a shouted high note. In a deft touch Hawkins reverses their roles here, the chorus first setting forth the lyric ("He taught me how . . .") and Morrison responding with her own melodic commentary. The chord changes move only half as fast in this stanza, abandoning the back-and-forth motion of the refrain, and the characteristic syncopated refrain rhythm is likewise smoothed out. The formal structure of this stanza is **a a′**, with longer musical phrases repeated to two rhyming poetic lines ("He taught me how to walk right and pray / And in rejoicing every day").

The song as a whole is made up of these two stanzas, repeated in the following order: refrain, refrain, verse, refrain, verse, and an extended concluding section based on the refrain. Rejecting the contemporary fade-out technique for ending the song, the group begins this conclusion with a long and exciting vamp, featuring classic gospel backbeat clapping by the chorus, jubilant alternation of choral refrain and Morrison's improvised interjections, and the soul-inspired accompaniment with its seventh chords

Stanza line 1

CHORDS			I								IV					
BEATS	x	4	x	1	x	2	x	3	x	4	x	1	x	2	x	3
SOLO	Oh		hap	py	day											
CHORUS						Oh		hap-	py		day					

Stanza line 2

CHORDS			I								VI7					
BEATS	x	4	x	1	x	2	x	3	x	4	x	1	x	2	x	3
SOLO	Oh		hap	py	day											
CHORUS						Oh		hap-	py		day					

Stanza line 3

CHORDS			IIm								V					
BEATS	x	4	x	1	x	2	x	3	x	4	x	1	x	2	x	3
SOLO	When	Je	sus		washed											
CHORUS						When		Je	sus	washed						

Stanza line 4

CHORDS			IIm								V					
BEATS	x	4	x	1	x	2	x	3	x	4	x	1	x	2	x	3
SOLO	Oh				when	He washed										
CHORUS								When	Je	sus	washed					

Stanza line 5

CHORDS			IIm								V					
BEATS	x	4	x	1	x	2	x	3	x	4	x	1	x	2	x	3
SOLO	When	Je-	sus		washed								He	washed	my	sins
CHORUS						When		Je	sus	washed						

Stanza line 6

CHORDS			I								IV					
BEATS	x	4	x	1	x	2	x	3	x	4	x	1	x	2	x	3
SOLO		a-		way,			Lord.								Ah,	
CHORUS						Oh		hap	py		day					

Stanza line 7

CHORDS			I								IV					
BEATS	x	4	x	1	x	2	x	3	x	4	x	1	x	2	x	3
SOLO				hap-	py	day										
CHORUS						Oh		hap-	py		day					

5.10. Chorus and solo lyrics, rhythm, and chord progression in the refrain stanza of "Oh Happy Day," as recorded in 1968 by the Edwin Hawkins Singers with Dorothy Morrison.

and relaxed instrumental embellishment. The music then subsides to a relatively quiet ending, via a restatement of the refrain stanza.

"Oh Happy Day" remains compelling from beginning to end thanks to its catchy rhythmic, melodic, and harmonic patterns, the extra excitement of its verse and conclusion, the fine singing of its choir, and perhaps above all the stunning solo voice of Dorothy Morrison. Her lines are always rather brief, alternating as they do with the choral lines, but they are marked by rich, sometimes rough tone, a full and consistent vibrato, a remarkably wide vocal range, a fine sense of swing, and a power that easily matches the chorus at full tilt. Her rhythmic sensibility is illustrated in the initial refrain stanza (shown in Ex. 5.10), where she consistently syncopates the downbeat, attacking no strong syllable on it until the very last line ("*happy day*"); this is an approach close to the one we noted in B. B. King's singing. Also central to her style are added ornamental figures, improvised for the most part in a major-type pentatonic scale, with falling motives related to Clara Ward's though with less intense blue inflections. Most importantly, she sings her curlicues with flair, conviction, and musicality; in a lesser voice they might have sounded vain or superficial, but in hers they sound appropriate and entirely convincing.

6 "Black twice": performance conditions for blues and gospel artists

STEVE TRACY

The Blues started from slavery. MEMPHIS SLIM

Why was I born in Mississippi when it's so hard to get ahead?
Every Black child born in Mississippi, you know the poor child was born dead.
J. B. LENOIR

Any discussion that purports to examine the social, cultural, political, and economic conditions under which blues and gospel performers have had to operate must take as its own genesis the dawn of the North Atlantic slave trade, surely one of the bleakest sunrises in human history. Nearly 250 years of the enforced system of legal chattel slavery in North America established a network of laws, attitudes, and strategies, imposed with a frequently vigorous and hateful, sometimes paternalistic and condescending, or misguided benevolent force that contributed to shaping the physical, spiritual, psychological, social, and cultural lives of the enslaved and their descendants. Reconstruction brought hope, post-Reconstruction disappointment, and the Jim Crow-era dismay and anger as a result of the unfulfilled promises of one of humanity's most promising systems. "I got the back woods blues," sang Rosa Henderson in 1924, "but I don't want to go back home," the indignities of the Jim Crow cars[1] and southern mistreatment overwhelming her desire to visit her childhood abode. Cow Cow Davenport expressed the sentiment, too – "I'm tired of being Jim Crowed, gonna leave this Jim Crow town" – but he left room open at the end of his song to sing about coming back if the North did not fulfill its promise – an all-too-common occurrence.

Most blues and many gospel performers, after all, have been African Americans, the descendants of slaves, and heirs to this racism and discrimination in their myriad forms, from the far greater likelihood of existing below the poverty level, to discrimination in housing, employment and education, to discriminatory attitudes that associate the "race" with intellectual inferiority and intensified appetitive passions, to the subtle and not-so-subtle internalization of such attitudes to create at times a self-hatred or self-destructiveness. Racism and paternalism – northern and southern, liberal and conservative, radical and reactionary – frequently resulted in the objectification of African Americans as primitive, exotic, ignorant, violent, sexualized, degraded non-humans, forming a network of attitudes and values that protracted the brutalizing environment under which slaves labored in the peculiar institution. When African American singers sang of being poor and a long way from home or motherless children, they delivered a message that was a culmination of these various pressures and prohibitions shaped into the optimistic art of the creator. Optimistic because it was implicitly or explicitly a defiance of defeat through the acts of creating and performing themselves; optimistic in its assertion of voice and humanity in a world that restricted or denied them both; optimistic in its utilization of a syncretistic African American style that would eventually transform American culture; optimistic in the ultimate philosophical assertion that "the sun is gonna shine in my back door some day."

Rural blues singers, whether playing on porch, at a house party or country supper, in the juke joint, on the street corner, on the circuit with a medicine or stage show, carried this with them. Urban blues singers, on the streets, in neighborhood clubs, on the road, in larger theatres, carried this with them. Performers both rural and urban "adopted" by Leftist political organizations who put them in the Café Society or From Spirituals to Swing or political rallies or in "folk" gatherings, or "rediscovered" and marketed to coffee houses, colleges, and international and domestic folk, jazz, and blues festivals, carried this with them. And they all carried this with them as entertainers whose aesthetics, demeanors and recordings were shaped in part by these attitudes. Black, frequently poor, sometimes illiterate, often self-taught or informally trained rather than conservatory graduates, they suffered the prejudiced standards of elitist social and cultural arbiters with a hardihood that bespoke their faith in themselves, their talent, their tradition, and/or their God as they persevered in creating a body of work that was its own most effective response to a warped hegemonic imposition of values. The difficulties for black performers were such that B. B. King often asserted, "if you was a black person singing the blues, you black twice" (Kostelanetz 1997: 174).

If we believed Blind Willie McTell's response to John Lomax's queries about the mistreatment of African Americans in the South in 1940 – "They haven't much trouble, the people, nowadays . . . Cause the white peoples mighty good to the Southern people, as far as I know" (McTell 1940) – we might think that social conditions had been greatly ameliorated less than halfway through the twentieth century. However, as Lomax presses McTell, it becomes clear that McTell is uneasy with Lomax's probing, unwilling to discuss the situation honestly with a white man – a situation that likely contributed to self-censorship in a variety of performance situations, though not always. A year later, Son House recorded "County Farm Blues" for

John's son Alan, describing with certitude the fate of a black man who did "anything that's wrong" in the South: a sentence to the county farm, where the bossman Captain Jack would "write his name up and down your back." Neither was this mistreatment limited to the South: Rosa Henderson bemoaned the demeanor of Chicago policemen, who "can't police at all" and "send you 'way for absolutely nothing at all." Other songs such as Blind Blake's "Third Degree Blues" make clear this constant threat of violence and incarceration under which blacks (performers included) existed. The connection in Blake's recording is made explicitly to the slave past:

> But they put me in jail, didn't give me no bond.
> It made me think about my people's that's dead and gone.

Obviously the problems faced by African Americans in hometowns, where they might be better known to the local authorities, would be present, even amplified, in unfamiliar settings, where charges of vagrancy might be applied to a likely worker who could be pressed into cheap labor by local enforcement officials.

Such a long history of enforced labor sometimes provoked a weariness that was vented with bitter humor: "I wouldn't tell a mule to get up, Lawd, if he set down in my lap," Big Bill Broonzy exclaimed in "Plow Hand Blues," lamenting a controlling system that treated him more like an animal than a man. It prompted him to attempt to break the cycle of discrimination by rejecting his rural enslavement: "Now I declare I'm through with plowin', that's what killed my old grandpap." But how to escape sweating back of a mule's behind from sunup to sundown? A number of people were drawn to the options of becoming a preacher or a musician, or both. As Son House sang in 1930, "I'm gonna be a Baptist preacher, and I sure won't have to work." But just because they were no longer snuffing up mule manure did not mean the air was clear – or the water tasted like wine – for performers in their chosen professions. The lives of blues and gospel performers were still fraught with specific professional dangers and indignities peculiar to the lives of African American performers.

"When I first started to hoboin', I took the highway to be my friend," sang many an itinerant blues and gospel performer about the optimistic beginning to their ramblings. Whether they were walking or riding their thumbs, or braving the more dangerous route of riding the "blinds" or the rods of a train, where the dangers of exposure to the elements, loss of limb – as in the case of Furry Lewis – and falling to their deaths were ever present, they were exercising their post-Civil War right to increased geographical liberation in large numbers. Unfortunately, the road can be a very fickle friend to the traveling musician, and many a blues and gospel singer has lamented the rigors of the road, from transportation to accommodations to law enforcement to club conditions and crowded itineraries. In the words of John Cephas:

> But I think it takes a certain kind of person to handle the aggravation of being on the road so much. Its definitely a strain. I mean, we've been on the road so long that I keep a bag packed all the time. When I come home, I just take out all the dirty clothes and put in some other clothes and set my bag by the door.... People don't really realize how much work goes into being a musician. They just see you on stage and naturally they think that playing music is easy for you. And usually it is, onstage. But they don't know how far you've driven to get there or how far you have to drive after you leave or that you have to play some more gigs the next day.
> (Pearson 1990: 185)

In the post-war era, most professional blues and gospel groups used "a large automobile or touring limousine [as] the usual mode of transportation," as Kip Lornell points out concerning sacred vocal harmony quartets in Memphis (1995: 87). Booking agencies did not always supply the most comfortable or reliable transportation, as H-Bomb Ferguson, traveling in a rented station wagon with B. B. King, lamented:

> All of a sudden we saw smoke coming from under the hood. And I can't drive, it looks like 4 in the morning.... Next thing I knew the motor was on fire. And we saw it, and I shook B. He was in on the seat sleeping. I say, "B., the wagon's on fire, let's go." We jumped out and got out – it burned up.
> (Ferguson 1984)

In fact, the travel itineraries were frequently so packed that the transportation was literally run into the ground, and The Spirit of Memphis Group traveled "at least half a million miles in one decade," so much that "no group member can recall the number or model of cars they used" (Lornell 1995: 87). Group member Jethro Bledsoe's travel itinerary for April 1952 lists seventeen appearances in nine states between April 3 and April 27, including appearances in Newark and Philadelphia on the same day (Lornell 1995: 203). While some groups, such as B. B. King's at the apex of his popularity, sometimes toured in a bus, the hard grind of driving all day and playing all night must have been grueling, particularly when it was sometimes a group member who had signed on to drive. Still, Horace Boyer points out that automobile travel was viewed as preferable, since "riding buses or trains meant having to travel in the 'colored' section" (Boyer 1995: 55). When blues performers sang "I'm gonna build me a railroad of my own," it was in part in response to these intolerable situations and lack of control and power over them that prompted their vow, just as the religious singer's gospel train bound for glory indicated a desire for a decent ride as well.

Rampant discrimination added to the pressures of the road. H-Bomb Ferguson described his experiences on his first tour of one-nighters in the 1950s:

> Macon, Georgia, North Carolina, Wheeling, West Virginia, the restrooms and the restaurants – BACK DOOR. We did. We even play a dance – most of it be in a barn, big old barn. The band would play, when you get through, you get something to eat, you go to the back, you get a sandwich to go. They had the "colored" and the "white" signs. And you couldn't come in the front door. But here's what really got me: the dance would be mixed, but you couldn't go over there and eat with them. They would go to the front, I had to go around the back and get ours. . . . We would get the sandwiches, jump in the wagon, and eat it on the way. And you had your little problems. A lot of times that we played in the Deep South, the sheriff would escort you out of town. Make sure you leave. The dance was over at 1, "You guys gonna get something to eat before you go?" We say, "Yes sir." He say, "Well I'm gonna take you to the restaurant. You go in the back door and get your food, and you hit the road. I'm gonna put you on the road." And they would. They would take you right on the highway and tell you, "Take so and so and get out of here." You figure everybody's enjoying theyself, why would they do that? See, I went along with everybody else. Otherwise, you might not be here today.
> (Ferguson 1984)

That threat of violence, and the hostility of law enforcement officers who anticipated the molestation of white women – "I don't want you hanging around here. You might fool with some of these white women," one Alabama sheriff said to Ferguson – was what prompted B. B. King to carry Winchester rifles with him on his bus on later tours (King 1996: 179).

Ferguson also described the extremely low pay for performances – "about 10–12 bucks for the whole show" – and poor diet and living accommodations:

> We wasn't making much money, so we would go in and check in a hotel together. And he said, "Hey H., how much you got?" I said, "I got about 7 bucks." He said, "We get a room together." So we would tell the lady, "We just want a room with a single bed, you know, full-size bed." He sleep at the foot, I sleep at the head. We eat sardines and crackers, get a pop. It was bad.
> (Ferguson 1984)

Not only that but, as Tony Heilbut reports, such simple tasks as laundry could become difficult to impossible to accomplish on the road: the Dixie Hummingbirds acknowledged, "when a shirt got dirty, they'd wear it inside out" (Heilbut 1971: 76). For all the deprivation and low pay, the group continued the tour, for as B. B. said, "You have to learn to crawl before you can walk. I know they're robbing me. We ain't making much money.

But we getting a little publicity out of it" (Ferguson 1984). That publicity, along with the pride of the performing artist intent on providing the best presentation of his talent and professionalism, made many a show far better than conditions would allow it to be.

For female artists the difficulties could sometimes be magnified. Rhythm and blues star Ruth Brown recalled "[d]ressing in sheds and outhouses by candlelight," narrowly avoiding a riot when she "tried to hang her gowns in a dressing room on the white level," and "red paint on the seats and flour in the gas tank" in Macon, Georgia. One would expect that encountering such hostility, suffering "Hey, bitch, what are you doing in this neighborhood" as part of the rocks and gravel of Jim Crow travel, would exact a heavy emotional price, and Brown acknowledges the "hurt in her soul" from such mistreatment (Goode 1969). B. B. King recognizes its effects as well: "After you have lived in the [Jim Crow] system for so long, then it don't bother you openly, but way back in your mind it bugs you" (Haralambos 1970: 374). But just as surely, H-Bomb Ferguson stated matter of factly and proudly, he would not allow it to have any effect on his performance. In response to the low pay and high prices – financial and emotional – he offered, "We split it, but nobody know. We come on the stage, you think them guys are millionaires! Half the time they be hungry as hell. We keep singing. We did that for about two years" (Ferguson 1984).

Long trips and low pay, of course, fostered conditions where marital fidelity could be severely tested. When Sonny Boy Williamson sang "I don't believe you really really love me, I think you just like the way my music sound," he was acknowledging the difficulties of performers beset by problems with groupies as well as doubts about their own value separate from their performing status. Sometimes there were practical professional advantages to illicit relationships, as Heilbut reports concerning the travels of some male gospel singers, and disadvantages for females:

> [T]here's a hard, practical reason for the promiscuity. The quartet
> singers need their women to help pay their hotel bills, cook for them,
> and treat them nice. Since most are family men, the eighty or ninety
> dollars they clean up on the road would make them candidates for
> welfare if gospel groupies didn't come to their rescue. Things are less
> easy for female gospel singers – the sexual double standard brands her a
> "whore" if she entertains protectors ...   (1971: 287)

B. B. King dedicated his autobiography *Blues All Around Me* to his fifteen children, many of them born in the 1950s to different mothers, admitting that he was an absentee father who found various women who comforted him: "These were women who understood me, women I tried to understand, and women I wanted to love. . . . I didn't think of the consequences of having children" (1996: 156). He regrets missing out on parts of their lives, but not pursuing his dream of making music, and takes pride in remaining in touch and supporting his children in the ways that he can. Twice married, he was also twice divorced, his marriages victims of separation produced by the rigors of travel. The loneliness that young women faced on the road was bemoaned by gospel singer Willa Ward-Royster, sister of Clara Ward: because Clara's mother "had imposed upon her an abstinence and loneliness that was intolerable," Clara dealt with her separation from men by dabbling "in homosexual activities," which prompted vehement mini-sermons from her mother when the activities came to light (Ward-Royster 1997: 68–9). Whether or not this homosexual activity resulted from Clara's enforced isolation from men or was an already present proclivity, surely it was exacerbated by a frequently hectic and demanding schedule.

Of course, there was also sometimes a burden for the African American performer with regard to the image it was necessary to project in public and on the stage. After all, in American society, high profile blacks were frequently held up as representatives of their race by whites, and expected to uphold the image of the "race" by black leaders. This responsibility was one often taken very seriously by musicians intent on projecting a sophisticated and responsible image, for both personal and racial reasons. Mahalia Jackson, for example, was told by a voice professor, "Young woman, you've got to stop that hollering. That's no way to develop a voice, and its no credit to the Negro race" (Boyer 1995: 88). Leaving the South for a broader touring schedule, southern quartets "presented themselves not only as upstanding and talented members of the community, but as a group of African American men who could and did serve as role models for other African American men" (Boyer 1995: 93). The Fairfield Four, for example, maintained strict by-laws in the 1940s specifying the number and times of business and rehearsal meetings, and rules for punctuality, speaking in public, drinking, accepting drinks from strangers, chewing gum in church, cursing, and showing up for broadcasts, with established fines for each infraction (Boyer 1995: 148–9). R&b saxophonist Earl Bostic was described as "always a gentleman . . . he stayed in his tux" (Tracy 1993: 133), and trumpeter Aaron Izenhall recounted restrictions in Louis Jordan's band:

> Louis couldn't stand any monkey business or sloppy playing, and if anyone smoked pot or took drugs they were fired on the spot. . . .
> Everyone had to behave like gentlemen, be clean, be smart and behave themselves. . . . But you couldn't fool him; if you'd been up all night at a party or had too much to drink, he'd know it. (Chilton 1992: 116)

While not all blues bands worked under such highly formal rules, especially if they played in smaller clubs or juke joints, some band leaders like Albert

Washington maintained a sartorially impeccable personal standard no matter where he played in public. For him, it made both the music and the musicians special, setting them apart from some ratty old amateur playing around rather than playing.

The performance venues, of course, differed in size, acoustics, and social milieu, each presenting distinct advantages and disadvantages with regard to the musician's experience. On famed Beale Street, the scene was virtually bursting with activity:

> the Monarch, the Midway, Pee Wee's Saloon, and the Hole in the Wall;
> the Palace and Daisy theaters; the One-Minute Cafe, the riverfront area
> at the foot of Beale with its carnival-like allure, its hucksters peddling
> fried fish, watermelon, and other fresh fruit, its hognose restaurants
> offering barbecue, pigs' feet, and, yes, chitlins, the tantalizing odors
> attracting the riverboat roustabouts sweating and swearing as they
> wrestled with crates ...   (McKee 1981: 8)

But all that neighborhood energy, which helped generate the visceral power of the blues, could also generate a level of violence and hostility that was dangerous for musicians and patrons alike:

> I was always afraid of that Hole in the Ground. . . . There's some old
> ladies was there, they was bad, they was just mean. They're old grown
> women but I was a young fellow. One of them called me. "Come here,
> Red," she say. Say, "You like me?" I say, "Yeah, I like everybody." Half
> scared. And she just taken her teeth and got a good mouthful of my
> forehead and she just worked, she just bit, just left a bad place where she
> just taken her teeth and just worked it up in there.   (McKee 1981: 138)

Big Bill Broonzy recalled the honky tonks in Charley Loran's camps, where men too short to reach the craps tables would "[p]ull that dead man up there, and stand on him and still keep shooting dice, see" (Lomax 1993: 464). Muddy Waters carried a gun for his own protection at the Club Zanzibar in Chicago (Tooze 1997: 89), and pianist Lonnie Bennet recalled nearly having his fingers shot off at the Vet's Inn in Cincinnati. In virtually every city, one could find a club officially named or unofficially nicknamed "Bucket of Blood," acknowledging, sometimes in an almost celebratory fashion glorifying the "outlaw" in a hypocritical environment, the violence found within the dim confines of the establishment. Of course, the club environment was not always unremittingly violent: blues performers frequently describe with great joy their performance experiences with patrons and other musicians, but that constant threat of violence was a situation with which musicians had to live, along with the possibility of being cheated with regard to door receipts, rate of pay, and drink charges.

Such clubs might frequently be without adequate ventilation or safety exits or equipment, making them hazardous for both musicians and patrons. One celebrated fire in Natchez, Mississippi, sparked blues recordings by Gene Gilmore, Baby Doo Caston, and Howlin' Wolf, describing the 1940 tragedy precipitated by a management decision to barricade the windows to prevent non-paying customers from getting a free look at and listen to Walter Barnes' band:

> Lord and the peoples all was dancin', enjoyin' their lives so hard,
> Just in a short while, the dance hall was full of fire.   (Caston 1974)

A fire resulting from a brawl in a Twist, Arkansas, club almost burned up B. B. King and his guitar, which he promptly named "Lucille," after the woman who precipitated the blaze. Clearly, where economic motivations rule, aesthetic and human considerations are among the early casualties.

Nevertheless, once artists made it to the stage in whatever venue, they frequently described a sense of strength, control, and fulfillment as they were finally able to do what they had put up with all of these various impediments for: perform. Some entertainers, for example, were not above "clowning" for their audiences, while others adopted what they considered to be a more "dignified" performance demeanor: "[R. H.] Harris refused to 'clown,' to leap off stage or run down aisles," preferring to "sing the folks happy" (Heilbut 1971: 116). Sterling Brown's poem "Ma Rainey" explores Rainey's symbiotic relationship with her audience, describing how her connection to "the people" and the folk roots informs her artistry, attitude, and subject matter, allowing her to help sustain those who have inspired her to her heights of musical greatness. As early as the 1920s such commentators spoke of the performances of blues singers as "strange rites" and of singers such as Bessie Smith as "priestesses" and "conjure women" (Van Vechten 1926: 67). If such descriptions were obviously influenced by the exoticization of the African American, they clearly also reflected a realization that the performances of blues and religious music were clearly more than mere entertainments, though highly entertaining they were. The performance of blues and gospel music, in fact, have been compared by a number of commentators, Charles Keil, James Cone, Paul Garon, and Jon Michael Spencer among them, who find similarities in style and function.

To some, such a discussion of the theological and religious ramifications of the blues seems anathema, since there are those in the Christian religious community who see the blues as the "Devil's music" and hence having nothing to do with religion as they know it. Clearly the origins, conditions and situations in performance venues, and frequently frank and earthy language and philosophy of the blues, have a great deal to do with this image. Still, we encounter in the history of the blues a variety of performers – Charley Patton, Blind Lemon Jefferson, Willie McTell, Rosetta Tharpe, Wynona Carr, and B. B. King among them – who have included blues, spirituals, and gospel music in their repertoires, though frequently discreetly and with particular audiences in mind. At times Son House would refuse to play the blues on Sundays, and Sam Cooke suffered embarrassing rejection when he tried to return to his religious audience once he had recorded the blues:

> While the Soul Stirrers were on stage, they called Sam up. . . . Somehow when Sam hit the stage, the crowd went dead and stayed dead till Jimmy Outler and Paul Foster came back. Folks were hollering, "Get that blues singer down. Get that no good so-and-so down. This is a *Christian* program."
> (Heilbut 1971: 121)

While there were those who maintained, even insisted upon, the separation of sacred and secular music, there is no denying that the symbolic functions of the musics can accomplish similar climaxes and ends, connecting Ira Tucker's comment that he feels himself to be head of the house in church – "And I've *always* been the head of my house," he adds (Heilbut 1971: 86) – to the role Charles Keil describes Bobby Bland fulfilling in his own performances. Bland uses melisma of the type "derived directly from the intensely emotional services of the Negro fundamentalist churches" (1966: 124), and through his "moralizing and preaching not from any superior vantage point but out of empathy" and use of church-related call-and-response patterns, puts "the audience in the palm of his hand" and makes himself and his listeners "one unit" (1966: 137). African American sacred and secular musics have always shared similar modes of performance – vocal timbres and patterns, the use of "blue" notes and melisma, percussive elements and syncopation, for example – that made distinguishing between them sometimes merely a matter of listening to the lyrics, as Langston Hughes pointed out in *Tambourines to Glory*: to Big Eye Buddy Lomax's assertion that "them gospel songs sound just like the blues," a sister responds weakly, "At least our words is different" (1968: 126–7). Actually, both can accomplish similar ends in terms of identifying and exposing problems to community consideration, providing a communal common ground for discussion, providing some sort of catharsis and relief, and giving the community itself a greater sense of coherence and cohesiveness, even if for only a brief space, and sometimes, in the cases of blues performers, only incidentally. After all, for the blues performer this was a job, not necessarily a calling, and the sometimes dissolute and promiscuous lives of blues singers did not always lend themselves to an exemplary moral higher ground – though, of course, the same could be said for some preachers as well. Ultimately, there are blues performers such as Big Joe Duskin who insist on the distinction: expressing displeasure at the fact that a recording company had released his material under the title *Boogie Woogie is My Religion*, Duskin retorted, "Boogie woogie ain't my religion, I'm a member of the Church of God." Still, performers such as Duskin would not deny not only the sociopolitical but also the moral accomplishments of the blues, as Ralph Bass explained:

> I'll tell you the major contribution. Without getting up on the soap box, without having marches, we brought blacks and whites together with music. I remember in Atlanta, Georgia, when "The Twist" came out. Hank Ballard was the featured act at this big club and they were lined . . . the whites were lined up, they were lined up, blacks and whites together, all down Auburn Avenue, to try to get into this club. The police came, man, and they said "We'll have a riot. Let 'em alone. Let 'em go." So here, whites and blacks together. We gave them a common denominator, a common love. We appealed to the one emotion that law couldn't do a damn thing about, their common love of music. And so, I think, through King and other labels, this was the great contribution: to break the shit down . . . especially in the Deep South. Break it down. (Fox 1987)

Eddie Boyd described one of the musical experiences that made it impossible for him to be a racist, despite a great deal of mistreatment at the hands of whites:

> So they had a little dressing room out back of the club, and this white man, he put a strand of hay-baling wire across there and hung a whole string of potato sacks up there and put on one side "Niggers" and (on the other side) "White Folks" (laughs). Those white boys took a knife and cut that sack down from end to end and piled it up in front of that nightclub and poured kerosene on it and set it afire . . . He said, "What the hell this son of a bitch talking about? Putting a damn sheet up here between us and y'all. It ain't hardly steppin' room in here. We play on the same stage. He don't know music is natural international, don't give a damn what color he is." I say, "Hello, brother, welcome to the club." (Boyd 1977: 15)

And just as performers have frequently described the ways that audiences segregated by ropes in dances found blues and r&b to be a rollicking impetus to jostling and finally trampling on the cords of division, so they have also seen blues and gospel music slowly over the years attract a diverse audience as well as performers from outside the African American community. After all, appearances at New York's Café Society and Carnegie Hall in the 1940s by such performers as Sonny Terry, Big Bill Broonzy, the Boogie Woogie Trio, Rosetta Tharpe, and the Dixie Hummingbirds, and performances by groups like the Soul Stirrers for Roosevelt and Churchill on the White House lawn, introduced the music to a whole new audience that responded enthusiastically to its artistry, even if it was in a rarified setting that did not always help produce performances in their most unadulterated form. Lena Horne's scripted introduction of Ammons and Johnson in the film "Boogie Woogie Dream" – "It has always been their greatest desire to play their music to a select society in a café like this" – feels rather condescending and disingenuous, yet such venues were the gateways to mainstream acceptability and greater economic success. Additionally, the airwaves provided unrestricted access to radio shows such as Joe Bostic's "Gospel Train" in the 1940s; Mahalia Jackson's C.B.S. radio program, which premiered on September 26, 1954; the sounds emanating from W.D.I.A. in Memphis and from their Goodwill Revues; as well as appearances of performers on such programs as The Ed Sullivan Show and the Dinah Shore Show, and numerous other radio shows featuring blues and gospel talent, which made white presence at live appearances inevitable. Just as inevitably, as racial barriers relaxed, integrated bands emerged as more common, especially beginning in the 1960s, sparking occasional cries of "nigger lover" on the one hand, and charges of pandering to whites on the other as blues performers attempted to negotiate the racial divide and "legitimize" their decisions to alter the complexion of blues bands. White performers have frequently enjoyed greater access to higher-paying venues and record contracts and sales that have prompted frustration among black performers; on the other hand, there are some facilities that have expressed an unwillingness to book white performers, feeling their audiences would prefer "African American originators" to "white interpreters." Increasingly, however, "mixed" audiences seem to have become more comfortable enjoying the music alongside each other. Although there have occasionally been efforts to "explain" references to African American culture to white audiences or legitimize the blues tradition in reference to the lives of whites, as in B. B. King's "Lucille" or Albert King's "Blues Power," in general the music now seems to speak naturally and unselfconsciously to its audience. Paradoxically, churches seem to be far less integrated than blues clubs and festivals, so gospel performances are more likely to reach an audience a higher percentage of which is African American, possibly in part due to the personal nature of religious affiliations on the one hand and the role that religion plays in establishing and maintaining group identity and cohesiveness on the other, though inevitably an element of racism is also reflected in such willful separation. The entry of blues and gospel directly into the mainstream of U.S. culture – as opposed to indirectly through cross-cultural influence – has seen the blues leave juke joint and back porch for tours such as the American Folk Blues Festival in the 1960s and early 1970s, and events sponsored by large tobacco and alcohol companies anxious to cash in on the blues' appeal. Nevertheless, one can encounter blues and gospel in small, informal venues where it continues to serve its intimate, personal functions unconnected to the commercialism that sometimes threatens to engulf it.

As John Cephas pointed out, the catalog of performance conditions for blues and gospel performers includes a wide variety of elements, most of which pre- and post-date the actual performance itself. When the blues come falling down like dark night showers of rain, after all, they fall on musicians who are, as B. B. King says, black twice, meaning that to all of the conditions and pressures of being black in America are added the special difficulties faced by musicians working their way through a world sometimes hostile to the mobile and public creative artist in an undervalued idiom. The performance should be understood in the context of all of these experiences, notable for its grace, power, and validity both because of and despite the many impediments facing blues and gospel performers out to provide a bit of consolation for the weary in the wee wee hours of the dark nights of their souls.

7 Vocal expression in the blues and gospel

BARB JUNGR

The human voice is like a thumb print, aurally and spectrally identifiable. The extraordinarily affecting voices of gospel and blues singers have, in their recordings, given us access to those singers' deepest emotions and, in so doing, allowed us to glimpse their individual and common struggles for dignity and freedom in an often terrifyingly hostile environment. Unlike other instruments, the voice emanates from and is played inside the body. In this respect it is unique. Contemporary understanding of "voice" must therefore incorporate the connection between the personality, physicality, spirituality, individual experience and social history of each singer. For the listener, description of these singers' vocal production is fraught with difficulties not least because the plethora of interpretations reflect individual singers' personal expression, as well as their commonality of experience in African American culture and society pre- and post-slavery. My own responses to this work emerge from my love of these musics and singers, and are subject also to my own cultural understanding and experience as both listener and singer/teacher. There are so many elements to "voice" that this brief chapter may only scratch the surface of the many extraordinary vocal performances in these genres. Each individual "voice" has its own story, its own personal history. I have focused on particular singers and examples in an attempt to raise some of the aspects of these relationships, personally, stylistically and in the context of their culture and society, but the voices I omit are by no means less important. Their omission is due to constraints of space and does not represent any aesthetic judgment on my own part. Furthermore, there is an established body of work in both African American cultural history and blues and gospel, on which I have drawn in an effort to be sensitive to the relationship of voice to personal and communal history.

The heritage of the great blues and gospel singers is largely and uniquely preserved on recordings, giving us access to performances by singers many of whom are now dead.[1] Some recordings are "acoustic" – that is to say, the performance has been recorded in an ethnomusicologically "authentic" manner, in the field (for example the many recordings made by Alan Lomax on porches, in churches and around campfires across the southern states). Some are studio based, wherein the voice may have been treated or modified by post-recording techniques (such as the more recent recordings of Sweet

Honey In The Rock, where voices have been overdubbed to create certain effects, or the contemporary recordings of Sounds Of Blackness with complex studio production). Some are so old that microphones and recording techniques used were too insensitive to give anything other than an approximation of the singer's "real" voice (Marie Bradley's blues singing is almost obscured by the surface recording noises of her 1927 recordings). It is evident from almost everything written about Bessie Smith that what she was doing in performance and what has been preserved in recorded sound are two quite different phenomena. Smith's work is variously described as being almost mesmerizing, as being so commanding and loud she didn't need a microphone even in a big hall, and is perhaps best summed up by a comment by the late Frank Schiffman, owner of Harlem's Apollo and Lafayette Theatres when Bessie appeared there as a headliner. "Whatever pathos there is in this world, whatever sadness she had, was brought out in her singing – and the audience knew it and responded to it."[2] The literature on both genres is filled with what the voice analyst Laver (1980) has called "the adjectival approach": voices are vaguely described as "pinched," "strained," "rasping," "full," "thin," and "nasal," to note a few. Terminologies are confused and further complicated when different listeners hear the same singer, for their perceptions of the performance are filtered through a wealth of associations, cultural aesthetics and personal preferences for the sounds to which they are listening and to which they ascribe meaning.

Using three approaches, the question of "voice" in the analysis of blues and gospel vocal production (timbre or vocal tone, ornamentation, vocal and performance aesthetic, and characteristic stylistic features) is identifiable and can be discussed in terms of the relationship to African American society and culture.

The Lomax approach

Alan Lomax, folklorist, ethnomusicologist and major archivist of American musics, played a central part in recording performances by many African Americans in the rural South, and assisted and actively promoted the careers of many artists including Leadbelly, Jelly Roll Morton, and Muddy Waters. Lomax identified stylistic traits using an analytical system to code songstyle and vocal production in the *Cantometrics* project. Traits particularly relevant to this discussion include vocal group, vocal organization, range, interval width, embellishment, volume, rubato, glissandi, melisma, tremolo, glottal effect, register, vocal width, nasality, vocal noise, accent, and consonants. These were assessed aurally and thus graded graphically. Lomax identified certain features of songstyle identifying the "gospel" tradition.

Unsurprisingly, he found strong similarities in songstyle features from African and African American examples particularly those pertaining to vocal parameters. Working with the Alabaman singer Vera Hall, Lomax observed that "components of this spiritual style reinforce its cohesive effect,"[3] noting that the songs were refrain-based and that melodies were "brief and repetitious" affording easy participation, that strong beats and pulse allowed everyone to follow the meter and, interestingly, that "it is mellow voiced – a psychological cue inviting and welcoming others." Lomax's work has been heavily criticized, but he proposed that "music expresses emotion; therefore when a distinctive and consistent musical style lives in a culture . . . one can posit the existence of a distinctive set of emotional needs or drives that are somehow satisfied or evoked by this music" (Lomax 1962: 125). In terms of the relationship of the "voice" to both the blues and gospel, encompassing the individual singing, the group singing, the expression of otherwise suppressed narrative, spiritual, sexual and emotional information, the individual physical act of making sound, the psychological implications of that, and finally the political expression of the community, Lomax was identifying a quite contemporary view of what "voice" in blues and gospel may, indeed, be "voicing."

Using Lomax's analysis, specific features help define the singing style of both gospel and blues singers. These are chiefly centered in ornamentation features:

- embellishment (very clearly displayed in Carolyn Bolger-Payne's version of "Precious Lord");
- vocal width: use of falsetto in male singers (Houston Stackhouse singing "Cool Drink Of Water") and vocal "jumps" from lower to higher register in women singers (Marie Bradley's glissandi into the soprano register from the modal voice[4]);
- melisma, rubato, and glissandi (a dominant feature of Jessie May Hill's performance as she slides between mid-line pitches).

Slides, wails, sobs, whooping and vocal sounds used in singing but originating in expressive speech are also definitive as in Robert Johnson's whoops between the text, and John Lee Hooker's spoken delivery. Indeed, the line between preaching in recognizable rhythms and pitch inflections and singing is often very thin. However, nasality, register, tremolo, range, glottal, vocal noise, accent and consonants are also displayed by all singers to a greater or lesser degree.

"Nasality" as Lomax understands it is more evident in John Brim's and Memphis Slim's voices, less in Chuck Berry and Howlin' Wolf's. Register is high for Buddy Guy, who moves into falsetto singing at the top of his lower range, often ending a raised note in a little cry. Etta James' voice becomes lower throughout her career. On her 1967 recording of "Tell Mama" she sings in a mid-modal register sliding into falsetto for effect, while she sings in a progressively lower modal voice on her recordings twenty years later. Robert Johnson uses the jump into falsetto with effect in his 1936 recording of "Kindhearted Woman's Blues." In gospel harmony groups the full ranges of registers are in evidence – no one register or range determines the styles.

As for vibrato, Ruth Brown has hardly any in her shouting rhythm and blues, whereas La Vern Baker uses fast vibrato on sustained notes, as does Bessie Smith. Lomax uses "glottal" to mean glottal shake which is not used extensively in either genre but is evident at times in the individual singing of John Lee Hooker. However, glottal attack varies greatly between individual singers. Some singers use a marked degree of vocal noise or "raspiness" (Clarence Fountain of The Five Blind Boys of Alabama, Howlin' Wolf, Blind Willie Johnson), some have a purer vocal timbre (some of Mahalia Jackson's performances, and the many exponents of the concert gospel tradition including The Princely Players, The Fisk Jubilee Singers and the many other African American U.S. university and collegiate choirs whose vocal training was greatly influenced by the Western classical model).

In features such as melodic shape, phrase length and text load there is no central model (while the descending vocal lines of blues singers have received attention, this is by no means definitive), but vocal group and vocal organization are found in the sub-groups of gospel choirs and jubilee harmony groups. Definitively the blues singer is a soloist, even if working with a band of supporting musicians, and the gospel singer may sing alone (Mahalia Jackson), with a group (Sam Cooke and the Soul Stirrers), or in a group with textural blending (Sweet Honey In The Rock). Comparing the use of this model in the songstyles of classical North Indian, or Western classical vocalizing many parameters would clearly be positively marked as defining features of both.

The Estill approach

Using the vocal model proposed by the voice specialist Jo Estill raises other possibilities.[5] Estill separated six specific and audible vocal parameters: *opera, twang, belt, speech, sob,* and *falsetto* (the meaning of this is distinct from that of male vocal register in Western classical terminology). Singers usually use more than one quality, while some are often found together: *opera* includes a quality of *twang,* as does *belt.* Conversational and more relaxed singing uses *speech* and sometimes *falsetto* qualities. Tommy Tucker and Elder Charlie Beck use both *speech* and *twang,* Michelle Lanchester's voice displays a quality of *falsetto* in which the back of the vocal folds is open but not adducting, creating a sound which might otherwise be incorrectly described as "breathy." *Cry* is a variation of *sob*, using a higher larynx position: the larynx is not tilted in *speech* or *falsetto*; here the larynx is in a mid-position, sitting neither high nor low. The key difference between *cry*, *speech* and *falsetto* is the postural change in the larynx, i.e. the thyroid cartilage is titled forward.

Twang and *cry* are heard frequently in gospel and blues singing. They both include in their physical set a tilted thyroid which stretches the vocal folds to thin them, while vibrato is a feature of the vocal production. *Twang* is evident in most of the blues and gospel singers' vocal deliveries. *Cry* is a distinctive quality heard as a sweetness in the voice and is audible in Joshua White, Bo Diddley, Otis Rush, Buddy Guy, Howlin' Wolf, Bessie Smith, Sam Cooke, Dorothy Love Coates and Brother Joe May.

Kayes describes the *opera* quality as characterized by a tilted thyroid and a low larynx position. She notes that (as in *belting*) a high degree of physical "anchoring" is necessary in the body to provide the physical support in the back, neck, spine and torso to produce high sub-glottal pressure and "support" loud and full vocal tone projection. In addition, the vocal folds are thick and the closed phase of the folds is long. *Opera* and *belt* are complex voice qualities that include *twang* in their "set up." Western classical training emphasizes register definition into soprano, mezzo, alto, tenor, baritone and bass with a corresponding use of a lower, tilted larynx position and with emphasis on a "clear" vocal timbre with vibrato and legato singing supported by particular breathing techniques.[6] *Opera* is clearly audible in some singers' voices, most particularly those "schooled" in the Western classical tradition, evident in the late nineteenth-century collegiate choirs.[7] Gifted musicians such as Harry T. Burleigh (himself a baritone) trained singers in conservatoire environments and this work was clearly audible in the singing of arranged spirituals. As composers learned the form of and wrote for Western classical registers, tutors taught the vocal requirements for this style of singing. These styles sometimes influenced show and musical singing, with performers moving between each, and can in turn be heard in the recorded performances of blues singers who "crossed over" genres in the early twentieth century (for example in the modal or contralto singing of blues recordings of the successful show performer Josephine Byrd). Some writers infer that singers such as Bessie Smith used elements of Western classical technique in her controlled legato phrases and breath use and control. Well, singers learn by imitation. If they can duplicate what they hear, they may appropriate vocal techniques into their own singing, and with the explosion of performance possibilities for African Americans in the early part of the last century where singers moved between engagements in vaudeville, tent shows, musicals, theatre shows, concert, clubs and roadhouses, a fertile ground was provided for vocal performers to enhance their crafts by providing many diverse examples of delivery. Fashion also played a part in this, particularly in the recording industry. Many early female blues recordings display more than a passing nod to show and vaudeville traditions both in the texts sung and in the vocal deliveries. Singers who used *cry*, providing sweetness of tone, moved quickly into vaudeville and shows, and were recorded easily. Bessie Smith's supported style of singing was suited to recording and concert. In other words the type of singing delivery correlated with the performance environment. A "shouter" would gravitate naturally through performance opportunity to r&b, a sweet singer to cabaret and vaudeville, a big-voiced singer would be better able to work in tent shows, where the capacity to *belt* would be an asset.

Belt is a full-throttle sound and is very evident when singers seem on the edge of their voice and emotion: one can almost hear the physical effort employed to make the sound, and it is a quality that would have been very valuable before amplification as it enables high-powered sound to be made and heard over other instruments. When gospel singers appear to be "upping the ante" with a highly exciting sound they are *belting*, usually also employing *twang*. Koko Taylor sometimes uses *belt*, as does Bessie Smith, Etta James, Sam Cooke, Dorothy Love Coates, and Gloria Griffin. When a gospel choir "takes off," the exciting sound is heard as and partly created by many singers *belting* simultaneously (Michelle Lanchester, Bernice Johnson Reagan and Yasmeen singing together, Sam Cooke with the Soul Stirrers, The Clarke Sisters and Dorothy Love Coates with the original Gospel Harmonettes all demonstrate this very effectively).

Kayes listened with me to a variety of recordings and in discussion identified *twang* as present in almost all examples of the blues and gospel singers we heard. *Cry*, *belt* and *speech* were used by most singers in various combinations. *Falsetto* was rare and *opera* quality not in evidence with the exception of those aforementioned singers schooled in a Western classical tradition. Some singers (Brother Joe May, Screamin' Jay Hawkins, Blind Gary Davis) produced a sob-like quality which is the quality of *cry* but with a lowered larynx and some used a constricted throat to produce what Lomax would have called raspiness and what is also heard as vocal noise or disruption. Estill's model reveals *twang* as a central component of vocal tone in blues and gospel, used most frequently in conjunction with *speech*, *cry*, *sob* and *belt*.

The Wolfsohn approach

Alfred Wolfsohn's pioneering work linking vocal timbre to physical, psychological and emotional states was developed both by Paul Newham to be used in psychotherapeutic voice work, and by members of the Roy Hart Theatre for use in a theatrical context to produce very extreme and affecting vocal production.[8] Focusing on the width and length of the vocal tract and linking psychological states to specific vocal productions, this method (like Estill's) is taught in praxis. Practitioners learn to identify emotional states by mimicking the vocal tract settings of the client thus empathizing physically, which enables them to diagnose accordingly. In respect of blues and gospel singing, put simply, if a singer uses a vocal setting that creates an exciting sound, the sound will be heard as such by the listener and will, more importantly, create an "excitable" emotional state in the body and being of the singer. These "effects" seem to be felt across cultural and aesthetic boundaries without respect to the listener's cultural competence, although there is no available research on this. There is considerable evidence linking elements of vocal production with psychological state[9] and this is important in the discussion of the vocal productions of blues and gospel singers, given the developments of these genres within the social, historical and political contexts of African American communities.

Melanie Harrold has studied extensively with voice and psychotherapy and in discussion with me provided observations of these states in the timbres of various singers of the genres. Chuck Berry's non-threatening, warm tone suggests "come here," when coupled with lyrics such as those of "In The Wee Wee Hours." With his easy glottal attack and speech-like delivery and relaxed intrinsic muscles, we sense a mother need. Compared to Muddy Waters' sexual singing, with the voice emanating from deep inside his being, we have a full sense of his "embodied" voice. His singing is not intellectual, but entirely responsive to his body need. Buddy Guy's shouting suggests a need to be heard, almost a desperateness. With his higher middle register tipping into occasional *falsetto* with small cries, there is a "lost" quality to him. Elmore James, with his high, thin tenor voice using a high larynx position with a lot of *twang*, accesses his heart in his singing, and uses a great deal of forward resonance. Little Walter uses the harmonica as his voice, the harmonica becoming a mother's nipple, a pre-verbal and oral experience of nurture. In contrast, Otis Rush seems to be "reaching," up and over his middle register into his *falsetto* voice, towards heaven. As he sings "So many roads, so many trains" crying "oh" in *falsetto* he holds the tension of his high notes collapsing into his lower middle voice.[10]

The *speech* factor is very illuminating. There is considerable research linking certain vocal traits with sexuality (Laver 1980). In his spoken delivery in "Walking The Blues," Willie Dixon's voice is experienced as deeply sexual; easy, low in pitch, he seems relaxed and inviting. John Lee Hooker singing "Sugar Mama" again uses the narrative voice, the speech-like quality Estill identifies, but Hooker moves from *speech* into a resonant singing voice with the quality of *twang* and the sweetness of *cry* moving onto *sob* when the larynx lowers. His singing is technically proficient as he allows his resonance to work for him. Howlin' Wolf "asks for water"[11] moving from deep in the throat into a *falsetto* cry, then again collapsing down into the lower register. Wolf's constriction of the throat gives a vocal noise quality, a rumble of a barely emerging growl.

The use of vocal noise by singers as an effect in the blues allows access to deeper feelings of emotion, both for singer and listener alike. Etta James on "Tell Mama" shows a strength, that of the "total" woman, working against what seems to be a weight on her chest and abdomen, and shouting, pushing through the masculine force she finds herself surrounded by – not least of all the full r&b arrangement. Her clear *falsetto* voice expresses her anger. Koko Taylor uses constriction to suggest her strength and anger, her voice is clear when she tells the story of "Wang Dang Doodle," but when she becomes active, singing of "kicking down doors" a barely suppressed rage emerges form the tight vocal noise she makes, a growl lending force to her lyrical interpretation. In blues singing we as listeners experience the singers' "reaching" inside for expression in each individual's style, reflecting a personal inner emotional state, but one we share through their performance. There is often a vocal muscular contact of the active emotional centers, focused around tension and release.

Gospel singing, whilst employing the same varieties of individual vocal timbres, looks "up," outwards, reaching as if towards salvation, a better life, and heaven. The gospel singer affirms existence, often in collective and openly participatory singing, but exhibits the same sense of tension and release, directed towards a different end. The gospel singer finds catharsis by releasing emotion through the expressed voice, towards a spiritual union with God. The Soul Stirrers provide almost a "spiritual backbone" for soloist Sam Cooke, a spine onto which he as the lead voice can fall back and feel supported allowing him full vocal, musical and emotional freedom of expression. This is evident in all of the harmony groups where a soloist "takes off" held up by the constant driving harmonies of the group.

Personal history and delivery

The human voice is completely connected to the physicality and psychology of the person singing, so much so that it is impossible not to take this into account when examining the idiosyncratic timbres present in both blues and gospel singers. The work both of Estill and the schools of voice and bodywork suggest that the singer operates stylistically through the form of gospel and blues, expressing recognizable individual manipulation of the musical forms, and also through the singer's personal "sound," which is intimately connected to their personal and communal experience. The personal histories of performers documented by such scholars as Heilbut (1997) indicate the depth of these relationships.

Julius Cheeks joined the Nightingales Gospel Group in 1946, and they soon became The Sensational Nightingales due to Cheeks' ability to take the crowd "up" with the hard gospel style of singing characterized by Boyer as "energetic and extremely intense solo and background singing, a preaching style of delivery, and exaggerated physical gestures" (2000: 204). The hard gospel style incorporates *belt* much more frequently than the softer gospel style which Boyer characterizes as "close harmony, precise attacks and releases, and underestimated – yet firm – rhythmic accentuation." Both employ *twang* and *belt* to a degree, but there is more use of growling, crying, and the kind of unrestrained shouting associated with preaching and sermonizing in the harder style. The effects of this kind of singing are powerful, and drawn from deep roots within the singer's psyche:

> At the other end of the post-war quartet spectrum stood the Sensational Nightingales and another legend – Rev. Julius Cheeks. Where the (Swan) Silvertones and the Spirit of Memphis captivated audiences with exquisite understatements, the Sensational Nightingales devastated them with diamond hard harmony and the primeval roaring lead of Julius "June" Cheeks. Jo Jo Wallace, who sang tenor with the Nightingales for thirty years, was brought up on the softer jubilee stylings of the Golden Gates and the Jubalaires and remembers the shock of joining the Nightingales: "It was almost like pulling my insides out, trying to sing behind Cheeks. I'd be hoarse every night. I nearly killed myself trying to make it with the Nightingales! I wasn't used to that style." Julius Cheeks was born into grinding poverty in the same South Carolina town Ira Tucker comes from. "It were bad, man. We didn't have a clock, we told time by the sun. We didn't eat right, we lived off fat-back and molasses. All us kids worked in the cotton fields, and Mama would whip me every day ... but she kept us straight." No proper schooling meant that he couldn't read or write, but he got himself a recorded Bible when he was twenty-four and played it to death ... Julius "June" Cheeks died in 1980, having left instructions that his body not be taken further South than the Fourteenth Street Bridge in Baltimore, signifying his fierce hatred of southern racism. His voice was lacerated from his twelve years on the road with the Nightingales and some say he just about sang himself to death, impervious to the warnings of doctors, until his voice – never a refined instrument at the best of times – began to sound like gravel in a tin bucket. His was the rawest of gospel's baritones – moving and painful in its evocation of the roughest side of the mountain. Listening to the Nightingales, it's possible to understand that Cheeks wasn't simply indulging in nostalgia when he said towards the end of his life, "I sit here sometimes and play my old records. I just cry. It'll make you cry, you know."
>   (Broughton 1996: 85–7)

The narrative style of delivery through which preaching becomes sermonizing becomes singing, moving into technically different deliveries, is present in both blues and gospel. The movement of singers between the genres reflects these similarities. With respect to the "hard" gospel sound, there is a correlation with the tenor of much of the Old Testament, with an angry, vengeful God who is to be celebrated and feared. Coupled with the day-to-day dehumanizing effects of racism and abject poverty, expression like Cheeks' is fueled by deep rage and a primal need to vocalize, to let this out, to drive these emotions into something outside, something other than what is. This is represented in this most powerful vocal delivery, where singers are not performing, but connecting to deep feelings and expressing them (like Cheeks), without thought of the subsequent consequence on their voices. Where singing is not, for the vocalist, simply performance, this affecting delivery is most manifest, and is felt alike both by singer and listener. The Five Blind Boys of Alabama, also characterized by Boyer as "hard gospel," sent members of their congregation to hospital rendering them so over-excited by raising "the spirit"; some participants, it is said, went into comas when they were playing, so powerful was the effect singing on their audience (Broughton 1996). One must also be aware of the relationships here of music to "trance" behavior, again in which the voice is a central component.[12]

For those singers whose work was not only about the gospels but was also about consistent performance, the change into high gear with *belt*, shouting and screaming are more infrequent during recorded performances and probably during live appearances. Since the blues does not demand the same specific performance aesthetic as gospel, blues singers *belt*, growl and shout for effect correspondingly less, and as performers, in a more "controlled" manner clear from recordings of singers whose style employs such deliveries, for example, Koko Taylor, Etta James, and Sippie Wallace. However, a similar relationship between personal story, voice and shared cultural and societal experiences is clearly evident.

Other factors

The concept of learning in terms of style and timbre also merits comment. In the early days of blues and gospel, singers learned from those in their immediate vicinity, giving rise to geographical "schools" of vocal styles recognized by blues scholars. The identification of geographic styles also raises questions about the effects of dialect, local rhythmic and speech qualities on singing styles, which demand more intensive analysis. The movement between performance arenas allowed singers to see, hear and learn from one another. Boyer notes that The Blind Boys Of Alabama were influenced by The Golden Gate Quartet's radio broadcasts, on which the Blind Boys modeled their early sound. Then, hearing that Archie Brownlee's Five Blind Boys Of Mississippi were "tearing up churches" with their shrieking and screaming style, they also adopted this means of vocalizing; finally when they toured together both groups were singing "hard gospel" (Boyer 2000: 202–3). The growing accessibility of recordings provided another means of "schooling" – that of imitation from recorded sources, which has influenced generations of younger vocalists far beyond the shores of North America. Jimmy Rushing's "shouting" style of blues singing was an influence on Walter Dallas and Jimmy Witherspoon (Oliver 1997: 75). There is an acknowledged understanding that the "gospel schooling" has been responsible for the basis of the vocal inflections and mannerisms which moved beyond gospel and provided the basis of vocal deliveries in early soul music and into contemporary genres. The connection between the vocal deliveries, styles and general performance aesthetic of blues and gospel is clear, without this singers from Thomas Dorsey, Johnnie Taylor, Rosetta Tharpe, Sam Cooke, to Aretha Franklin to name the more prominent could not have moved so effortlessly between the sacred and the secular. Paul Oliver writes:

> An early connection with the church was common to a very large number of blues singers and musicians, whose ability to play an instrument or sing at all was often due to their parents' religious associations: the mother who played the organ, the father who preached and lead a gospel choir are familiar in the backgrounds of innumerable blues singers, from T-Bone Walker and Lightnin' Hopkins, Yank Rachell and Otis Spann to Chuck Berry and Junior Wells. Not only were a large number – perhaps the majority – of blues singers raised in God-fearing families, but a high proportion of them also had their first experiences of singing, and sometimes playing, in public in the churches of the South. Singers whose careers were as varied as those of Bukka White, Sunnyland Slim, Jimmy Witherspoon, B. B. King, Magic Sam and Little George Buford commenced in this way.   (1968: 84–5)

The frequent use of the male falsetto register is also indicative. In Malawi high tenor to falsetto male voices are found in traditional music and in Christianized choral work, where high register male singers will sometimes sing in the soprano section of a choir.[13] Male falsetto voices in gospel and blues have elements of *cry*, *sob* and *twang*, and individual timbres. In other styles employing falsetto, there has been a prevalent tendency to regard the high male white voice as "woman-ly." This happens in Western classical music where register is, as Newham suggests, read culturally and as Frith proposes for pop, gender may be mapped onto it. However, the timbre and songstyle of the blues and gospel falsetto singer is highly individualized, and is related to and emerges from the use of falsetto in some sub-Saharan African cultures; its affect is read somewhat differently, and the vocal elements of *cry* and *sob* (in, e.g., Marvin Gaye, Jackie Wilson) suggest the caring side of heterosexually expressed "female-ness."

The microphone has had a profound effect on the vocal performances of blues and gospel singers. Frith talks at length about the importance of the microphone in popular music, which allows the voice to be heard in "close up," providing a new intimacy which hitherto had been impossible through the demands of rendering vocal projection in a manner that allowed the voice simply to be heard (Frith 1998: 187–9). The development of the blues as a musical form from the "shouting" style of the field hollers is well documented by Oliver, Baraka and others. Equally, the influence of the preaching style of delivery within the gospel tradition has affected vocal performance (the development of Aretha Franklin's distinctive phrasing is clearly influenced by the preaching style of her father, Rev. C. L. Franklin). The vocal requirements of pre-amplification deliveries demand a large physical component and certain vocal qualities render the voice more audible in an acoustic environment where the singer may be required to project over a group, sometimes in the open air. Here, elements of *belt* and *twang* may be deliberately employed to aid projection in the way that specific techniques support projection of the voice in opera and musical theatre. Memphis Minnie's voice clearly exhibits *twang* in her performances, and there is a clear sense of power and physical support. In the rural blues, preaching blues, and gospel recorded in churches before amplification became commonplace, vocal deliveries often incorporate belting and some voices reveal an amount of vocal noise caused by friction of the vocal folds in order to meet the demands of constant high-pressured singing under adverse performance conditions. The 1928 sermonizing combining singing and preaching by Rev. Johnny Blakey of Chicago is almost painful to listen to, for the singers are at the edge of their vocal limits and are actually shouting, Blakey's voice growling the sermon. Amplification and microphone-singing developed alongside the growth of radio as a popular medium, and the blended vocal sound of the "soft gospel" jubilee harmony groups effectively exploited this in their close-harmony singing. Groups such as The Golden Gate Quartet were perfect for radio, and radio was perfect for disseminating their distinctive styles and sounds across the continent. The microphone allows the spoken delivery of John Lee Hooker, or the easy vocal quality of Willie Dixon, to be heard over the amplified blues. It's unlikely that Bessie Smith would have been heard over these sounds without a PA, despite her legendary massive singing voice. The microphone is an essential ingredient to the vocal production of amplified blues, some gospel singing, and influenced directly the vocal style of specific performers and some harmony groups.

Conclusion

Dunn and Jones (1994) note the use of the word "voice" by feminists has come to "refer to a wide range of aspirations: cultural agency, political enfranchisement, sexual autonomy, and expressive freedom" historically denied to women and it may be argued, to the emergent post-slavery African American community. "Voice" in this usage has become a metaphor for textual authority, and alludes to the efforts of people to reclaim their own experience through writing, or to the specific qualities of their literary and *cultural self-expression*. Evolving from their African cultural history through slavery and post-slavery in North America, the blues and gospel created a "performance" (in the widest sense of the word) arena in which that "voice" could be "embodied" to produce vocal expression in culturally constrained and defined ways within blues and gospel which, simultaneously, encouraged full individual and personal expression. Thus all timbres were acceptable, from the Western classical to the most raw. Each singer who makes the transition from porch or yard to regular (as in the Church) or professional (staged) performance, either by being so elected within her community or by making the performance of blues and gospel a "profession," displays a "grain" of voice,[14] a vocal timbre or tone and style of vocal performance and indeed "embodied" physical performance that is recognizable to the listener. In the context of blues and gospel, analysis of the vocal productions of specific singers shows that there are no overriding specific techniques in common use to such an extent that one can describe them as vocal production "norms" for the genres. Indeed, general vocal deliveries of blues and gospel singers are not clearly defined as separate stylistically or tonally. Gospel and blues singers draw from the same well of singing and timbral possibilities and uniquely manipulate those elements individually. Embellishments, in Lomax's terminology, including melisma, sounds originating in vocal expression and glissandi, are almost always in evidence. The ability to improvise rhythmically and harmonically and to inflect notes is part of this aesthetic, as many writers have noted. The "voices" of blues and gospel singers, the physical individual sounds they make, are as numerous as the performers of these genres. And if there is a commonality in the vocal production, it is in a far deeper place than that measured by any analysis of sound. It is rather in the nature of tropes like "sincerity" and "transformation" (both of the self and the listener) which cannot be discussed without taking into account the backgrounds of the performers against a wider understanding of the development and history of the African American community in the political landscape of North America. Both blues and gospel are stylistically still contemporary musical forms – that is to say, they are present today in many parts of the world. But in describing the vocal productions from record of those originators of the forms, contemporary singers *must* display the same understanding of inner emotional commitment to the singing of the material, not the collection of ornamentations which define the singing style. These factors, appropriated by many popular music forms, and some non-African American performers are often, though by no means always, superficial. It is in Krehbiel's quotation at the front of Oliver's *Screening the Blues*[15] that the underlying quality of voice in the performances of the great singers of both genres can be identified, "the spiritual." This is elusive, but audible. For, *without* the singer's spiritual commitment, though the voice may praise the Lord, it won't get the congregation's plane off the runway. Though it may describe the pain of living or the joy of sex in words, it will not be "singing the blues."

8 The guitar

MATT BACKER

Of all the instruments associated with the blues, the guitar is predominant. And of all the instruments associated with popular culture, the impact of the blues on the guitar – be it in the hands of Jimi Hendrix, Eric Clapton, or Kurt Cobain – is incalculable. But where did it all start? Can you really make a link between the psychedelic explosions of a pop icon (albeit one who would regularly include blues standards in his repertoire) and a lay preacher from the Mississippi Delta like Blind Willie Johnson? And what about the link between the sacred and the secular forms of the music? Today we tend to see blues and gospel as two distinct genres or, as is the case in today's commercially driven world, two separate markets. As we shall see, it wasn't always thus. The two branches share the same roots.

"You know, the blues come out of the field, baby," Sam "Lightning" Hopkins told Sam Charters in 1964. "That's when you bend down, pickin' that cotton and sing 'Oh Lord, please help me'." Always a secular performer, he was nonetheless at pains to acknowledge the important role of religion, underlining the way in which the line between blues and gospel is often blurred. "The blues is a lot like church ... when a preacher's up there preachin' the Bible, he's honest to God tryin' to get you to understand these things. Well, singin' the blues is the same thing" (Charters 1965: 375).

The legendary Texan could, and did, sing about different things. Fifty years of performing seasoned, rather than altered, his particular blues and he was emblematic of the rural origins and popular development of the music and the guitar. Essentially a solo performer occasionally accompanied by bass and drums, he almost invariably played a six-string flat-top acoustic guitar, trademark thumb pick providing a constant rhythm, bare fingers stroking the treble strings. He was discovered playing at a church social gathering by the legendary Blind Lemon Jefferson, and Hopkins spent time in prison, on chain gangs, rode boxcars, played at hobo camps and juke joints and, by the late forties, had hit records. He found a new white audience in the sixties and seventies, performing constantly until his death in 1982. Thus he is a link between the pre-war Delta traditions and the modern age, not unlike his contemporary, John Lee Hooker, but a more useful example due to his direct contact with people like the aforementioned Jefferson.

Blind Lemon Jefferson is perhaps best known as the template for the joke which states that in order to be a blues man one needs a handle that is comprised in equal parts of: an affliction, a fruit, and the surname of a U.S. president. In his time he was a star in both sacred and secular fields. He saw himself first and foremost as a preacher, spreading the word both on and off the pulpit. He would travel from church to church and hundreds of people would flock to watch him perform. In a pre-mass media age, these meetings were essential not only to the dissemination of the gospel, but also to the music in all its variegated forms.

His technique incorporated a loose rhythmic feel and quite an inventive and active instrumental approach, responding to accompanied vocal phrases with single-note runs. There was none of the rhythmic strength of, say, Robert Johnson whose grooves by comparison seem etched in stone. Jefferson, like many of his contemporaries, sacrificed the structure in order to accommodate the performance, his single-string breaks providing a further breathing space in an already flexible sequence. His 1920s recording of "Black Snake Moan" is typical of many rural blues pieces in that, although following a repeated sequence that occurs every twelve bars or so, it does not adhere to the traditional twelve-bar chord progression. Rather than rising to the subdominant on bar 5, it drops down to a dominant chord based in the sixth degree of the major scale in and around bar 7, returning to the tonic at around bar 10 for the duration, before repeating (in the loosest possible sense) the pattern. His single-note runs do not have the clarity of his protégés', Hopkins appearing to have greater dexterity. No matter.

In an era when we have become accustomed to rigid computerized rhythms, it is sometimes difficult to appreciate the somewhat elastic sense of meter used by some of these players. But we can still enjoy the contrasts between players like Jefferson and contemporaries like Mississippi John Hurt, whose ornate and consistent finger picking sounds folksy and Celtic by comparison. Jefferson stroked groups of strings with the flesh of his fingers whereas Hurt would use alternating picking patterns more common to classical guitar or, as mentioned earlier, folk. His 1928 recording of "Stack – O – Lee" (better known as the standard "Stagger Lee") evinces an unusual degree of instrumental articulation for the genre and the period, probably achieved through the use of fingerpicks (plectra worn on the thumb and fingers of the picking hand) or very strong nails. Not long after this recording Hurt slipped back into obscurity, only to reappear almost thirty years later and be embraced by proponents of the folk craze. A late fifties recording of "Candy Man Blues" from the Newport Folk Festival shows that the voice, as you would expect, has been somewhat seasoned, but the picking remains as sprightly as ever. One can only imagine what fans of Peter, Paul, and Mary made of the bawdy lyrics.

Blind Willie Johnson shared an infirmity, a Founding Father's surname, and a vocation with Jefferson. Both were preachers and would have thought themselves out-and-out gospel performers, possibly regarding music as a sideline to their church work. Johnson would have been unlikely to consider himself a virtuoso slide guitarist, responsible for some profound and moving recordings.

Slide guitar is often identified with the blues, but is reckoned to have originated in Hawaii. Towards the end of World War I a Polynesian craze swept the United States, and touring troupes of Hawaiian musicians played to full houses across the country. Performing traditional songs, they utilized "slack key" guitar, wherein a metal bar was slid across raised strings tuned to an open chord – a sound quite familiar now, but revolutionary then.

Common tunings included, and still include: open D (strings tuned D–A–D–F♯–A–D – lowest string to highest), open E (which consists of the same intervals a tone higher), open G (which is D–G–D–G–B–D low to high – this tuning is responsible for a disproportionately high number of songs by the Rolling Stones) and open A (which again is the same tuning a tone higher). Various players adopted favorite tunings. Blind Willie McTell appeared to be fond of D, Robert Johnson of G. I say, "appeared" because of the lack of specific information; other than a few recordings, our only evidence is anecdotal and aural.

Knowledge of the Hawaiian craze would have been likely to have seeped into backwaters of the Deep South, and to have adapted itself well to the sort of instrument likely to have been owned by an itinerant sharecropper, one rather difficult to fret with a warped or broken neck. Techniques associated with the Diddly Bow (from whence Elias McDaniel derived his pseudonym, Bo Diddley) would have applied. This simple instrument was created by stretching a piece of wire or string over a nail hammered into a board, box, or even the side of a house. A piece of metal or glass, such as a bottle or can, was then used to touch the string at various points along its vibrating length to create different pitches while it was strummed, plucked, or picked (Palmer 1991).

The term "bottleneck guitar" describes the preference some players had (and have) for breaking or sawing off the neck of a bottle and wearing it over a finger. Others would use a piece of copper or chrome tubing, bone, and socket wrench or, in Blind Willie Johnson's case, a pocket knife. Sliding produces vibrato, glissandi, bends, and microtonal inflections that can emulate a human voice. In the correct hands, it is an extremely expressive instrument.

Johnson was possessed of such a pair of hands. His 1929 recording of "God Don't Never Change" is inspired and inspiring. Evoking the omnipotence of the Almighty in an almost laconic way, he ignores any standard chord progression instead relying on eight-bar phrases repeated over a monotone, alternating a verse and refrain. He provides a solid bass groove whilst doubling the vocal melody with the slide. Fans of guitarist and sound-track composer Ry Cooder would particularly enjoy it. Indeed Cooder cites Johnson's 1927 recording of "Dark Was The Night, Cold Was The Ground" as the inspiration for the memorable theme to the Wim Wenders film "Paris, Texas." Richard Spotswood says of "Dark Was The Night":

> I'll resist the temptation to match the emotional eloquence of this performance with words of my own; certainly it belongs on any list of the greatest records ever, powerfully illustrating the spiritual appeal the slide guitar has in the hands of a master . . . a nearly wordless prayer in the form of an intimate dialogue between Johnson and his instrument, assuming the status of performance only through the presence of a microphone.
>
> (Spotswood 1991)

The difference between him and his namesake, Robert Johnson, who Charles Shaar Murray calls "the most mythically correct" (Shaar Murray 1999: 399) blues artist, could not be starker. Whereas Blind Willie sang of the Lord's intransigence, Robert sang "If I Had Possession Over Judgement Day" or "Me And The Devil." His songs could be roughly divided into the secular, the misogynistic, and the blasphemous: his impact on rock music is incalculable. Led Zeppelin famously cribbed his line in "Travelling Riverside Blues" in which he suggests that his intended might like to "squeeze my lemon 'til the juice runs down my leg," the Rolling Stones covered "Love In Vain" and "Stop Breakin' Down" and Cream's version of "Crossroads" brought the story of Johnson's alleged pact with the devil to an audience of millions. We have twenty-eight songs and one photograph of him – in which he is dressed in a snappy suit, wearing a wide brimmed hat, and holding an expensive Gibson guitar – not standard fare for an itinerant blues man. Not unlike Christopher Marlowe, the exact manner, place, and reason for his death are shrouded in mystery.

He must have been the Jimi Hendrix or Charlie Parker of his day. The recordings indicate a finesse and swagger unequalled (to the best of our knowledge) by his peers. He is recorded solo, but making enough noise for several men. The rhythm is solid. One could even describe it as funky. Using what sounds like his bare fingers alternating with his thumb, he clearly articulates slide phrases that have now become staples of the musical diet, such as the signature riff to "Travelling Riverside Blues" or emulating the sound of the famous squeezed lemon in the same song.

Alan Lomax, the Library of Congress musicologist who documented Johnson and many others with his field recordings, recalls that the sessions took place in his hotel room and that Johnson was so shy that he faced the wall. Ry Cooder, in a 1982 BBC radio interview, believes that this was not due to timidity at all, but was Johnson utilizing a technique called "corner loading" which entails playing towards hard surfaces, which are at right angles to each other in order to increase ambience and bass response. The quality of the recordings is remarkably good, as are the performances. The playing is assured; the time is solid although the tempo increases. This has the effect of building excitement as the acceleration is gradual and consistent, and the instrument is well in tune and, at a guess, outfitted with new strings.

Unlikely as it may seem, Johnson had a mentor in the form of the singer, preacher and slide guitarist Son House, whose devotion to his calling would ensure that his secular performances would remain sporadic until his death in the sixties. Another of his protégés was Muddy Waters, to whom we will return later, and yet another associate was a little-known preacher and guitarist, Will Moore. It is not surprising that many of the principal characters in the story of the blues first encountered each other in the Mississippi countryside, and there are many minor players who were important ingredients in the area's rich musical stew, and in some ways were patrons of the arts. Moore is such an example, who would no doubt have been forgotten but for the exploits of his stepson, John Lee Hooker.

The stepfather seems to have been eager to protect his charge from the pernicious influences of the world of music, teaching the young Hooker the songs and techniques of his contemporaries yet forbidding him to perform. This merely strengthened the boy's resolve, and he proceeded to move north in and around 1933 (exact dates are never a forte of blues chronology).

His apprenticeship was long, and not necessarily easy. His moves, first to Memphis, later to Cincinnati, and finally to Detroit (but, interestingly enough, not to Chicago) seem to reflect the migratory patterns of rural black America in the years leading up to and including the war. He played in clubs and juke joints, solo and accompanied, worked as a janitor, cinema usher and in a car factory, all the while maintaining his primordial Delta style. Whether he played electric or acoustic guitar, he never abandoned the bare-fingered strumming interrupted by occasional single-note bursts that remains his stock-in-trade.

By 1948 he was popular enough in the Detroit area to come to the attention of a white record producer, Bernard Besman. In those days, producers did little more than try to capture a live performance as quickly as possible. Besman was unusually experimental, using techniques which would not become commonplace for another two decades, although his motivation was purely fiscal – the budget did not extend to paying for a band: the producer recalls trying to fill out the sound as much as possible (Shaar Murray 1999: 131–3). He put a cardboard box beneath Hooker's stomping foot in order to re-create something akin to a rhythm section and placed a microphone very close to his guitar and overloaded the input channel of the recorder, creating a deceptively electric sound. A speaker was then placed in front of a toilet bowl, recorded, and mixed in with the original signal, producing a revolutionary slapback echo. One song from these sessions, "Boogie Chillun," went on to sell a million copies, and Hooker's journey to international stardom had begun.

Whether alone in a recording studio in the forties, or duetting in the nineties with Bonnie Raitt, Carlos Santana, or Keith Richards, his approach remains remarkably consistent: seated, foot tapping, thumb-down stroking the bass strings, index finger stroking the treble strings, rhythm occasionally broken by flurries of higher-register notes. An open string will often drone the tonic throughout, and Hooker's tendency to avoid chord changes or to change in unusual places (in the great Delta tradition, ten-, eleven- and thirteen-and-a-half-bar phrases are not uncommon) adds to the exotic quality of his music. His favored tunings are either standard or open A, which many blues players refer to as "Spanish" tuning. Whoever sits in with him has to adapt to his way of doing things, and he has produced a surprising number of successful recordings with guest stars, like "Hooker n'Heat," "The Healer," and "Mr. Lucky," where the guests never swamp or dilute the artist's identity. Comparison between the performance of "I Cover The Waterfront" on his mid-sixties album *The Real Folk Blues* and the same song on his 1991 album *Mr. Lucky* is instructive. The former is remarkably sparse, accompanied only by the artist's foot and some spare strummed electric guitar. Using first-position open chords and strumming using the flesh of his fingers or thumb, the result is truly an example of the dictum "less is more." The more recent version, a duet with Van Morrison, has the backing of a full band including Hammond organ, bass, drums played with brushes, and Morrison playing the guitar part, an insistent sixteenth-note triplet part on electric guitar, probably played using a plectrum and down strokes (at least that's what he did when I played with him). While this version respects the artist's integrity and approach, it somehow is less evocative, coloring in as it does the spaces left blank on the original version.

While Hooker was developing his electrified swamp shuffle in Detroit, another transplanted Deltan was making significant waves in Chicago. McKinley Morganfield, better known as Muddy Waters, is best remembered as a singer, bandleader and songwriter – songs like "Mannish Boy," "Hootchie Kootchie Man," and "Seventh Son" are now standards, and popular culture would be very different if he had not written "Rolling Stone." His influence as a guitarist cannot be underestimated either, bearing in mind his utilization of a particular twentieth-century commodity – electricity.

Until the late 1940s, with the possible exception of modern classical composers and/or boffins like Leon Theremin and Pierre Schaeffer, technology had not altered the sound of music significantly since the invention of the saxophone. Forms were changing in classical and jazz music, but instrumental timbres remained unaltered. Whatever squeaks and scrapes might be coaxed from, for example, a violin, it remained a violin, be it in a piece by Schubert or Schoenberg, and one can argue that, addition of valves notwithstanding, there isn't a great deal of difference between the instrument used in "Trumpet Voluntary" and that played by Dizzy Gillespie.

Amplification was used sparingly in the late thirties, and allowed certain revolutions in technique. Frank Sinatra would not have been able to develop his singular phrasing without the aid of a microphone, and Charlie Christian's guitar would never have become a lead instrument in Benny Goodman's band. These were, however, amplified sounds in the true sense of the word – a human voice made audible over a big band, the sound of an arch-top guitar increased so that single notes could carry. Up until the 1970s, jazz guitarists like Wes Montgomery, Jim Hall, or Kenny Burrell continued to use the technique pioneered by Christian, using a naturalistic clean sound, particularly suited to sophisticated chord voicings.

As bands like Muddy Waters' or his contemporary Howlin' Wolf's played to increasingly full rooms in an increasingly loud world, they had to increase their volume in order to compete, and in so doing, taxed their equipment to the limit. The distortion that results from an amplifier being overdriven compresses the signal, producing increased sustain and frequency limitation. The combination of electric guitar and an amplifier behaving in such a manner produced something akin to a new instrument, so far removed from its origins that classical guitar maestro Andres Segovia would describe it as an abomination.

This meant that when Waters sang, "I'm a King Bee," he could produce an onomatopoeic sound with his slide on the upper register of his guitar, which would have been untenable on an acoustic instrument. Similarly, his band mate, the harmonica player Little Walter, would amplify his instrument resulting in a sound akin to an entire horn section. Using techniques such as note bending and crossing (using the tonality produced by inhaling as opposed to exhaling as the root) and playing through a distorted amplifier produced a powerful new lead instrument which, when allied with the electric guitar, took the music out of the swamp forever.

The tonality of an overdriven amplifier is not unlike a human voice or a horn. Inflection and phrasing oddities like glissandi and vibrato become more apparent. Notes take longer to decay, facilitating string bending. B. B. King, often considered to be the string-bending pioneer, claims that ignorance and a certain lack of technique forced him to emulate the sound made by his cousin, Bukka White. King was apparently unable to get to grips with a slide, and found other ways of producing a similar sound, and made the world a better place. As regards his technique, he says:

I felt that when I trilled my hand, I got this sound that my ears say was
similar to using a bottleneck, because I never could do it the usual way.
Like I say, I've got stupid fingers that just won't work.

(Tobler and Grundy 1983: 14)

His stupid fingers helped produce a creamy, vocal tone that is probably the
most influential sound in the history of the electric guitar, as is his unique
quick vibrato, achieved by using the knuckle of the left-hand index finger as
a fulcrum and letting a rocking action of the hand move the string from side
to side. Combining a Gibson 355 model (he favored ES 5 s and L5s in the
fifties, switching to the semi-hollow 300 series upon its introduction in 1958)
with a Fender Twin Reverb amplifier, his tweaks, trills and sustained notes
have ensured that the voice of his guitar, named Lucille, is as prominent as
his own, and has wormed its way into the sound and technique of countless
others including Eric Clapton, Carlos Santana, and Peter Green. Again, the
combination of guitar and amp is of paramount importance here, as well
as learning the dynamics of both. Dr. King, again:

That's technique, which comes from practising, and it also comes from
having a pretty good ear that's able to work with the volume and
feedback of the amp in such a way that it eventually becomes
professional. What I'm trying to say is that anybody can just turn the
guitar up and scream, but to be able to control it without going to your
volume controls, but using your ear to tell you when it's getting too loud
or not loud enough, takes technique, because you've got to work with
the frets there . . .

(Tobler and Grundy 1983: 14)

At the time of writing, King continues to record, and performs hundreds
of times per year. Most people are familiar with his soulful, horn-drenched
sound. Always the leader of big bands, his tight jazzy revue can be linked
to T-Bone Walker's, whose sophisticated brand of big band blues came out
of Texas at about the same time as Clarence "Gatemouth" Brown's, the
only blues artiste mentioned here that this writer has had the pleasure of
working with. Both owing a lot to singer and saxophonist Louis Jordan, they
would use horn sections and sophisticated chord voicings and substitutions.
In a 1997 interview with Jas Obrecht, Brown referred to his tendency to
view his guitar as part of the horn section, and to differentiate himself as a
performer:

I'm playin' them horn lines, and I come in and play horn solos. I play the
kicks with the band. It's a magical thing . . . and I got something else to
say; this record is starting to take me out of the blues scene. I hope so,
man, because when they talk about the blues, the whites think of
Mississippi and Chicago. Man, I can't stand that kind of stuff. I really
can't.

(Obrecht 1997: 88)

By the mid-1950s, the blues was reaching a wide audience, and crossing over into the white populace. The term "blues" was becoming as diverse and all encompassing as its cousin, jazz. Sub-classifications began to emerge, and old style Delta players like Mississippi Fred McDowell and Mississippi John Hurt began to be, as mentioned earlier, incorporated into the folk revival. Gospel became a separate entity. One of the few people to continue in the tradition of performing lay preachers was Elmore James, who believed that the blues was the devil's music, and that he was firmly in the hands of the prince of darkness when performing. Accordingly, he described his guitar tone as "the gates of hell opening up" (James 1969). The author of what is probably the best-known slide guitar phrase in the history of the genre, he tuned his flat-top acoustic guitar to open D or open E, fitted a magnetic pickup to it and put it through an amplifier set on "stun." The aforementioned lick, which opens "Dust My Broom," consists of a fiery sixteenth-note triplet double-stop consisting of the root and the dominant, sliding down to the third and then to the root, all of the notes that would be arrived at naturally by laying a slide across the twelfth fret of a guitar using this tuning. The full band, augmented by a horn section (on some recordings of this often re-recorded song) change on time, follow all the rules and, as you would expect with an aggregation led by Beelzebub, rock.

The guitar tended to feature less in straight gospel performances, providing a more supportive role in songs that were based on hymns and spirituals. One exception was Sister Rosetta Tharpe, who was unusual in that she was a solo female performer who played the electric guitar, by the fifties well on its way to its current position as that most testosterone fueled of instruments. Another influential player in that field was Clive "Pops" Staples, paterfamilias of a group of girls with truly divine voices. His subtle use of tremolo (an electronically produced modulation in volume), rhythmic accents and chord voicings would become a staple of the guitarist's vocabulary, as evinced in the group's hit records in the late sixties and early seventies. Other guitarists who would incorporate this styling would include Curtis Mayfield and Jimi Hendrix.

By the later part of the 1950s, a number of small specialty labels emerged from various regions, but none was as important to the dissemination of the blues as Chess records in Chicago. Including all of the pre-eminent performers of the era: Muddy Waters, Howlin' Wolf, Willie Dixon (who also served as in-house songwriter, musical director, and A&R), they were able to take some of their artists to a wider audience when, as Muddy Waters put it, the blues had a baby and named it rock'n'roll. While Elvis and Carl Perkins and Bill Haley terrorized God-fearing people everywhere, imagine the effect provided by Bo Diddley, whose showmanship and tremolo-drenched guitar playing was accompanied by maracas and a high-speed mambo that sounded like an American's idea of jungle drums. The emulations of human speech on "Mumblin' Guitar" would be studied and emulated by the aforementioned Hendrix, and the sexual innuendo of "Mona" and "Who Do You Love" would be copied and redefined by The Doors and The Stones, among countless others. In 1979, British punk super group The Clash would insist on him as their support act on their debut American tour. But Chess had an ace in the hole, a remarkably influential guitarist, singer and songwriter who was also a powerful entertainer, and one of the few black performers to cross over onto white radio and television.

It has often been suggested that had Chuck Berry been born white, he'd have been bigger than Elvis. He might even have obviated the need for Elvis and the Rolling Stones. His distinctive duck walk and rapid-fire double-stop guitar phrases mesmerized audiences everywhere, and he was in the tradition of crowd pleasers like Guitar Slim and T-Bone Walker. But he took the traditions of the twelve-bar blues – apparent in down-tempo tunes like "Wee Wee Hours" – to new lengths, wedding driving, blues based, up-tempo stompers to knowing, witty, literate lyrics. Equally familiar with blues, jazz and country, he told complete stories in three verses, accompanied by guitar phrases that are inseparable from the song. The slid major-sixth chord which heralds the opening of "Memphis, Tennessee" wedded with the Jimmy Reed inspired rhythm track (faithfully duplicated in covers by, among others, Lonnie Mack, and The Faces) evokes the story of lost love leading up to the punch line "Marie is only six years old . . . " The sixteenth-note triplet augmented chord that starts "School Days" is as ugly as any alarm clock can be at the crack of dawn. Each sung phrase is answered by a double-stop down-stroke guitar phrase, ending in the chiming chorus "Hail, Hail Rock and Roll" answered by a line evocative of a school bell at the end of a long day. This call and response is rooted in the Delta tradition, but paints a picture a world away: of bobby socks, blue jeans and burger joints that will forever be innocent 1950s America. The fact that the author was a black man in his thirties makes it all the more remarkable.

By the beginning of the sixties, the influence of the blues guitar was all pervasive. Performers like Buddy Holly were taking the influence of Bo Diddley to white audiences through songs like "Not Fade Away," and California surfers found a soundtrack in guitar instrumentals like Dick Dale's "Miserlou" and The Ventures' "Pipeline." Texan blues artist Freddie King recorded an album of instrumentals and found himself with a crossover hit. Signed to Chicago's King records, his recordings with a band of seasoned professionals took the blues format a little bit further. "The Stumble" weds a memorable melody to a chord progression which departs from the standard twelve-bar format – starting on the IV, returning to I on bar 3, up to IV on bar 5, and then to V on bar 7, before arriving at a stop-time break in which a diminished chord leads to a I–VI–II–V turnaround, a jazz staple. "Driving Sideways" stays on I for four bars, reverting to V on bar 5. "Hideaway" is more of a standard twelve-bar, but with added stop-time sections and time changes to keep the listener interested. It was a huge hit in 1961, and found another audience when John Mayall's Bluesbreakers covered it on their debut record. Their guitarist, Eric Clapton, saw a photograph of King playing a Gibson Les Paul, and decided that he had to have one too – although by the time he finally obtained one, his hero had switched to a Gibson 345 like his namesake, B. B. Despite using finger and thumb picks, his technique owed little to people like Lightnin' Hopkins, being another player who was inspired by the saxophone. "I play my guitar like Louis Jordan used to play his horn," he said in an interview with *Guitar Player* magazine not long before his death in 1976. "That's the same sound that I get" (F. King 1976).

The third of the Three Kings was Albert – like the other two, no relation. A native of Mississippi, he achieved his biggest success in the sixties when he recorded in Memphis for the legendary Stax label, home to such soul stars as Otis Redding and Sam and Dave. The fusion of blues and soul was made in heaven, with the peerless house band of Booker T. and the M. G.s (purveyors of the classic "Green Onions") and the Memphis Horns providing a funky foundation for King's razor-sharp tone and wide bends. These were achieved by playing a conventionally strung guitar left handed, and not re-stringing, as other left handers like Charlie Christian or Jimi Hendrix were wont to do. Having the highest string at the top of the fretboard not only gives it a great range, but pulling from above rather than pushing from below (the most common string-bending technique) enables other strings to be bent simultaneously, allowing for King's remarkable multi-timbral phrasing. His choice of guitar – a Gibson Flying V – allowed unprecedented access to the upper reaches of the fretboard, too. Eric Clapton brought him to the attention of a wider audience in the sixties when Cream covered his classic "Born Under A Bad Sign," and his influence on players like Jimi Hendrix, Robert Cray, and Stevie Ray Vaughan is incalculable.

In Britain in the late fifties and early sixties, blues aficionados like Alexis Korner and John Mayall would find a willing group of young acolytes who may not have been aware of the rich cultural traditions of the music they loved, but just loved the sound. Sonny Boy Williamson is reputed to have said of the Yardbirds, his backing group on an early sixties U.K. tour, "They want to play the blues so bad . . . and they do!" but others, like Muddy Waters, John Lee Hooker and Bo Diddley were more encouraging of their young European admirers. Upon arriving in America for the first time, the Rolling Stones could not believe that their American idols were not household names – after all, they had played to the same young audiences in Britain night after night. When their American popularity ensured a spot on the popular teenage show "Shindig," one of the Stones' provisos for appearing was that Howlin' Wolf open the show. This provided a bemused wide American television audience with their first exposure to their own legacy. To this day, many Americans make a pilgrimage to Liverpool because they think it is the birthplace of rock'n'roll.

It wasn't purely down to longhaired British art school students to educate white America. In Chicago, middle-class white boys like Michael Bloomfield and Paul Butterfield honed their skills on guitar and harmonica by watching, and copying, artists like Buddy Guy and James Cotton perform in South Side clubs. The Butterfield Blues Band would approach their subject with the same missionary zeal as John Mayall's band in Britain, or Al Wilson's Canned Heat in northern California. A pair of albino brothers must have been quite a sight in Texas juke joints when Johnny and Edgar Winter popped in to listen or play. Parts of the Butterfield Band would join Bob Dylan for his legendary electrification, Canned Heat would be a huge hit at Woodstock, and Johnny Winter would be the most expensive signing in the history of Columbia Records in 1969. Blues – whether interpreted in the form of meandering jams by the Grateful Dead in San Francisco, or loud riffs by the Earth Blues Band in Birmingham (who would find greater success when they changed their name to Black Sabbath) – had been subsumed into the mainstream.

As the seventies grew to a close, people began to get used to the idea of rock stars being elder statesmen as their heroes stumbled out of drink or drug rehabilitation programs. Some of them chose to use their lofty position to thank some of the people who provided them with the cash flow that nearly killed them. Johnny Winter produced Muddy Waters' "Hard Again," an epochal return to the rawness of the fifties Chess recordings. Keith Richards put together an all-star band to celebrate Chuck Berry's sixtieth birthday, filmed as "Hail, Hail Rock and Roll" and Eric Clapton's blues nights at the Albert Hall are almost as regular a part of the social calendar as the First Night of the Proms. John Lee Hooker would have to wait until the nineties for his much-deserved Grammies and all-star duets, but the blues would never again be part of the mainstream.

Gospel became a marketing term, but the influence of earlier performers like Sister Rosetta Tharpe and Aretha Franklin became apparent in mainstream successes like Whitney Houston and Mary J. Blige. Out-and-out gospel choirs like Sounds of Blackness would find a large and affluent black audience, but the role of the guitar would be marginal.

As Punk, New Romanticism, Hip-Hop and Dance infatuated the public, a younger generation of blues guitarists would return to different eras in the history of the music. Stevie Ray Vaughan would reacquaint his audience with the work of Guitar Slim, Buddy Guy and Albert King as well as establishing Jimi Hendrix in the blues pantheon before joining it himself courtesy of a helicopter crash. His brother Jimmie, a long-serving member of The Fabulous Thunderbirds who kept alive the work of arcane artists like Slim Harpo and Lazy Lester, would play at the inauguration of president George W. Bush. So too would fellow hirsute Texans Z. Z. Top, who allegedly provided funds to turn the shack in which Muddy Waters was born into a national monument. In America, there is a chain of restaurants and venues part owned by veteran rockers Aerosmith and comic actor Dan Ackroyd called "The House of Blues," which combines an upmarket Planet Hollywood approach to soul food (the cuisine of the Deep South) and decor which resembles a highly decorated rural shack. Performing at the New Orleans branch, located in the French Quarter, is a surreal experience.

Others have persevered in a more low-key way. Johnny Winter has recorded for blues labels like Alligator and Point Blank, and has been a fixture on the blues circuit for over twenty years, abandoning the capes and rhinestone suits of the seventies. Younger performers like Eric Bibb, Ben Harper, Sonny Landreth, and Keb Mo' explore all areas of the blues, from Delta-influenced musings to reinterpretations of Led Zeppelin's "Whole Lotta Love." Olu Dara does what Taj Mahal has been doing for thirty years, which is exploring roots and branches of the blues in African and Caribbean music. Ry Cooder recorded with Malian guitarist Ali Farka Toure, who in turn has been assiduous in showing the world the African origins of the blues.

There are a few survivors of the old days in the Mississippi Delta. Henry "Mule" Townsend spent the early years of the twenty-first century touring the U.S. and Europe – seventy-two years after making his first commercial recordings. Along with Honeyboy Edwards, Homesick James, and Robert Lockwood Jr. (who spent his early years playing with Robert Johnson), they called themselves the Delta Blues Cartel and played as they always have. At the other end of the spectrum, little-known Mississippi guitarist R. L. Burnside found unlikely collaborators in the form of the Jon Spencer Blues Explosion, who despite their name are New York post-punkers who mix deconstructed riffs with break beats and samples. Their late nineties album, *A Ass Pocket of Whisky*, led to Burnside recording with younger producers who have worked with alternative rock acts like Beck and Liz Phair, who utilize contemporary sounds and techniques. Unlike other anachronisms – Muddy Waters' late sixties foray into psychedelia *Electric Mud* springs to mind – these recordings actually work. Burnside's *I Wish I Was In Heaven Sitting Down* is one of the best albums of 2000, in any genre.

Whatever happens to the blues guitar, it is clear that we are at the end of an era. As Robert Palmer says in an article on the Delta Blues Cartel, which could easily apply to any of the old masters, they are "better understood as deans of the old school who helped to author its code . . . when they pass, so go the mysteries . . . and all the wisdom that lay within" (Palmer 2001: 48).

9 Keyboard techniques

ADRIAN YORK

In the late nineteenth and early twentieth centuries, many of the itinerant pianists working in the whorehouses, gambling dens, bars and lumber camps of the American South played in a style known as barrelhouse. Blues, gospel and boogie-woogie piano styles all emerged from barrelhouse and so to understand the roots of these styles it is to the early days of barrelhouse that we must turn. The "race" recording industry was not underway until the 1920s and so the only sources that we have for studying the pianists of the pre-recording era are the occasional piano roll and the written and recorded recollections of a younger generation of "piano professors." Therefore this chapter can only recount a partial history, trying to draw together fragments of a much deeper culture into something coherent. This I have done by examining the playing techniques that unite and separate these interwoven styles, their genesis, transformation and cross-genre transplantation that has so informed the development of popular music through the twentieth century.

The early rural and urban barrelhouses, juke joints and honky-tonks were bars where entertainers sporting exotic-sounding stage names such as Papa Lord God, No Leg Kenny and Drive 'Em Down would play on "honky-tonk" sounding pianos. Some pianists only played barrelhouse blues in their performances, others would combine blues with ragtime, popular songs and classical pieces. These piano "crushers" or "pounders" had to make themselves heard over the noise of the bar often at the expense of accuracy and certainly without much in the way of formal technique. Combined with the function of providing dance music, these conditions helped to form an aesthetic that was quite unique. Barrelhouse was pianistically innovative in the use of grace notes, a technique that uses the same finger to slip from the note a semitone below to the intended note, three- or four-note glissandi and one- or two-handed tremolandi as embellishments. It is very probable that the barrelhouse pianists were trying to imitate similar effects used by the early rural blues guitar players. Meter varied between a steady $\frac{4}{4}, \frac{2}{2}$ for more up-tempo tunes, and $\frac{2}{4}$ for a two-step feel. Left-hand patterns could be as minimal as a root note on beats 1 and 3 sometimes ornamented by an ascending grace note or three- or four-note glissandi. The addition of a fifth above the tonic points the way to the early boogie left hands.

The early barrelhouse feel was a simplified version of the ragtime left hand. The ragtime "boom-chick" consisted of a low register tonic or chord tone in octaves on beats 1 and 3 going to close-position triads voiced around middle C on beats 2 and 4. The barrelhouse version could be as simple as broken-octave quarter notes starting with the lower octave, often adding in the fifth to the higher octave on beats 2 and 4. When this voicing is played with a eighth-note feel, it again points the way ahead to boogie-woogie. Another left-hand option was the walking bass where you move to adjacent scale tones or chromatic passing notes in a four to the bar quarter-note feel.[1] Eighth-note triplets or syncopated eighth-notes supplied rhythmic momentum in the right hand. As with the early blues guitar players, the harmony could be as straightforward as a tonic drone with the occasional foray to chords IV and V or a blues turnaround. Chords would mainly be majors and minors with their sevenths, major sixths, and the occasional passing diminished chord. Chord voicings were much less full than those of the ragtime pianists with the open fifths and fourths in the left hand creating a hollow-sounding harmony. Soloing was generally restricted to decoration around the vocals. The most common scales were the blues and myxolydian[2] which were often used simultaneously, allowing for the flattened and natural thirds to be used as adjacent notes and sometimes "crushed" together creating a major/minor harmonic ambivalence. Although eight-, twelve- and sixteen- bar blues forms were common, song structures reflected the informal setting and players often threw in extra beats or bars.

One early development of barrelhouse was boogie-woogie, a repetitive eight-to-the-bar left-hand pattern with both the rolling left-hand patterns and right-hand effects being influenced by the sound of the railway. The style was popular by the late 1890s for as Eubie Blake said about a pianist named William Turk:

> He had a left hand like God. He didn't even know what key he was playing in, but he played them all. He would play ragtime stride bass, but it would bother him because his stomach got in the way of his arm, so he used a walking bass instead. I can remember when I was thirteen; this was 1896, how Turk would play one note with his right hand and at the same time four with his left. We called it "sixteen," they call it "boogie-woogie" now.

Roy Carew, a New Orleans music fan, said in a telling assessment of the early style: "I would say that boogie-woogie was the bad little boy of the rag family that wouldn't study. I heard crude beginnings of it in the back streets of New Orleans, in those early years following 1904, but they were really back streets . . . such music never got played in the gilded palaces."

Previously known by a variety of names such as "dudlow joe," boogie-woogie did not go under that name until 1929 with the release of Clarence "Pine Top" Smith's "Pine Top's Boogie-Woogie." Initially the boogie left hand was introduced several choruses into a performance as a way of giving added rhythmic impetus. Whilst it is probable that the various bass lines were linked with particular dance steps there is some speculation that some of the bass lines may have originated in the vaudeville theatres as a way of providing accompaniments to various novelty acts. The earliest-known recording featuring boogie bass lines was Clay Custer's version of George W. Thomas' "The Rocks" recorded in New York City in 1923. It starts with a rolling swing-feel bass changing to a rolling straight[3] feel and straight broken octaves in the left hand. The right hand part consists mainly of arpeggiated flourishes and melodies in octaves that are rhythmically staid. His younger brother Hersal's piano roll of "The Fives" from 1924 has a pounding eighth-note right hand underpinned by straight eighth-note left-hand broken octaves and a repetitive boogie eighth-note left hand going from the chord root and fifth (played twice) to root and sixth and finally root and flat sixth. The right hand also uses the idiosyncratic sixteenth-note tremolandi that is part of the Texas piano sound. The ill-fated prodigy Hersal, who died aged only twenty in 1926, also influenced later blues pianists with tracks like the 1925 "Suitcase Blues" with its proto-shuffle opening left hand, right-handed eighth-note triplet and sixteenth-note thirds and octave tremolandi. Despite coming from a through-composed formal composition, these are all elements that are still present in contemporary blues and rock'n'roll playing.

If the Texas influence was important in the development of boogie-woogie, the state was also a home to some of the most idiosyncratic barrel-house stylists. Robert Shaw's composition "The Ma Grinder" is a rhythmic mix of ragtime, barrelhouse and blues, with an exaggerated use of grace notes and glissandi, propelled along using the New Orleans habañera feel. A similar mix is present in the early sanctified singing and barrelhouse/rag/gospel piano playing of "Blind" Arizona Dranes. Born *c.* 1905 she performed in the Pentecostal and Holiness churches in the Dallas/Fort Worth area and became the first well-known gospel piano player. She defined the essential elements of the gospel piano style: the left hand plays the bass, the middle register supports and harmonizes the melody and the upper end adds fills and countermelodies. The harmony is straight from the Protestant hymnals, diatonic with diminished passing chords, but with an added blues influence; the rhythm can be straight or swung with much use of syncopation. She recorded tracks for the Okeh label in Chicago such as "In That Day" (1926), "I Shall Wear A Crown" (1928) and, prefiguring the $\frac{12}{8}$ feel of the 1950s, the $\frac{3}{4}$ "He Is My Story." Her left hand plays octave eighth notes with sixteenth-note syncopation in both hands. Her right hand plays eighth-note triads in the middle register, pounding sixteenth-note patterns that sound like Jerry Lee Lewis, and offbeat sixteenth-note riffs. Dranes fills between vocal lines with her version of the Texan right-hand tremolando, coming in on the second sixteenth-note in the bar over a major triad.

Another successful Dallas gospel musician of this early period was Washington Philips (1891–1938) who on his recordings accompanies his heartfelt vocals with the "dulceola," a very rare keyboarded dulcimer. With his left hand he plays either a simplified ragtime left hand or arpeggiates the left hand while the right hand "plucks" swung syncopated sixteenth-note lines, often moving from major triad to major sixths. The right hand doubles the vocal melody and also fills in with chiming right-hand lines, either single note, in sixths, or in octaves. The extraordinary sound made by Philips in recordings such as "Mother's Last Word To Her Son" and "Denomination Blues" is strongly reminiscent of the sound and tonality of kora music from Senegal, Mali, Guinea and Gambia mixed up with a hillbilly feel and a blues tinged vocal!

If Washington Philips created a sound fit for the ears of angels, Luther Magby's recordings "Blessed Are The Poor In Spirit" and "Jesus is Getting Us Ready For The Great Day," bring us closer to earth. Accompanied by a syncopated and busy tambourine the wheezing sound of his two-manual harmonium gives these energetic two steps great momentum. His left hand sticks to tonic and dominant onbeats while the right hand breaks up the diatonic triads into sixteenth-note responses to his gruff vocals.

The influence of the early barrelhouse and boogie styles was felt in New Orleans where Jelly Roll Morton was codifying the early jazz style. From the recordings Morton made for the Library of Congress in 1938 he brings to life the playing styles of some of those early unrecorded pianists. The four to the bar opening feel of Morton's version of Tony Jackson's "Michigan Water Blues" begins with triads in both hands voiced tonic, fifth and flat seventh on the first beat. The upper two notes then descend chromatically over the four beats of the bar ending on tonic, third and fifth. The left hand moves into more traditional territory with an octave walking bass that turns into split octave eighth notes, and he then plays a series of tunes that came from the "lower-class districts." The two versions of the twelve-bar "Honky Tonk Blues" feature either the simplified rag or broken octaves left hand. The eight-bar "Levee Man Blues" has an even more basic left hand, four-in-the-bar tonic and dominant to tonic and submediant, perhaps to reinforce the rural setting of the composition. In "New Orleans Blues" and "Low Down Blues" Morton demonstrates how in New Orleans the tango rhythm is fused with the blues. The accuracy of these performances is uncertain, however there are clear variations between the different styles that he presents and these recordings remain a tremendous resource for the jazz and blues historian. In his own compositions and arrangements Morton offers a more sophisticated take on the blues than some of his less-schooled peers. His playing is more pianistic, harmonically adventurous and uses more complex voicings whilst retaining many of the early barrelhouse stylistic elements.

The success of the blues divas in the early 1920s created recording opportunities for the barrelhouse, boogie and early gospel pianists. It is these recordings from the 1920s and 1930s that give us the first contemporary impressions of the stomps, boogies and blues being played in the barrelhouses and the city rent parties. Until this point the pianists would have learned tunes from each other, adapting them with their own trademark riffs and introductions, creating a shared localized repertoire that would have to be mastered by any pianist trying to break into the local scene. A case in point is the "Vicksburg Blues" which was developed around 1922 by "Little Brother" Eurreal Montgomery and various other pianists in the Vicksburg area. He taught it to Lee "Porkchops" Green who subsequently taught it to Roosevelt Sykes. In 1929 Sykes then proceeded to record it (as "44 Blues") as did Green ("Train Number Forty-four") and eventually "Little Brother" himself. Little Brother's version has a slow half-note left-hand walking bass each note being anticipated by chromatic glissandi whilst the right hand plays eighth-note chordal patterns and supports and answers every vocal phrase with a fast repetitive note that seems to merge with his adenoidal vocal. In Roosevelt Sykes' version that answering phrase is pitched in a much lower register and the whole performance feels as if it is teetering on the edge of rhythmic collapse.

The tension between sacred and secular is a defining characteristic of African American society but once we move away from the machinations of church politics and examine the process of cultural exchange we see that the relationship between gospel and blues piano is one of symbiosis and not of conflict. It is in the music of Georgia-born Thomas A. Dorsey that we see the clearest example of this process. Dorsey started off by playing blues and barrelhouse at local rent parties eventually graduating to working with blues diva Ma Rainey. Using the stage name Georgia Tom he formed a duo with guitarist Tampa Red and in 1928 as "The Hokum Boys" they had a hit record with the seminal hokum blues "Tight Like That." Dorsey's piano playing on the hokum tracks is in a gently rocking barrelhouse style which he claimed was effective for not annoying the neighbors at rent parties. After a religious conversion in 1921 at the National Baptist Convention in Chicago he turned to composing and performing gospel blues compositions, and by the early 1930s had given up secular music for good. Despite initial resistance, partly due to his racy hokum background, Dorsey ended up as the revered father figure of American gospel music having made a neat switch of careers as the blues industry hit bad times with the Depression of the 1930s. What he achieved was not just the integration of his barrelhouse feel into newly composed gospel/blues compositions, but the business and creative vision to understand that his songs and style could be popular with the northern churches. Until that point they had rejected the downhome southern style of worship in favor of Western classical music. They were, however, forced to respond to demand for this new gospel sound. His style became well known as the "Dorsey Bounce" and his feel was fully formed by the time of his 1934 recordings "If I Could Hear My Mother Pray Again" and "Singing In My Soul." The octave left hand emphasizes the tonic and dominant on beats 1 and 3 with eighth-note runs linking the chord changes while the right hand supports the melody with syncopated triadic chords and embellishes with high-register major pentatonic fills. It was of course another musician from Georgia, Ray Charles, who in the 1950s reversed this process transforming the gospel music of his childhood into secular r&b.

By the late 1920s we can see the development of barrelhouse into a number of distinct stylistic and regional archetypes. St. Louis was a city with a strong tradition of ragtime piano and the ragtime sense of restraint and control was clearly present in the playing of pianists such as Wesley Wallace and Henry Brown. They had a reputation for playing slow to mid-tempo blues with Brown in particular using hollow sounding open fifth four-to-the-bar figures in the left hand. However there is a danger of simplifying the regional issue and not taking into the account the diversity of feels that each pianist could play. Wallace impresses with his unusual $\frac{3}{4}$ train boogie "No. 29" and Brown shows the clear influence of the stride and jazz pianists in "Twenty First St. Stomp." Also active during this period in St. Louis were Sykes, who achieved fame in early 1940s Chicago with his rocking boogie basslines and right-hand blues and boogie licks, and Peetie Wheatstraw (*b.* William Bunch in 1902), who was born in Tennessee but moved to the East St. Louis area. He was best known for the up-tempo "stomp." This approach had moved beyond the drone bass parts of the earlier barrelhouse stylists to either a straight four-in-the-bar feel, with the simplified ragtime bass or basic boogie figurations, or a $\frac{2}{2}$ feel with a single-note bass lines on the first and third quarter-note beats of the bar. His songs such as "Peetie Wheatstraw Stomp" transplant the rural barrelhouse feel into an urban context.

The transition from barrelhouse to boogie-woogie can be traced in the 1925 recording of Charles "Cow Cow" Davenport's influential "Cow Cow Blues." This piece features a pounding left-hand octave eighth-note bass line, strong two-handed riffing, repetitive right-hand single-note or broken-triad licks and a turnaround that is still heard in the playing of contemporary New Orleans pianist Dr. John. "Cow Cow Blues" is one in a line of train blues including the first great boogie masterpiece, Meade "Lux" Lewis' 1927 recording of "Honky Tonk Train Blues." Against a steady rocking triadic left hand that shifts from the second inversion tonic to the subdominant first inversion, Lewis pulls off a virtuosic series of riffs, single-note/thirds/sixths tremolandi, and runs off and against the beat that leave the barrelhouse behind. In the following year Pinetop Smith, who was Lewis' and Albert Ammons' flatmate, recorded the first boogie-woogie hit. "Pinetop's Boogie-Woogie," the tune that gave the genre its name, features a rolling boogie left hand, a catchy melody in thirds and sixths and the infamous "lick" turnaround made famous by Ray Charles.[4]

The boogie-woogie craze started in 1938 in New York when Chicago pianists Meade Lux Lewis and Albert Ammons teamed up with Kansas City-born Pete Johnson for John Hammond's "Spirituals to Swing" concerts at Carnegie Hall. Ammons provides a link to the r&b of the 1940s with his 1936 recording of his version of "Pinetop's Boogie-Woogie" which goes under the title "Boogie-Woogie Stomp." The track features a rhythm section and brass and is driven along by Ammons' "hucklebuck" left hand.[5] The same left-hand pattern drives Pete Johnson and singer Joe Turner's 1938 "Roll 'Em Pete" but it is Johnson's almost continuous eighth-note right hand in thirds, fourths and triads and the use of chromatic passing notes, which anticipates later rock'n'roll styles. Chicagoan Jimmy Yancey is the final key figure in the mid-1930s resurgence of boogie-woogie. With his rolling triadic left-hand patterns, his style was closer to that of the older generation of barrelhouse pianists, his playing often being slower and more pensive than that of his pupils Ammons and Lewis.

Despite the importance of Chicago as a location for the development of boogie-woogie, it was a resident of Indianapolis who provides the link between the rural and the urban Chicago blues style. Pianist/singer Leroy Carr and his musical partner guitarist "Scrapper" Blackwell recorded extensively for the Vocalion and Bluebird labels from the late 1920s until 1935. They set a new standard of interplay between piano and guitar with Carr's driving four-to-the-bar left hand providing a solid rhythmic bed for his gentle, melancholic vocals and Blackwell's piercing single-note guitar lines. Their biggest hit was their first version of Carr's "How Long-How Long Blues," an eight-bar medium-tempo blues that hinges around Carr's open fifth quarter-note left hand with the guitar and right-hand piano providing the decoration. Although there is nothing innovative about the individual elements of their playing, Carr and Blackwell created a rhythmic and structural template that greatly influenced the Chicago sound.

The differences between the blues and barrelhouse tradition during the Depression years can be heard in the work of two Chicago players who were both recording in the mid-1930s. On Eddie Miller's recordings from 1936 such as "I'd Rather Drink Muddy Water" or "Whoopie" the left-hand parts are either stride or walking bass with boogie elements being restricted to fills. However George Noble's style on tracks such as the 1935 recording of "TB Blues" has both hands being boogie-based with the tempo being slower, the articulation much heavier, a looser sense of metrical structure and the left hand often playing a boogie-based drone throughout most of the composition. The right hand either plays blues answering phrases in octaves, single-note fills in the manner of "Vicksburg Blues," tremolandi or triadic riffs with crushed thirds.

The best-known exponent of piano blues in Chicago in the 1940s was Big Maceo Merriweather whose style became the model for the urban blues pianists in the city. Originally born and raised near Atlanta, Georgia, once in Chicago he teamed up with Thomas Dorsey's ex-guitarist Tampa Red recording a succession of hard-driving duets such as their 1941 classic "Worried Life Blues." This is a mid-tempo eight-bar blues typical of their output with a heavy four in the bar feel. From the same session "Ramblin' Mind Blues" shows the influence of older players such as Little Brother Montgomery and Roosevelt Sykes and the rocking boogie of "Can't You Read" with its hard swinging broken-octave left hand predates the sound of Ray Charles. The boogie-woogie element was key to Maceo's style and having been born left-handed can have only given added strength to his bass lines. In 1945, Maceo recorded the classic boogie-woogie "Chicago Breakdown" which again featured a hard-swinging broken-octave left hand as well as idiosyncratic right-hand diatonic chordal patterns and eighth-note left-hand riffing. The strength and quality of his playing attracted several students including Otis Spann and his cousin Johnny Jones, who integrated Maceo's style into the larger units typical of the urban Chicago sound of the 1950s.

It was Muddy Waters who integrated the piano and harmonica into the electric urban blues units saying, "Another change was the piano. If you get the piano in there you get a full bed of background music . . . I kept that backbeat on the drums plus full action on the guitar and harmonica and the piano in the back, then you've got a big sound." Waters occupies a parallel position to that of Duke Ellington or Miles Davis in jazz, all inspired bandleaders who developed their sound around key personnel in their bands. Otis Spann grew up in a small town called Belzoni, Missouri, where he had tuition from a local player called Friday Ford. After coming to Chicago he became Waters' piano player waxing seminal tracks such as "I'm Your Hoochie Coochie Man," "Got My Mojo Working" as well as recording with other artists on the Chess label such as Little Walter ("Key to the Highway") and Bo Diddley ("I'm A Man"). What Spann achieves is a total integration with the guitars, harmonica and drums, embellishing "I'm Your Hoochie Coochie Man" with fast repetitive high register seventh voicings and, on "I Just Want To Make Love To You," taking over the role of the guitars by providing the main riffs. Johnny Jones worked with Tampa Red after Big Maceo's premature death and then went on to play in slide guitarist Elmore James' band. He also recorded "Little Red Rooster" with Howlin' Wolf and composed the blues classic "Big Town Playboy."

1930s Chicago was not only the city where the blues was becoming urbanized, it was also the center of the burgeoning gospel scene. Thomas A. Dorsey founded one of the first gospel choirs at Chicago's Pilgrim Baptist Church in 1932. His protégé Roberta Martin started her career playing the piano for Dorsey's choir, eventually branching off to form her own Roberta Martin Singers. Martin brought elements of a Western classical music sensibility to gospel both through her piano playing, which is characterized by both a lightness of touch and richness of tone, and her harmonic knowledge through which she developed a series of chord substitutions and harmonic cadences that are still part of the gospel sound today. For instance instead of cadencing from a I chord to a V and then back to a I, Martin would start on a I second inversion, then go through a VI^7, II^7, V^7 ending on the I. Martin favored slow tempos with compound-time signatures such as $\frac{6}{8}$, $\frac{9}{8}$ and $\frac{12}{8}$ so developing the gospel waltz style of composer Lucie E. Campbell. Martin placed her right-hand chords around the middle register of the piano often anticipating each chord change by playing any new chord two eighth notes before its actual entry followed by a move to the chord a fourth away returning to the new chord on the downbeat. For the rest of the bar Martin would often move her right hand to the higher register putting in fills in octaves, broken octaves or thirds, which would act as a "response" to the "call" of her downbeat. Endings would be slowed right down with right-hand arpeggios going up the keyboard.

If Martin defined the harmonic structures of gospel it was another Dorsey protégé who added the rhythmic elements that energized the gospel music of the big urban gospel choirs through the 1960s and 1970s. Singer and pianist James Cleveland's piano playing is described by gospel scholar Anthony Heilbut as being "sensational" with "strong, clanking chords, the heavy pedal alternating with the limp, lyric right hand." His powerful sound may have emerged from his enforced practice method. As he told Heilbut "My folks being just plain, every day people, we couldn't afford a piano. So I used to practice each night right there on the windowsill. I took those wedges and crevices and made me black and white keys. And baby, I played just like Roberta." When he became director of the radio choir at Bethlehem Baptist Church in Detroit where the Rev. C. L. Franklin was pastor he took the young Aretha Franklin under his wing coaching her in both piano and vocals. Aretha's pure gospel piano playing and singing is at its purest on recordings made in 1956 at her father's church when she was only fourteen years old. On tracks like "Never Grow Old" and "There Is A Fountain Filled With Blood" we hear dramatic confirmation that Aretha's style was fully formed by this time. She mostly plays with a slow rubato feel articulating each chord change with a mid-register right-hand chord and octaves in the left hand. At the end of every line she puts in a right-hand fill, often ascending spread inversions of the chord or major pentatonic octave lines. Left-hand octave tremolandi or right-hand single repetitive notes that have their roots in the blues support moments of tension. When Aretha chooses to emphasize the rhythm she does it with a swung right-hand octave motive on the tonic that takes us straight to her soul recordings for Atlantic in the 1970s.

Aretha is accompanied on these recordings by the Hammond organ, which supports the harmony with mid-register chords without adding any rhythmic interest. But it was many years earlier that the organ was introduced to gospel music. In 1937 gospel diva Mahalia Jackson, yet another Dorsey collaborator, had her pianist Estelle Allen use a church organ to accompany her on two tracks, "Keep Me Every Day" and "God Shall Wipe All Tears Away." Allen sticks to simple accompaniments that followed the chords without adding any embellishments. It was two years later in 1939 that composer and music publisher Kenneth Morris introduced the Hammond organ and piano combination to gospel. If the organ played sustained chords then the piano could be more rhythmic or vice versa; the organ could match the vibrato of a choir whilst the piano had a driving attack to its sound. Western art music organ techniques were integrated into the gospel sound by Detroit musician Alfred Bolden who tried to establish the organ as a solo instrument. Organist Billy Preston began his career playing for James Cleveland's Gospel Chimes group alongside pianist Jessy Dixon. Preston went on to become the top soul organist/keyboard player of the 1960s taking his gospel styles and enriching the sound of the Beatles and other pop artists before establishing a successful solo career. The piano/organ combination went on to be the foundation of the gospel sound until the 1970s when the synthesizer came into gospel and pop music production techniques became the norm. The organ of choice was the Hammond B3 organ with Leslie rotary speaker cabinets. The Leslie had a rotating horn on top of the main speaker that could spin at different speeds providing a different level of effect. The swirling sound of the Leslie added an emotional excitement to the sound of the organ and it would be brought in and out to match the mood of the music.

The movement of artists across the secular/sacred divide had been well established by the 1960s, but in 1969 the cultural pendulum swung the other way with a record being released that introduced a white pop sensibility and the white pop market to the gospel choir format. Without the vocals

The Edwin Hawkins' Singers' recording of "Oh Happy Day" could be a great piece of soul-inflected pop. The piano ripples rather than drives with accents on the third and sixth eighth note of the bar opening the door for the soul/pop piano work on Aretha Franklin's "Say A Little Prayer" and the feel and sound of George Harrison's "My Sweet Lord." From this point on the crossover between the gospel and r&b/pop sounds has become less distinct. Gospel-influenced artists such as Andrae Crouch, The Winans, The Sounds of Blackness and Destiny's Child have either crossed over completely or else present a gospel/lite message with the production values reflecting the commercial imperatives of the day.

Both gospel and blues piano and keyboard styles have influenced artists working in many other genres. Big band swing artists such as Count Basie as well as pop singers such as the Andrews Sisters jumped on the boogie-woogie fad. The Louis Jordan "jump" sound of the 1940s and r&b of the 1940s, 1950s and 1960s were based on the boogie-woogie feel with added blues and swing elements. Jazz musicians in the 1950s and early 1960s revisited their blues and gospel roots in compositions such as Horace Silver's "The Preacher." Ray Charles, the first great soul star, integrated the cocktail blues ballad style of Charles Brown with the gospel and boogie-woogie sounds of his childhood in Georgia. In 1951, the blues and boogie right-hand figurations of Ike Turner enlivened the proto rock'n'roll of Jackie Brenston's "Rocket 88," creating a model for Johnnie Johnson's playing with Chuck Berry later that decade. In New Orleans, a distinctive regional piano style developed with its roots in Jelly Roll Morton's "Spanish tinge," barrelhouse and boogie-woogie. Pianists such as Professor Longhair, Fats Domino, James Booker and Dr. John created an easily identifiable sound that expressed the "good times" feel of the city. In England, Graham Bond introduced the Hammond organ into pop music paving the way for its use in progressive and hard rock and in piano and organ combinations in groups as diverse as Bruce Springsteen's E Street Band and Ian Dury and the Blockheads.

The journey from the barrelhouse to the digital locations where much contemporary music is made encompasses an intriguing history of racism, poverty, social progression, technological development, religion, and the music business. Despite these elements it is these pianists and their creativity that have helped to create the diversity of popular music culture in the twentieth century.

10 Imagery in the lyrics: an initial approach

GUIDO VAN RIJN

Both blues and gospel are strongly formulaic in many respects. One area in which songs demonstrate the degree of originality necessary for them to become memorable to a particular audience is in the types of images to be found in their lyrics. This chapter is not therefore concerned with the description of everyday events, or the way narratives are created,[1] but with the use of the imagination to render the commonplace in some way extraordinary.

Blues and gospel music belong to the oral tradition. Access to these lyrics can, therefore, be highly problematic. Record transcriptions present a great many difficulties both because of the condition of the often very rare records and the highly idiomatic articulation often employed. Early folklorists and publishers printed many lyrics from songs that were sung to them. The pioneer of recorded blues lyric analysis is Paul Oliver, but his 1960 *Meaning in the Blues* and his 1968 *Screening the Blues* contain only isolated stanzas. The same holds good for Samuel Charters in his 1970 *The Poetry of the Blues*. Paul Garon's surrealistic approach to blues lyricism in his 1975 *Blues and the Poetic Spirit*, while a controversial but stimulating effort, does not lay the groundwork for a comprehensive study.

To analyze the use of imagery in blues and gospel songs an accurate written corpus with complete transcriptions is required. In 1969 Eric Sackheim published his *The Blues Line: A Collection of Blues Lyrics from Leadbelly to Muddy Waters*. At the time this was a breakthrough publication and although the (complete) transcriptions in it are more than adequate, there are many lines in italics, which indicate phrases Sackheim could not hear. In 1983 Michael Taft published *Blues Lyric Poetry*, a computer-generated anthology of 2,000 (complete) lyrics. However, the expensive publication contained so many inaccuracies in its transcriptions that it has never been a really useful tool.

An audacious attempt to transcribe the pre-war lyrics is now being made by R. R. Macleod in his series on the *Yazoo*, *Blues Document* and *Document* reissue labels. The early Yazoo volumes are notoriously inaccurate, but when Richard Metson, Bernard Holland and later John Newman joined the author, the accuracy of the transcriptions improved greatly. At the moment of writing Macleod has reached DOCD 5280 and a prospective table suggests that, from the frequency with which the books are appearing, he should have reached the end of the Document Series by 2010. Next the enormous task of all the subsidiary and competitive labels will have to be accomplished and then we begin on the thousands of unissued and unreissued pre-war recordings that are among the *c.* 20,000 songs listed in the standard discography by Dixon, Godrich, and Rye. The massive number of post-war recordings has not received any systematic transcription approach at all so far.

A comprehensive approach to the use of imagery in blues and gospel lyrics is therefore currently impossible because of the paucity of accurate lyric transcriptions available. However, a first exploration of a possible framework and the fruits that may be picked from a systematic approach are possible within the limitations of this chapter. The results of this limited survey are nonetheless highly likely to be replicated as a greater number of transcriptions become available.

As a framework I have borrowed the system so successfully employed by Caroline Spurgeon in her classic 1935 study *Shakespeare's Imagery and What It Tells Us.* She used the term "image" to connote "any and every imaginative picture or other experience, drawn in every kind of way, which may have come to the poet, not only through any of his senses, but through his mind and emotions as well, and which he uses, in the forms of simile and metaphor in their widest sense, for purposes of analogy."[2] In one of the charts at the back of her book Spurgeon divides imagery into eight categories and a large number of sub-divisions. After a painstaking counting of the range and subjects of the images in Shakespeare's plays the resultant chart shows, for example, that Shakespeare employs no fewer than 245 images from "sports & games." After an analysis of them the writer concludes that Shakespeare must have been very interested in sports himself and that his favorite games may have been tennis, football, fencing, tilting, wrestling, and especially bowls. This could therefore be a way to learn more about frequently recorded blues and gospel singers as well. In another chart Spurgeon compares Shakespeare's use of imagery to that of his contemporary dramatists and concludes, again as an example, that Shakespeare, Marlowe and Massinger use no images from "town life" at all, whereas Jonson, Chapman and Dekker do. In this way we might also compare, say Lightnin' Hopkins and John Lee Hooker, both artists with an enormous recorded output.

Other approaches are also possible. In his 1951 *The Development of Shakespeare's Imagery*, Wolfgang Clemen analyzed the development of Shakespeare's imagery as seen against the background of the growth of his dramatic art. In this way blues scholars could compare the early period of, say, Big Bill Broonzy with the mature artist. However, in this chapter, I loosely follow the Spurgeon classification of images to try to achieve a more or less systematic survey of the imagery employed by a range of blues and gospel artists. Only isolated stanzas will be used in this essay. The reader is referred to the sources (*Roosevelt's Blues,* the *Agram* sleeve notes and the later (and more accurate) volumes of R. R. MacLeod's *Document Blues*) for the complete lyrics. Only by studying the complete lyric will the suggestions made for the interpretations of the imagery become fully clear. When no suggestion for an interpretation is made I hold the imagery to be self-evident. It is not easy to bring gospel fully into the picture, owing to the greater scarcity of accurate gospel transcriptions. These are represented where possible, while further reference is made in the conclusion.

Nature

A surprising number of images have been derived from "nature," suggesting that artists had been in close contact with it. Plant life provides an important category. Katherine Baker uses the constancy of nature to stress her determination in "Mistreated Blues":

> Just as sure as the leaf grows on the tree,
> I'm goin' to treat you mean, just like you treat me.[3]

Luella Miller compares the fate of the mistreated woman to the "weepin' willow" in her "Dreaming Of You Blues":

> Oh, you weepin' willow grows in the swampy land,
> That's the way with a sad woman when she's got a triflin' man.[4]

In his 1931 "Starvation Blues," Arkansas-born guitarist Charley Jordan sings:

> The grass is all dying, the rivers all dripping low,
> Do you know what is the matter? Starvation is at my door.[5]

Jordan describes Nature itself on the brink of death. Just as the artist has no food and drink, nature is no longer nourished by the rain. Jordan was one of the premier commentators on the hardships of the Depression. In the midst of a crisis in the recording industry Jordan kept making records.

Alice Moore compares "grass" to pubic hair twice, first in "Grass Cutter Blues," next in "Telephone Blues":

> And I woke up this morning, and the rain was falling fast,
> And I began to wish that, I had some good man to cut my grass.[6]

> I tried to satisfy my man, and I nearly broke my back,
> Now he's gone around here, pickin' this wild old grass.[7]

In "Smiling Rose Blues" Luella Miller pictures the "street girl" as a "smiling rose" who does not show the hardship that she is living in:

> You see them smilin' and lookin' like a rose,
> The troubles that they have, there's nobody knows.[8]

Images from the weather and the elements are also found. On October 2, 1941, Rev. J. M. Gates from Atlanta, Georgia, preached a remarkable sermon for the R.C.A. microphones entitled "Hitler and Hell":

> I can't help thinkin' about Hell: "Hitler and Hell,"
> They tell me that he's a man who lives in a storm.[9]

Gates here aptly describes the hell of the Second World War that caused the deaths and ruination of millions of innocent people. Like a storm that wreaks havoc on the land, Hitler ruins the world.

Like many of her fellow blues singers Lizzie Washington compares the blues to "showers of rain" in "Mexico Blues":

> When your troubles come, they pour just like the showers of rain,
> But your worst trouble come when your man get a new jane.[10]

The blues also come down like showers of rain in Tampa Red's "Stormy Sea Blues":

> Rainin' on the ocean, stormin' on the sea,
> Blues and that shower is showering down on me.[11]

The imagery in the Edgewater Crows' "No Bonus Blues" of 1936 (Edgewater is situated on the outskirts of Mobile, Alabama) is of fire rather than water:

> Bonus money like fire, and it sure will burn your hand,
> I didn't get me no bonus, but I'm gonna spend some other man's.[12]

In January 1936 the American Congress had finally decided to make bonus payments to the World War I veterans. In the Depression this was a rare windfall. For poor people who have suddenly received a substantial amount of money the bonus is certainly like fire that will burn your hand. The bonus money taught many veterans who their real friends were and the unknown vocalist of the Edgewater Crows showed some nasty intentions.

Other nature images originate in the seasons and, close to the land as so many of these singers were, farming. Spring is a time to make a fresh start. Scrapper Blackwell has put up with his woman in the wintertime, but now he has the "Springtime Blues":

> It's springtime now, the summer's gonna come,
> I've stood your jive all winter, now I've got some other one.[13]

Josh White (born in South Carolina) refers to the farming of cotton in his 1933 recording of "Low Cotton":

> When you're pickin' low cotton, you gotta get down on your bended knees,
> Wonder who plant this low cotton, that gave me such a dirty deal.[14]

On the surface, this of course means that the cotton plants are growing low, so that you have to get on bended knees to pick them. However, there is a double meaning to White's "low cotton." At the time prices for cotton were dramatically low because of overproduction and thus the low growing plants become symbolic of the low prices.

Katherine Baker describes her sexual attractiveness and availability through some apt farmyard imagery in "Wild Women Blues":

> Apples in my orchard, peaches on my shelf,
> I'm getting tired of bein' all by myself.[15]

Finally, imagery from celestial bodies does occasionally turn up. Walter Davis had to move back in the woods because his woman gave him so much trouble. Now he falls back on mother nature to comfort him in "Moonlight Is My Spread":

> The blue sky is my blanket, and the moonlight is my spread,
> The rock is my pillow, that is where I rest my head.[16]

Animals

In farmland communities, one might expect images of birds, domestic animals, and reptiles, and these appear in abundance. "Birds" occur in a typical Depression blues, Charlie Spand's 1931 "Hard Time Blues":

> Well, the time is so hard, the birds refuse to sing,
> And no matter how I try, I can't get a doggone thing.[17]

Nature itself is upset and as troubles never come alone Charlie also experiences some serious woman trouble because he cannot get a job:

> Lord, my woman is hard to get along with, as a sitting hen,
> And she ain't cooked me a square meal, honey, in God knows when.[18]

The marvelous image of the unapproachable woman as "a sitting hen" could only occur to someone who has grown up on a farm.

Mississippi guitarist "Big" Joe Williams very often employed stanzas about "a rooster and a hen." Here are two examples; the first one is from his strangely titled 1935 recording of "Providence Help the Poor People":

> Well, the rooster told the hen, said: "Hen, go lay,"
> She told him: "No, the provident gave me place to stay."

> She told him "No," she don't have to lay no more,
> Well, well, it may be tomorrow, ooh, Lord, I won't be back no more.[19]

In spite of the odd title "Big" Joe was referring to the provident/charity organizations that supplied food and shelter. The record company misspelled it as "providence." The hen refuses the rooster's command to "go lay," because she is no longer dependent on him. Thanks to the provident the woman now has a place to stay and she sees Poor Joe as a moocher. A second example of Williams' rooster/hen imagery is to be found in the 1945 "His Spirit Lives On," sung on the occasion of F.D.R.'s death:

> Well, now the rooster told the hen: "I wants to go crow,"
> Said: "Now president Roosevelt is gone, can't live in this shack no more."[20]

Williams sees Roosevelt's death as such a shocking event that even the animal kingdom is moved. Here he may express the fear that he will even lose his home now that his beloved president is no longer there to take care of him.

Two more "birds" are employed in Louisiana-born Leadbelly's 1940 "Red Cross Sto":

> She says: "Old cow died in the middle of the branch,
> Jaybird whistled and the buzzard danced."[21]

Excited about the large amount of carrion the "jaybird" whistles and the "buzzard" dances. The old "cow" has drowned, but in death her floating body provides food for the living. At first sight this stanza seems unrelated to a song about the Red Cross store, as does the following stanza from the same song:

> She said: "A toad frog jumped at the bottom of the well,
> And this poor boy, God, he done jumped in hell."[22]

Another dying animal, this time a "toad frog" who jumped to its death. As this song has its origin in the circumstances surrounding the draft for the First World War and as it was sung when the United States was preparing for the first-ever peacetime draft, it is perhaps possible to identify both stanzas as metaphors for the horrors of the battlefield.

After Pearl Harbor had been bombed on December 7, 1941, many blues lyrics contained anti-Japanese sentiment. "Doctor" Clayton was outraged in his "Pearl Harbor Blues":

> The Japanese is so ungrateful, just like a stray dog on the street,
> Well, he'll bite the hand that feeds him, soon as he gets enough to eat.[23]

Adolf Hitler is compared to another wild animal when he stretches out his "paw" in "Pearl Harbor – Parts 1&2" by the Soul Stirrers from 1947:

> Old Hitler from Berlin stretched out his paw,
> Brought the European countries into war.[24]

Only a close observer of farm animals could evoke a powerful image of a "billy goat" such as Georgia-born Barbecue Bob (aka Robert Hicks) uses after the 1929 elections in his 1930 "We Sure Got Hard Times":

> Just before lection, you was talkin' how you was goin' to vote,
> And after election was over, your head down like a billy goat.[25]

Evidently Bob's girlfriend had not voted for Herbert Hoover, the personification of the Depression to the blues and gospel singers, and not only to them. To the men born on the farm the image of the eating goats and hogs had become synonymous with dejection. When Rev. R. H. Taylor (who was recorded in Hattiesburg, Mississippi) recorded his 1936 sermon "The Bonus Have Found the Stingy Mens Out" [*sic*] he scolded the veterans who had spent their bonus too soon by comparing them to hogs in the same characteristic position:

> Don't call my husband a hog!
> Oh yes, he's hog! Or remind me of a hog. Under the acorn tree with his head
>   down.
> Gruntin' and eatin', never look up to see where it's coming from.
> I wouldn't say that!
> Possibly a limb would fall and break his neck. That's the way these bonus
>   mens are.
> Amen!
> They are with the head down, enjoying their blessings,
> Don't never look up to thank God for nothing he has done to 'em.[26]

Other animals familiar to such singers include squirrels, horses, and dogs. Here are two songs in which squirrel imagery occurs. The first one is Leadbelly's 1942 "Mr Hitler":

> He says if God rules heaven, he's gonna rule the world,
> But the American people say he will be shot down just like a squirrel.[27]

Squirrels are no farmers' friends. Out in the country Leadbelly must have seen squirrels being shot from the trees. In this song he predicts that Adolf Hitler will be killed off in a similar manner. The second song in which a squirrel is used as an image is Sonny Boy Williamson's 1944 "Check up on My Baby." In this song an imaginary conversation takes place between Hitler and Roosevelt. The former brags that he has "the fastest airplanes in the world." The latter retorts that his airplane can climb in the sky as speedy as a squirrel can climb a tree: We got a airplane that's built up like a squirrel.[28]

In "You Know That Ain't Right," Edith Johnson describes her lover's fancy woman as a "young colt," a term used for a debutant lover, who, confusingly in this context, is of the male sex:

> I pay rent, keeping food on the table,
> When I come home, he got a young colt in my stable.[29]

In "Telephone Blues," Alice Moore discards of her unfaithful lover in a drastic way:

> And he made me love him, now he's trying to throw me down,
> So I got a shotgun, hit him just like he was a hound.[30]

And in "Doggin' Man Blues" she again refers to the cruel ways that "dogs" are often treated by human beings:

> My man, he mistreated me, he treated me like a dog,
> But that lovin' he's got, made me fall just like a log.[31]

This sympathy for the poor "dog" is also expressed in Mary Johnson's "Muddy Creek Blues":

> I'd rather be in the muddy creek, floating like a log,
> Than to be in St. Louis, treated like a poor watchdog.[32]

At the end of Doctor Clayton's "Pearl Harbor Blues," he sings that the U.S. sold brass and scrap iron to the Japanese, which they had now turned into treacherous bombs. Just like the ungrateful stray dog with its full belly the Japanese "bites the hand that feeds him." Only a neglected "stray dog" will act so unnaturally, even a "rattlesnake" will warn you before it attacks. Not so the Japanese:

> Some say the Japanese is hard fighters, but any dummy ought to know,
> Even a rattlesnake won't bite you in your back, he will warn you before he
>   strikes his blow.[33]

Mary Johnson's "Muddy Creek Blues" contains an ominous meeting with a personified "tadpole":

> I went to the muddy creek this morning, with my razor swinging in my
>   hand,
> I said: "Good morning, Mr. Tadpole, have you seen anything of my man?"
> The tadpole vowed to me, before I raised my hand:
> "I'm telling you, dear lady, I'm not keeping up with your man."

"Muddy Creek Blues" ends with an unveiled threat emphasized by a blood red "wine" image:

> I say I'm black and evil, you sure don't know my mind,
> I'll cut your throat, Mr. Tadpole, drink your blood like cherry wine.[34]

Mary Johnson presents the "snake," which is often used as a phallic symbol, as a despicable, untrustworthy animal in "Rattlesnake Blues":

> You treats me like a rattlesnake, crawlin' on the ground,
> The better I try to treat you, the more you throw your mama down.[35]

In "Rattle Snake Groan," Luella Miller has the same opinion of a "rattlesnake," but in her case the mistreating lover is an even more severe case. In which the "boa constrictor" is called for:

> Rattlesnake, rattlesnake, what make you worry me so?
> I know that you are dangerous when you crawl at the front of my door.
> Must been a boa-constrictor, rattlesnakes don't bit so hard,
> And I know that he was dangerous, when he crawled up in my yard.[36]

Even insects and fish are employed for their apparently innate qualities. In "Spider Blues," Will Weldon imagines he is the spider that has cast his web to catch lovely females:

> Yes, I'm that spider, I build my web all over town,
> Yes, I'm gonna catch a butterfly, hoo, well, if she keep on hangin' around.[37]

In "I'm Going Fishing Too," Alice Moore uses an image from fishing to explain that she is ready for love, and that her sexual appetite is quite diverse:

> I believe I'll go fishing, at catfish, snipe or trout,
> There's some good fishes in my lake, all they need is pulling out.[38]

Very few images from "town life" are used, instead nature and the animals that are part of it are responsible for the majority of all the images used. Most of these artists had moved to the big cities (St. Louis, Memphis, Chicago and New York) at the time of recording but in order to respond to the experiences of their listeners, they did not forsake their country roots when they were inventing their poetic images.

Food

In a society where the tribulations of everyday existence were ever-present, focus on such a basic commodity as food is unsurprising. What is notable is the end to which such imagery is put. In "Red Cross Sto," Leadbelly tells the story of a man and a woman, the latter being described as follows:

> She was a good-looking woman, she had great big legs,
> She walks like she walkin' on a soft-boiled egg.[39]

The "soft-boiled egg" is a fine food image that pictures a well-built woman as she walks. The song continues:

> She come down here and she bowed down on her knees,
> I said: "You better look somewhere for your butter and cheese."[40]

She tries to persuade her husband to enlist in the army so that he will be able to support her with a bonus payment. The man obviously does not feel like it because the life of a soldier is too dangerous, and refuses to be her meal ticket. The phrase "butter and cheese" may also have sexual overtones. Leadbelly later explained that the story was based on a real event. The woman had left her husband and was now pleading to him in regret. The man does not want to provide for her anymore, either financially, or sexually.

Food images in the blues are notorious for their sexual overtones. Thus "butter" and "cheese" are often used as images for sperm. Sometimes the food/sex imagery develops into a sustained metaphor as in Louis Jordan's 1942 "Ration Blues":

> Baby, baby, baby, what's wrong with Uncle Sam,
> He's cut down on my sugar, now he's messin' with my ham.
> I gotta cut down on my jelly, it takes sugar to make it sweet,
> I'm gonna steal all of your jelly, baby, and rob you of your meat.
> They reduced my meat and sugar, and rubber's disappearin' fast,
> You can't ride no more with papa, 'cause Uncle Sam wants my gas.[41]

All the rationed goods mentioned in this hilarious song are images of a sexual nature. Thus "sugar" may stand for semen, both "ham" and "jelly" for the vagina, "meat" is sexually attractive female flesh, "rubber" is a condom, the "car ride" refers to sexual intercourse and "gas" might refer to semen again.

Another example of the use of "meat" with a sexual connotation is to be found in Sonny Scott's 1933 "Red Cross Blues No. 2":

> I saw two women, they was arguing on the street,
> They was talking about that Red Cross meat.[42]

As the rest of the lyrics make clear they may have something going with the head clerk of the Red Cross Store, who is identified as sexually attractive by the image "Red Cross meat."

A food image, for once without a sexual connotation (I think!), is the use of "kraut" in the 1936 song "Bonus Men" by Earl Thomas:

> Boys, I wonder what that girl's gonna do, when the bonus men's money play out,
> She'll be standing there round Black Avenue, looking like a barrel of kraut.[43]

An original image if ever there was one! It is hard to imagine, but we can be sure that the unfortunate girl will not have appeared to her best advantage in these destitute circumstances.

For women singers, food also serves as an effective and frequently used sexual image. "Nickles Worth Of Liver Blues" by Edith Johnson presents "(bird) liver," "stew" and "grease" all as images of female genitalia:

> Bring me a nickel's worth of liver, dime's worth of stew,
> Feed everybody on Lucas Avenue.
> Bring me a nickel's worthy of liver, dime's worth of grease,
> Whipped my man, he called all the police.
> When you see me worried, I'm thinkin' 'bout my bird liver,
> I'll kill you 'bout him, and my hand won't even quiver.[44]

When Edith sings "Honey Dripper Blues" she uses an unabashed food image that she no doubt learned from her accompanist Roosevelt Sykes, who was known as "The Honey Dripper" on his numerous Decca and OKeh recordings.

> Ah, he treats me mean, only comes to see me sometimes,
> But the way he spreads his honey, Lord, it makes me think I'll lose my
>   mind.[45]

In "Soothing Syrup Blues," a post-war recording, Edith used another sweet delicacy to describe a tender love encounter:

> If your baby twist and turn, won't let you sleep at night,
> All he wants is a little more syrup, then wants you to hold him real tight.[46]

These images show the persistent pleasure derived by blues artists from the use of food/sex symbolism.

Everyday existence

As is to be expected there are more domestic images to be found in female lyrics than in male ones. Key groups focus on images from around the house, on sickness and death, and on adornment.

In "Ain't No More To Be Said," Edith Johnson advises her lover how to keep her "stove" red hot:

> I just need plenty of coal, to keep my good stove cherry red,
> And if you keep the ashes shook down, Lord, there ain't no more to be
>   said.[47]

Lizzie Washington feels the same need and wants her lover to use his most efficient tool in "Skeleton Key Blues":

> Papa, they tell me you's a key man and keep plenty of keys in stock,
> It takes your long skeleton key to keep my soul unlocked.[48]

Luella Miller's love in "Wee Wee Daddy Blues" is readily available at every possible moment:

> I've got love like a hydrant, I turns it on and off,
> If you want me to steal, I swear your soul be lost.[49]

There are of course a great many images of "Death." One of them was encountered above when "Starvation" was knocking at doors. Another, very interesting one, is to be found in Jack Kelly's 1933 "President Blues":

> I believe, I believe, President he's alright,
> He kept me from goin', I say, to the Last Big Fight.[50]

For years this final image was misunderstood by all the blues experts who heard the record. An amazing number of suggestions for its transcription was offered. "The last big fight" surely must be "Death" itself. Here life is seen as a series of fights and the artist is saved from the final fight by the inspiration he received from Franklin D. Roosevelt.

To Luella Miller in "Tombstone Blues" a faithful lover is so essential in life that she would rather be dead if he mistreated her:

> If the tombstone was my pillow, and cold clay was my bed,
> If my daddy continue mistreat me, I would just as soon be dead.[51]

Many diseases are mentioned in the blues, tuberculosis being one of the most prominent, as in George Noble's "T. B. Blues":

> Mmm, T. B. is killin' me,
> Like a man when he's in prison, always wish he were free.[52]

One of the most inventive images is used by Alice Moore when she applies "jewel" imagery in "Blue Black And Evil Blues" to describe the clitoris and "the pearl diver" as a marathon performer, by analogy with the diver's ability to hold his breath and plumb the depths.

> Yes, my man is a pearl diver, and his stroking can't go wrong,
> And he puts it on the bottom, and all the breath's so doggone long.[53]

A variety of images relate to other aspects of daily life. One of the best-known blues images from the world of sports is the "jockey," here employed by Elizabeth Washington in her "Riot Call Blues":

> My man, he a jockey and he taught the little girl just how to ride,
> He said, when it gets tough in the middle, that he'd try it on the doggone
>   side.[54]

Professions also appear. One that may come in handy in a love scene is used in Alice Moore's "Push Cart Pusher":

> He pushes all day long, then he come in and push at night,
> I like my push cart pusher, 'cause he pushes them up for me.[55]

Money, of course, features prominently. As early as 1933 Memphis blues artist Jack Kelly sang the very first blues song about the new incumbent of the White House:

> I was walkin' around in Memphis, until my foots got thin as a dime,
> Don't be for President Roosevelt, I would have done a penitentiary crime.[56]

The thin dime, the American 10-cent coin, provides a wonderful image for the hungry vagrant, who was only kept from stealing food by his faith in the new President:

> Everybody cryin': "depression," I just found out what it means,
> It means a man ain't got no money, he can't find no big money tree.[57]

In the middle of the Depression the "money tree" is here used as a symbol for the non-existent source of income.

The itinerant lives of so many singers at different times give rise to imagery concerning travel, particularly concerning the automobile. In Edith Johnson's "Ain't No More To Be Said," "gas" stands for sexual energy or semen. The stanza describes male sexual appetite. Many female blues lament the speed that, it is claimed, often characterizes male love-making:

> A man is like a brand new car, always filled up with gas,
> Ah, they're willing to take any kind of road, Lord, and they'll take 'em down
>   real fast.[58]

A fine example of car imagery is to be found in Lizzie Washington's "Sport Model Mamma Blues." The "puncture" image is used as a symbol for penetration.

> I'm a sport model mamma, I'm out on the floor for sale,
> I speed with my tail light on so you can get on my trail.
> I'm just a plain little Ford, I have puncture every day,
> You may own a limousine, but they punctures the same old way.[59]

Learning and the arts

Images from these realms are extremely rare. Education for black people in the southern states was virtually non-existent at the beginning of the twentieth century. The only exception was the black preacher who was usually at least literate and had acquired some learning through his studies of the Authorized King James version of the Bible. An exceptional example of imagery from this category is to be found in the 1941 sermon "Hitler and Hell" by Rev. J. M. Gates:

> You is a standin' library for your peoples in Germany,
> You is a walkin' and talking encyclopaedia for your peoples in Germany.[60]

These remarkable images of a "library" and an "encyclopaedia" show Adolf Hitler as the totalitarian leader who is the only source of approved ideas for his people.

In "My Low Down Brown" by Lizzie Washington, a scientific image is used in praise of a good lover:

> My baby's long, my baby's tall, built just like a radio line,
> He keeps a good wavelength, I can tune in all the time.[61]

There are few images from the arts, as there are few from the sciences: a lack of formal education must be the main reason for this absence, although there is one clever use of a "musical instrument." In "You Ain't No Good Blues" Edith Johnson puns on the "organ" as a "musical instrument" and a "sexual organ":

> Oh, when you get a good woman, why don't you treat her right?
> 'Cause I flock at that old organ, play it morning, noon and night.[62]

Personifications

The final group of images take the form of "personifications." A personification is "a figure of speech in which inanimate objects or abstract ideas are endowed with human qualities or actions."[63] The two animal personifications, "the hen" and "the rooster," we have already discussed. There are also, of course, a great many personifications of "Death." One of them was encountered above when "Starvation" was knocking at doors.

Another omnipresent subject for personification is "Evil." A fine example is to be found in the sermon quoted twice already: "Hitler and Hell" by Rev. J. M. Gates from 1941:

> I'm thinkin' now of innocent children and women dyin' all over the land
>   and country,
> As you come crushin' through like the Demon of Hell on Earth.[64]

Adolf Hitler as the "Demon of Hell on Earth" who "comes crushin' through," drives the message home and must have had a far greater impact than the simple use of the personification "Devil."

To provide work for the unemployed during the Depression Roosevelt launched many so-called "alphabetical agencies," employment programs known by their abbreviations. These programs were often such a profound influence in the lives of the blues singer and his audience, that they were experienced as living persons. Joe Pullum's "C.W.A. Blues" from 1934 is about the Civil Works Administration:

> C.W.A., you're the best pal we ever knew,
> You're killing Old Man Depression, and the breadlines too.[65]

The C.W.A. was meant to help poor people through the bleak winter months of 1933–34. In its four-month existence it had provided work for more than four million people and had released them from the stigma attached to the welfare recipient. No wonder Pullum had come to know it as "his best pal."

The P. W. A., the Public Works Administration, was another such agency. Jimmie Gordon lavished praise on it in his 1936 "Don't Take Away My P.W.A.":

> P.W.A., you're the best old friend I ever seen,
> Since the job ain't hard and the boss ain't mean.[66]

Again the agency is seen as "the best old friend" by the singer. The P.W.A. (1935–41) was a successful agency that had spent $6 billion to provide money instead of relief. With the money they earned, the blues singers claimed they could support their women. No wonder the P.W.A. was such a popular agency.

A final image of a similar nature is provided by Charlie McCoy, who was saved by his only friend, called "Charity," in 1934:

> I said, Charity, Charity is my only friend,
> When I lost my job, the charity took me in.[67]

We have seen that the veteran bonus was an unprecedented windfall in the Depression. So much so, that "the bonus" was personified by Charley Jordan in his "Look What a Shape I'm In (Bonus Blues)" from 1937:

> So, bye, bye, Bonus, till we meet again,
> I know I have lost my only and best friend.[68]

Katherine Baker personifies the blues in "Wild Women Blues" by quoting a very old blues stanza about the inevitability of hardship in life:

> The blues jumped a rabbit, run him one solid mile,
> The rabbit got so worried, he cries just like a child.[69]

Conclusion

Finding a framework to make sense of the wealth of imagery in blues and gospel lyrics is a crucial issue: it would appear that the framework Caroline Spurgeon developed for Shakespeare's imagery is also applicable to the imagery in blues and gospel lyrics, much of it highly original within the language as a whole. As the use of imagery is one of the necessary ingredients distinguishing poetry from prose, this essay provides further evidence, for those who still need to be convinced, of the poetic quality of blues and gospel lyrics. Through lack of formal education the singers can hardly delve in the realm of learning. Instead they find their inspiration in nature and they do so with an uninhibited, pure sense of the powerful effect original imagery can achieve.

We have noticed that the popularity of the food/sex metaphor accounts for a large number of "food" images and that the most frequent type of image employed is the personification which emphasizes the powerful effect an organization, a system, a program, a nation or an abstract notion may have on the individual. They are felt to be alive and as a result are turned into human beings who make use of their five senses to experience the sensations of life on the planet Earth. From this initial survey, it would also appear that women singers use more imagery from the domestic domain and that men use more imaginative imagery in the form of personifications.

Much further research remains to be done in this field: I have only scratched the surface in this essay. It would, for example, be very interesting to see what development the use of imagery underwent in the post-war blues and gospel lyrics. Perhaps the increased possibilities for education in the second half of the twentieth century will produce a more significant number of images concerning learning and the arts. As I suggested above, individual artists can be compared by a study of their respective use of imagery. The same could be done to find differences between the various locally determined kinds of blues and between the religious and the worldly manifestations of the music.

Although more and more blues lyrics are published nowadays, the scarcity of transcribed gospel lyrics is quite striking. In slavery time spirituals are generally acknowledged to have often contained coded references to freedom, escape, and emancipation. This seems to continue into the era of recorded gospel, for the songs, unsurprisingly, share with the blues many images of being elsewhere or traveling there. The destination is Heaven in this case, obviously, rather than Chicago or other points on the map, which makes for both similarity and difference – whether by road:

> Well, I'm moving up the king's highway, well, I'm moving up the King's
>   Highway,

> Well, old Satan's on my back, trying hard to turn me back, but I'm moving
> up the King's Highway.[70]

by train:

> This train is bound for glory, this train,
> This train is bound for glory, and if you ride it, it must be holy.[71]

by aeroplane:

> Oh, Jesus is my air-o-plane, he holds this world in His hand,
> He rides over all, He don't never fall, Jesus is my air-o-plane.[72]

crossing the River Jordan:

> I'm gonna cross at the rivers of Jordan,
> Some of these days.[73]

or just rising to glory:

> Some glad morning, when this life is over, I'll fly away, I'll fly away,
> To that home on Christ's celestial shore, I'll fly away, I'll fly away.[74]

Images of fighting a Holy War are also common:

> I'm a soldier in the army of the Lord.[75]

while communion and communication with God are of course important
themes, the images sometimes drawing on modern technology:

> Telephone to Glory, oh, what a joy divine,
> You can feel the current ridin' on the line,
> When you call the number, be sure you get the throne,
> Then you can talk with Jesus on the royal telephone.[76]

Unsurprisingly, there's much biblical imagery:

> I want two wings to cover my feet, I want two wings to veil my face,
> I want two wings to fly away and this world can't do me no harm.[77]

(From Isaiah, 6:2: *"Above it stood the seraphims: each one had six wings; with
twain he covered his face, and with twain he covered his feet, and with twain
he did fly."*)

In this chapter, I have suggested ways in which imagery in blues and
gospel music can be analyzed. The results show an abundance of original
imagery. A sharp focus on the marvelous imagery in these genres will enhance the understanding of the lyrics and will provide even better ways to
enjoy the music by a celebration of the poetry of blues and gospel music.

11 Appropriations of blues and gospel in popular music

DAVE HEADLAM

Appropriations of blues and gospel – taking musical and textual elements and recombining them in new contexts – is a topic bound up with issues of race, identity, culture, and social and economic class, as well as music history and theory. Viewed benignly, such appropriations are part of the inevitable evolution of musical styles and cultural values, both within societies and between classes and races. In a broader view, however, they are emblematic of the exploitation found throughout history in encounters between groups of peoples. In the United States, black musical expressions in blues and gospel have been appropriated by the recording industry for the mass white audience throughout the twentieth century, in a tension between music as identity and culture and music as mass-marketed, profitable diversion. Of the many aspects to the role of blues and gospel in U.S. society, I am concerned here with their contexts within the legacy of slavery, and the appropriation of musical elements by other genres. How do blues and gospel songs give rise to styles – rhythm and blues, rock'n'roll, doo-wop, rock, heavy metal, soul, funk, disco, rap, ska, reggae, pop-gospel, contemporary Christian, and others – which continue to dominate all forms of media today?

Categorization, crossover, fusion

Writing about music involves categorization to facilitate comparisons of styles, but unless we discover a musical area equivalent to the Galapagos Islands, we inevitably find that musical styles result from many influences which defy clear boundaries. The terms "crossover" and "fusion," while useful, rely on such categorization and thus need qualification. The roles of Chuck Berry and Elvis Presley in the rise of rock'n'roll (r&r) in the 1950s are often cited in relation to appropriation, crossover, and fusion, and will serve as examples. In most writings, r&r is described as a crossover style – one that crosses over from one core audience to another to create a new, larger audience – emerging from a fusion of elements in music of the time:

(1) country and western (c&w) music, known earlier as "hillbilly" and "folk" music, and generally associated with a lower-class southern and western segment of the white population;

(2) the popular or "pop" style of mainstream white singers and Tin Pan Alley style tunes, associated with a mass white audience and;

(3) rhythm and blues (r&b) styles, labeled "race" music before 1949 and associated with a black audience.

The defining features of these categories are racial, regional, social, and economic: reference points are positions on the Billboard charts, a changing set of sales lists used by the music industry. However, r&r, c&w, pop, and r&b are interrelated, catchall terms for varied musical styles that feature interaction between white and black musical elements and which change over time. What distinguishes r&r is its economic impact, influence on subsequent musical styles, the social changes it reflected and fostered in relations between whites and blacks, and the large audience it created, which mark it as a music of crossover, fusion, and appropriation.

Chuck Berry, from a black, middle-class outskirt of St. Louis, developed his musical style from his own varied background, not only singing in a church choir and playing blues and r&b but also listening to pop and c&w. His genius was to create a fusion from these sources adding a faster tempo, increased emphasis on the guitar, a conversational and pure (white) sounding vocal style with purposefully "clear" diction, and lyrics that appealed to the growing population of white teenagers.[1] Writing new songs that draw on this background, he crossed over the boundary from a specialized black r&b market to the larger white, urban audience of the pop charts and emerging r&r. Elvis Presley, poor and white from Tupelo, Mississippi, in the "cat" mold of rebellious young whites who grew up amidst black influences, combined similar sources (and adding his abilities in gospel and r&b to a mix of pop and c&w styles) but in "cover" versions of existing songs. Covering songs in varying styles was a common industry practice at the time, as labels tried to find new audiences for the same material, rearranged to fit different tastes. With his distinctive vocal sound and style and charismatic stage presence, Presley broke through music industry categories, with songs such as "Hound Dog" of 1956 appearing on the r&b, pop, and c&w charts at the same time. Crossing over in his fusion of styles, Presley created a new, larger audience that fueled a huge expansion in the size of the recording industry.

From the point of view of race and class, which drove music industry categories of the time, Berry appropriated c&w, Presley appropriated r&b: they took musical elements from a different culture, mixed them with other elements, and made them their own. Berry's appropriation and his own additions resulted in a phenomenally influential guitar-based flavor of r&r, in which he was an original as a writer and performer. In the new context, the moderated black forms of expression in his songs moved closer to white listeners' tolerances – he was the "brown-eyed handsome man," marketed with strawberries on the covers of his second and third albums from Chess records in Chicago – and Berry, like Louis Armstrong in jazz, found a voice that sold well to whites (but was less welcome to black listeners). Presley's appropriation resulted in a new type of expression, a southern white who could combine r&b and c&w styles into "rockabilly" with an up-tempo urgency that defined a youthful mass white audience. Presley was not an original creator like Berry: rather, he fused and reinterpreted the styles he had heard in his life. In the new context he created, Presley combined the forbidden thrills associated with black expression and the rebellious image of white trash in a sexy musical package that proved immensely popular and influential.

Appropriation

The story of U.S. popular music chronicles the self-expression of smaller groups, defined by race, region, or class; the mixing and recasting of elements from this expression in local encounters between these groups; and the marketing, exploiting, and transforming of that expression for a national, mass audience. The personal nature, depth of feeling, and strong sense of identity found in many black blues and gospel songs historically have found only relatively small core audiences. To generate a larger audience, a musical and social balance was struck between the music's intensely authentic aspects and the broad tastes of the mass audience. This transformation took many forms – both Berry and Presley found ways to appeal to a larger audience by combining elements of white and black musics – and encompassed many styles. An inevitable by-product of this process, however, is that the original social and cultural meaning is lost as new contexts are imposed. When British guitarist Eric Clapton or folk-blues emulator John Hammond Jr. sing Robert Johnson's "Cross Road Blues" (1936) thirty years later, for instance, the meaning is significantly altered if not lost entirely under the new context of rock music and a museum-like re-creation, respectively. Even with good intentions, these white performers mimic a foreign expression and profit from it.

The white covers of black r&b and r&r songs of the 1950s are emblematic of the loss of meaning in such appropriations. Throughout this decade and previous ones, as noted, record labels released different versions of songs, trying to hit the mass audience or at least find a different niche audience. As black r&b became popular, covers took on a racial tone, as white performers recorded arrangements tailored for the large white audience. The case of Pat Boone's cover of "Tutti Frutti" by Little Richard is an example. Richard, like Chuck Berry, was an original in his own style of r&r, using piano instead of guitar from the New Orleans-based tradition. The song "Tutti Frutti" originally had bawdy lyrics full of gay sexual *doubles entendres*; while Richard's recording had rewritten lyrics to suit the target teenage audience, his outrageous demeanor and stage act relayed the meaning of the original version. But in Boone's wholesome cover version, on the infamous Dot label, the schoolboy presentation of the song reflects nothing of the original context, but maintains enough of the beat and style to appeal to the mass audience. The appropriation thus jettisoned the music's meaning and created a new one, in which a "Tutti Frutti" could be part of a Norman Rockwell-envisioned white 1950s teenage romance. Characteristic of the industry contracts of the time, Richard received a small fee and royalties on his own performance, and thus he did not profit from the cover versions. Boone initially outsold Richard and fellow New Orleans r&r star Fats Domino with his cover versions, but in a significant change emanating from the popularity of r&r among the younger audience, the originals began to sell more heavily than the covers and Boone, like Elvis, retired to more popular styles. This change, paralleling blacks' struggles for equality in the Civil Rights movement, was significant and pointed out the political and social effects of these musical developments.

Despite the extent of the literature on blues and gospel music and their influence, a question not generally asked in musical terms is "why"? Why are elements of blues and gospel so engaging, even when presented in watered-down form with their original meanings lost? Why do these elements stand as a wellspring for musicians in popular and even classical styles? A metaphor that I will use in this context is "grain," as in the "grain of the voice" from Roland Barthes.[2] This grain, or texture in the sound and the associated expression, is a human element interpreted as a physical and emotional effort that resonates with listeners, as they relate the emotions to their own lives. These feelings combine pleasure and pain in a familiar way: the lives of teenagers are obviously highly amenable to such feelings, as are people oppressed or down on their luck in love or in life, or people expressing religious feelings that tend to emphasize the sweet reward in heaven for the painful life below, as in gospel singing. Terms such as "bittersweet" and "soulful," and references to reaching, longing, and searching are found throughout the expression and literature on this music. It is perhaps these universal elements, which are transferred in performance but are difficult though enticing to emulate in appropriation, that are essential to understanding the continuing influence of blues and gospel music. However, while musicians have continually regenerated themselves by "returning to the roots" of the music – the original blues and gospel expression – the original performers and creators of the expression and its social meanings tend to be left behind in such cultural transactions.

Blues to 1950s r&b and r&r

In the 1940s, many blues-related music forms, categorized now as r&b, echoed city life, where the faster pace, electrified instruments, and an urban audience and setting prompted a wide variety of blues-derived styles. The recordings of this music generally come from small, independent record labels, as the big labels stayed with white pop. Most of the styles of r&b were based on blues forms, the twelve-bar format and variants, but in regularized, speeded-up versions, often with added "stop time" verses, where the entire ensemble would stop abruptly, leaving the singer to articulate a compelling lyric solo. Branches of swing jazz and ensemble blues-influenced music called "jump" and "shout" blues emerged, with main figures Louis Jordan, Joe Turner, Roy Brown, Lloyd Price, Wynonie Harris, and Fats Domino. Jordan, a singer and saxophone player, was known for his "jive" or jump styles, in a small jazz-style combo with witty lyrical *doubles entendres* that combined urban sophistication with down home references (e.g., "Saturday Night Fish Fry"). Jordan's style was altered in songs like Roy Brown and Wynonie Harris' versions of "Good Rockin' Tonight" (late 1940s) where the boogie shuffle rhythm is augmented by the "rockin'," gospel-influenced, emphasized backbeat "2 and 4" style characteristic of r&r.

At the same time, up-tempo, electrified updates of country blues songs emerged, with Elmore James doing updated, boogie-rocking versions (with prominent electric guitar) of Robert Johnson songs like "Dust My Broom," and Muddy Waters transforming country blues elements in Chicago with an evolving small combo eventually adding harmonica and blues piano to guitar, bass, and drums. In the small group format, more emphasis was given to the rhythmic elements and a defined beat in faster tempos; the twelve-bar blues form and variants with "stop time" recitative-like vocal breaks were, as with jump blues, standardized as the basic framework. The electric guitar gained in influence and not only replaced the saxophone but spawned its own unique forms: in Detroit, John Lee Hooker's solo guitar and voice song, "Boogie Chillun" (1948), maintains only the outlines of the blues form within its mostly riff and drone basis.

By the early 1950s, the transformation from blues to varying styles of boogie and rockin' r&b and electric blues was complete. It had a strong following in the black community but there was also some crossover interest as a young white audience responded to black r&b vocal group and solo styles. These events occurred, however, at a time when black performers were not allowed into clubs unless they were on stage and were generally ripped-off in their contracts, while whites and blacks could not even appear on the same stage or dance together in public venues in the South (although mixing and influence occurred in private or smaller settings). But DJ Allan

Freed noted that white teenagers were buying r&b records in Cleveland in the early 1950s, so he applied the term "rock'n'roll" to a wide variety of the music to give the songs a non-stereotyped identity, with the new audience oblivious to the connotations of "rockin' and rollin'" or "rollin' and tumblin'" or any one of many sexual metaphors.[3] With the incentive of selling records to the emerging teenage baby-boom generation, the search was on for the right mix of appropriated elements and ways around the racial problem of convincing a mass audience of whites to buy black music. While appropriations of black music had been an established practice from ragtime at the turn of the century, the economic and youthful population factors in the 1950s dramatically increased the pace.

The centers for music most involved in the appropriations of blues elements in the 1950s were Chicago, Memphis, and New Orleans.[4] In Chicago, electric blues recordings on the Chess and Vee-Jay labels, among others, featured Elmore James, Muddy Waters, Howlin' Wolf, Little Walter, and Willie Dixon. Chess recordings epitomized the vocal, lyric, and small ensemble aspects of the transformed blues, where the roles of Dixon as performer, composer, producer, and arranger added the type of studio production familiar from pop music. The other side of music at Chess was the r&b and r&r of Chuck Berry and Bo Diddley. Diddley's pioneering style of rhythm guitar playing was highly influential in Britain in the 1960s, but he never achieved the chart success of Berry. Diddley attributed his own music to the "Shout," an antecedent to gospel; his characteristic "Bo Diddley rhythm" ("shave and a haircut, two bits") has been variously related to sources ranging from Cuban clavé to ragtime Habañera. For white audiences, it was just a good beat for dancing; for Diddley, however, bitter about money, r&b was "rip-off and bullshit."[5]

In Memphis, B. B. King, Bobby Bland, and Junior Parker were among the blues performers, who were often from Mississippi, recording and performing in the late 1940s and 1950s at mixed race venues like the Palace Theatre. White record producer Sam Phillips exploited the local social mix by recording r&b and c&w by Ike Turner, Howlin' Wolf, Earl Hooker, and Rosco Gordon, and selling masters to labels like Chess. Phillips noted the increased buying activity around r&b, formed his own label, Sun records, and recorded Rufus Thomas among others, but, famously wanted to find a white performer who could sing in an authentic black r&b style. That singer was Elvis Presley. While not the first to combine black and white elements – Frankie Laine (1947 "That's My Desire") and Johnnie Ray (1951, "Cry") are often cited as earlier white singers who sounded "black," and "hillbilly boogie" songs had appeared from 1945 (the Delmore Brothers "Hillbilly Boogie") – his early exposure to church gospel, the personal quality in his voice with its rebel tone and gospel grain, and his charismatic persona

Ex. 11.1.

helped launch him as a superstar who generated a mass white audience.[6] Other similar white performers were Carl Perkins, Jerry Lee Lewis, Johnny Cash, and Roy Orbison, who all recorded at Sun Studios, and later Buddy Holly from Texas.

The third center for r&r was New Orleans, where, in the 1950s, Fats Domino and Little Richard emerged to represent two sides of black music and performers. Domino was presented as a non-threatening figure in the tradition of minstrel shows: a good time dance machine for white audiences. Working with white producer Dave Bartholomew, and session players like drummer Earl Palmer, Domino reworked Professor Longhair's (Henry Roeland "Roy" Byrd) traditional New Orleans piano style of rollicking gumbo boogie blues and high triplets to become one of the best-selling 1950s r&b and/or r&r artists. Little Richard, as discussed above, built on a long tradition of showmanship from vaudeville to influence musicians ranging from Mick Jagger and Paul McCartney to James Brown, George Clinton and Prince. That Richard turned to the church in 1958 revealed the gospel influences on his vocal style.

The sheer variety evident in lists of the "first" r&r songs indicate the extent of the crossover and fusion at the time.[7] "Rocket 88" by Jackie Brenston with Ike Turner, recorded in Memphis in 1951, is often cited in this context, and features a compendium of r&r-style elements in its lyrics, performance, and instrumentation. But the true economic impact of r&r came from white covers. A significant appropriation of the early 1950s was Bill Haley's cover of "Shake Rattle and Roll," originally by Joe Turner. Turner, from Kansas City, was a blues shouter who appeared with pianist Pete Johnson in one of the "Spirituals to Swing" concerts at Carnegie Hall (1938), and whose songs are quintessential turnings of r&b into proto-r&r expressions. In "Shake, Rattle, and Roll," based on an unwavering twelve-bar blues form, a boogie acoustic bass is doubled by the piano left hand under continuous right-hand piano licks, saxophones and electric guitar, and drums slapping the snare on beats 2 and 4. The bass is still mostly walking in a jazz style, but adds some characteristic rock'n'roll rhythms under syncopated accompaniment figures (see Ex. 11.1). Over a saxophone counterpoint in verses 3 and 7, Turner shows his vocal prowes: the power in the high register with a quick vibrato, particularly on the word "Devil." The text contains lots of sexual innuendo, of the "one-eyed cat peeping in a seafood store" variety, mostly too salty for a wide release.

Ex. 11.2.

Bill Haley, following earlier c&w crossover figures Jimmie Rodgers, who sang "blue yodels," and Hank Williams, a r&r forerunner, converted his western swing group into an r&b cover band, the "Comets." Haley's adaptation of "Shake, Rattle, and Roll," from 1954, is in a faster tempo, with the prominent guitar and saxophones playing short, rockin' riffs in call-and-response answers to the vocal phrases, a typical blues effect missing from the Turner version. The series of four solos ends with the famous fourth solo: electric guitar in a proto-Chuck Berry style with the virtuosic descending scale in quadruple plucking. Although the bass, now electric, still walks in a jazz-derived style, it also combines with the saxophones in the quintessential rock'n'roll rhythm (Ex. 11.2). The lighter tone of the voice, the greater use of the guitar and more filling in the higher-register space, along with the faster tempo gives Haley's version a lighter, r&r sound compared to the heavier, lower-tessitura Turner recording, and the text, altered but not completely devoid of *doubles entendres*, loses its meaning in the new context.[8]

The songs recorded by Presley at Sam Phillip's Sun Studios in Memphis and early on for R.C.A. Victor are all appropriations of different styles. Elvis was a master cover artist, but what separated him from Pat Boone (the two sold the most records in the 1950s) was his ability to reinterpret the songs adding his own "edge" to the sound rather than merely rendering a sanitized form. Hedging his bets but also anticipating the changing audience, Philips released Elvis records with one side r&b, the other side c&w, with crossover elements found in common between the two styles. Elvis' first hit song was "That's All Right," from a famous session where he fooled around during a break, imitating Arthur "Big Boy" Crudup's performance recorded for Bluebird in 1946, and the two accompanying musicians, Scotty Moore and Bill Black, both well versed in country music styles, accompanied him in a raucous "rockabilly" style derived from western swing.[9] Crudup never received any royalties from Elvis' recording and died penniless, his contribution to the music that started a marketing and recording revolution unacknowledged, his role in this famous appropriation emblematic of the fate of many original black artists in the sudden rise of r&r.[10]

Crudup's tune "That all Right, Mama," has string bass and drums in a swing jazz style, while the slightly distorted electric guitar chords and 2-3 string strumming solos are from an adapted country blues style. The form is in a modified blues form, a ten-bar setting, like a twelve-bar form with bars 7 and 8 omitted. In the setting of the lyrics, bars 1–4 are different in each verse, using stop verse form, with bars 5–10 setting the refrain, "That's all right, That's all right, That's all right now Mama, any way you do"; this refrain is thus a mini blues form within the larger verse. Crudup adds several irregular features: he compensates for the omitted return to I in the blues form by playing with the changes in his bars 6 and 7, adding a move to I and moving through IV–I–V in irregular durations, and adds and omits two beats in several places. Crudup also alters the form by extending the final vocal verse ("Dee dee") by two bars, so that the final "That's all right now Mama" is delayed for a greater effect when it comes.

Elvis' shorter version is at about the same tempo, but sounds more snappy because of the clearer bass attacks. The opening guitar strumming and the clean sound and country licks of the solo guitar section set an upbeat country atmosphere, rather than a jazzed-up country blues. The ambiguities of downbeats in Crudup's version are clarified with clear chord changes, but Elvis intensifies the song by shortening each verse to nine bars, omitting the balancing tenth bar on I; this omission propels the song forward after each verse. In the final "Dee Dee" verse, he also shortens the beginning to three bars, adding "I need your lovin'" to link the verse into the change of chord and refrain. In the intensification in the chorus section with the threefold "That's all right," Elvis extends the final "Mama" adding a country-ish slide up to the note in his characteristic seductive style. This inflection, also reflected in his interjected "I need your lo-vin'" in the final verse, changes the song from Crudup's declarative version to Elvis' highly suggestive one: that it may be "all right" for the woman involved to mistreat him, but she might want to reconsider. It is this element of a sly, sexy wink in the sound combined with the rhythmic drive from the omitted balancing tenth bar in the form that reflects Elvis' effect on teenagers, and the vastly greater success of his version over Crudup's.

Blues to 1960s rock and gospel to soul/funk

At the end of the 1950s and leading into the 1960s, a split occurred in the musical world viewed through the lens of blues and gospel appropriations. Soul music stemming from gospel supplanted blues-based r&b, as described below. Meanwhile, following the abrupt end of the first generation of rock'n'rollers in the U.S. by death, gaol, injury, scandal, and the army, the rise of Calypso from Harry Belafonte, and a few years of industry pap of the American Bandstand variety, white musicians in the U.S. and Britain became interested in r&r, r&b and Chicago electric blues. This formed the basis for four developments: the Liverpool bands in Britain, most notably the Beatles; London groups like the Rolling Stones, Cream, and Led Zeppelin influenced by Chicago and even Mississippi blues; their counterparts in the U.S., such as the Paul Butterfield Blues Band and Canned Heat; and a folk/blues movement in the U.S. featuring Bob Dylan, which had a psychedelic folk/blues rock aspect on the West Coast along with some Latin/blues mixes, in bands such as Santana. It took the entire decade for rock musicians and their critics to catch up to musical developments in the black music world, as most white rock groups went through their blues reworking years to eventually develop their own style. What made rock music different from preceding appropriations was the enormous wealth and influence that modern media exposure and the baby-boomer audience fostered.

The 1960s interest in blues-based music featured a group of white player-scholars – John Mayall, Eric Clapton, Paul Butterfield, John Hammond, and Al Wilson, among others – who sparked a blues revival, which revitalized the careers of many older black blues players. B. B. King, Muddy Waters and other blues players performed for adoring white throngs in the late 1960s, and as music critics and scholars became aware of the blues tradition and its influence on rock music, they began to document the blues and create a "museum exhibit" context valuing authenticity and originality. Older players, Son House, Skip James, Mance Lipscomb, Robert Pete Williams, Rev. Gary Davis, and Mississippi's Fred MacDowell and John Hurt, were rediscovered and brought back into the recording studio and onto the stage to play for white audiences. In general, the rediscoverers paid their debt to the original musicians and helped them to at least some proportion of recompense. Blues came to be highly valued in white venues, but not by black audiences. The scholarly and performance-based appropriation was largely based in Britain, and this trend has continued, as evidenced by this book.

In Britain, r&r and Chicago electric blues had a huge influence, primarily in the two centers of Liverpool and London. Visits by Big Bill Broonzy (1951), Muddy Waters (1958), Sonny Boy Williamson (1963), John Lee Hooker, and others, which included playing with the inexperienced white British players, inspired the nascent blues crowd. The groups that emerged – the Beatles, Rolling Stones, the Who, Cream, Led Zeppelin, and others – evolved rock music by combining elements of r&r, r&b, and Chicago electric blues with their own native influences. Commentators on the enormously successful British rock music scene were alerted to the origins of the music, and the Mississippi Delta original performers became legendary. With its appropriation of American blues, and a fusion of blues elements with other styles, British rock music raised the awareness of the United States to its own cultural heritage.

The musical rise of the blues and its transformation into rock music can be seen in the careers of two guitarists, Eric Clapton and Jimi Hendrix.[11] In

Britain, interest in blues and jazz was fostered by Chris Barber, Alexis Korner, Cyril Davies, Graham Bond and John Mayall in the early 1960s; these pioneers set the stage for Clapton and others. Clapton had a passion for Chicago electric blues and the earlier Mississippi Delta Blues, and found influences in Robert Johnson, B. B. King, Albert King, Freddie King, Buddy Guy, Otis Rush, and Magic Sam. Several group experiences playing in the Yardbirds and Bluesbreakers lead up to the "supergroup" Cream, which recorded rock versions of blues songs by Johnson and others.[12] Adapting blues to the power trio group of guitar, bass, and drums, Cream had a dual nature of reworked blues and newly composed songs, some in a transformed "psychedelic" style originating in the drug scene on the U.S. West Coast. The blues songs became the vehicles for extended, virtuosic improvisations in concert, and in songs like "Sunshine of Your Love," Cream prepared the ground for Led Zeppelin and later heavy metal. Here the blues progression became simplified into the blues riff, then the heavy metal riff, a single motive that constituted a reduction to one driving element. This emphasis on the riff, with minimal harmonic motion, can be heard in Hooker's "Boogie Chillun" and even earlier, in songs like "Spoonful" and the "Rollin' and Tumblin'" family of songs.[13] After Cream, Clapton's high point came with his personal blues transformation, the song "Layla"; Clapton has returned again and again to the blues, most recently in his *From the Cradle* (Reprise Records 1994), and with the authenticity bestowed by recordings with B. B. King and others, he has come to personify the British appropriations of blues.

The case of Jimi Hendrix is emblematic of the power of the "made in Britain" label to overcome racial barriers. An accomplished performer of all black styles in the States, playing with many of the black stars of r&r and soul – Little Richard, Sam Cooke, Jackie Wilson, B. B. King, the Supremes, Chuck Jackson, Solomon Burke, Muddy Waters, Albert King, the Isley Brothers – and influenced by Buddy Guy and others he heard while touring, he was largely relegated to black venues of the "chitlin" circuit of black bars and clubs in the South. Hendrix went to Britain at the behest of ex-Animal Chas Chandler and became an overnight sensation for his "authentic" (black) abilities. After an auspicious beginning jamming with Cream, Hendrix was fitted with a multiracial group, the Jimi Hendrix Experience, then returned to the States to achieve superstar status. A blues guitarist in the great tradition, yet at the same time a rock musician and innovative composer with all the psychedelic trappings of the 1960s, Hendrix brilliantly combined the technological and musical trends of his own heritage and British music developments to create a music in which the blues elements are thoroughly assimilated, yet remain distinctive. His emphasis on the sound of the guitar helped usher in the era of rock as timbre music. His best-known song, "Purple Haze," combines a potent opening lick with the famous "Purple Haze chord," a jazzy dominant ♯9 (E–G♯–D–G), in a sixties, LSD-filled statement of the blues. Hendrix and soul singer Otis Redding, both headliners at the Monterey International Pop Festival of 1967, where Hendrix ended his set by setting his guitar on fire, were at the pinnacle of the blues/rock and gospel/soul reworkings of the 1960s. Critical and audience reaction was mixed to Hendrix, however, particularly among the black audience, who didn't identify with his rock leanings; to the largely white audience at Monterey and at his other shows, he was the personification of the exotic black other, "superspade," and the pure, uninhibited emotion that was considered a caricature of the black performer by blacks.[14] Hendrix was at the end of the black rock guitar tradition leading through John Lee Hooker to Chuck Berry; with the notable exceptions of Vernon Reid, Lenny Kravitz, and Prince, following black guitarists like Robert Cray have tended to stay within the traditional blues camp, while white guitarists like Stevie Ray Vaughan and Eddie Van Halen have emulated Hendrix and continued his legacy.

Musically, the transformation of blues into rock is largely a reduction, in instrumental forces, rhythmic complexity, harmonic motion and form, with a simplification to a basic riff amidst a syncopated rock beat. The rock combo, with its basic guitar–bass–drums–(keyboard) setup simplified the textures of the urban blues models. The biggest change, aside from the volume, is in the rhythm: from a fluid, jazzy or bluesy shuffle rhythm, to the emphasis on backbeats 2 and 4, to an unwavering straight eighth-note rock rhythm with emphasized beats and syncopations. The rhythms of Cream's "Crossroads" (from Robert Johnson's "Cross Road Blues") and Zeppelin's "Whole Lotta Love" (from Willie Dixon's "You Need Love") are representative.[15]

The rise and transformation of rock music from its blues-based beginnings is contrasted between the Beatles, who continued to evolve, and Rolling Stones, who largely stayed within their style of blues-rock. The Beatles, part of the r&b and r&r-influenced music scenes in Liverpool, England and Hamburg, Germany, in the late 1950s, started playing songs by Presley, Berry, Little Richard, Perkins, Holly, Gene Vincent, Eddie Cochran, as well as by vocal groups the Shirelles and Isley Brothers, taking songs by Leiber and Stoller and others and thereby appropriating the appropriated styles. They also sang show tunes and pop songs, foreshadowing their own eclectic output. While big sellers in Britain in the early 1960s, the American label Capitol owned by British EMI passed on their early records, and so the Beatles' initial songs came out on the black Vee-Jay label from Chicago; within a year, Capital realized their mistake and squeezed Vee-Jay out. This industry action was emblematic of the effect of the Beatles: their appropriated style squeezed out the original black artists and they provided a model for the "rock group" in which black performers have had almost no part. One of the Beatles' early hits was "Twist and Shout," originally by the black vocal group the Isley Brothers. The Isley Brothers had first recorded "Shout" in 1959, a gospel-type celebration song, then added the popular "twist" dance element, from Chubby Checker's 1959 cover of Hank Ballard and the Midnighters tune called "The Twist," to the formula in 1962. The Beatles' version is characteristic, with excellent production in the guitar sound, and high-energy vocals and arrangement. The tension in the Beatles between the bluesier Lennon and pop-leaning McCartney went mostly in the latter direction until the group split in 1970, with a legacy as the most influential popular music group of all time.

The Rolling Stones started in the Crawdaddy Club in London playing their own versions of r&b: their first five albums included covers of Buddy Holly, Chuck Berry, Muddy Waters, Howlin' Wolf, Garret Strong, Jimmy Reed, Willie Dixon, Slim Harpo, Rufus Thomas, Marvin Gaye, Valentinos, Drifters, Coasters, Wilson Pickett, Solomon Burke, Bo Diddley, Otis Redding, Sam Cooke, Don Covay, and Arthur Alexander. Their recording of "Little Red Rooster" in 1964, from a Howlin' Wolf version of 1961, and "Good Morning Little Schoolgirl," vastly outsold the originals, but, unlike Led Zeppelin and other groups, the Stones followed Clapton and their American counterparts Canned Heat and others in acknowledging their debt and supplying royalties to the original blues performers, such as Muddy Waters and Howlin' Wolf. Their own style emerged in the song, "(I Can't Get No) Satisfaction," a riff-based reworking of Muddy Waters' "I Can't Be Satisfied," originally from 1948 (adapted from a church-inspired song, "I Be's Troubled").[16] Along with the riff and guitar timbre, they substituted the banalities of American advertising for the blues male macho sentiments of the original. This loss of meaning in British reworkings of American blues was a necessary part of the reason for its success with white audiences in the U.S.

Gospel to 1950s and 1960s vocal groups, and 1960s soul

Gospel, like jazz, has a mixed-race heritage, with parallel streams of black gospel, from Thomas A. Dorsey, Mahalia Jackson, and the Johnson Gospel Singers and Dorsey Trio from the 1920s, and white Christian gospel, starting from James D. Vaughan, who published his *Gospel Chimes* songbook and organized The Vaughan Quartet, the first white, all-male, professional gospel quartet, in 1910. These two tracks continue to the present day. In the 1940s, as jump blues took on a wider audience, Mahalia Jackson had a gospel million seller on the Apollo label with "Move On Up a Little Higher" and in the 1950s signed with Columbia to become a crossover success. Elvis

Presley, who solidified the move to white r&r, also ushered in the contemporary white gospel sound, with "His Hand in Mine" (1960), demonstrating the gospel source of his vocals in the process. The r&r era features two important developments in black music styles. First, black vocal groups, based in gospel "Jubilee" quartets, jazz vocals, and popular groups of the 1940s, created the "doo-wop" and more up-tempo r&r vocal styles that predated the mass crossover appeal of solo r&r. Second, black solo artists, particularly Ray Charles and Sam Cooke, appropriated gospel elements into r&b, and r&b elements into gospel, to create soul music. In the 1960s, both solo artists and vocal groups developed soul, which combined r&b, gospel, and popular styles in Detroit's Motown, Memphis' Stax and from Muscle Shoals, Alabama, Fame, then took two routes: a more sophisticated, orchestral sound in Philadelphia smooth soul leading to the crossover disco styles; and a harder rhythmic edge as funk in James Brown's music.

The elements of gospel featured and appropriated were:

(1) the *a cappella* style vocal groups, originating in Jubilee quartets;
(2) the call-and-response "preaching" style drawn from the church;
(3) the showman aspect of costumes and dance routines from the church;
(4) the syncopated dance rhythms of the hand-clapping and body-shaking rituals of church participation; and,
(5) the virtuosic use of ornamentation in solo singing, particularly in female solo voices.

While gospel music flourished in cities alongside blues, in Detroit, Chicago, and Philadelphia, and a tradition of white Christian music existed alongside black gospel for much of the century – as white folk and c&w existed alongside black blues – the appropriation of gospel was largely by black artists. Only relatively recently have white singers found a mass pop audience using gospel styles.

If the guitar is the quintessential blues instrument, the voice is the gospel instrument. Gospel expression stems from worksongs, church singing, camp and revival meetings, and encompasses spirituals and other religious styles including the choral jubilee singing. The rhythm of gospel is a vocal rhythm, in the tradition of church preaching, where hand clapping sets the beat. The vocal style and body rhythms of gospel are difficult to emulate: whereas there have been many white blues guitarists, there are few white gospel singers of similar stature. Singers, particularly female, of jazz, blues, and gospel, borrow from one another yet are distinctive in the approach to articulation, the bend in the pitch, the continuity or break in the release, the amount of breath in the sound, and the inflections of the lyrics.

The male vocal groups in the 1940s were one of the initial gospel-related venues for black performers to cross over to the larger pop audience. The

Soul Stirrers, formed in 1934, were recorded by Alan Lomax for the Library of Congress in 1936, but later began singing newly composed gospel songs with lead singer Rebert H. Harris. Harris ad-libbed in syncopation against the group, setting the stage for the 1950s style, and his successor Sam Cooke. Cooke became a sex symbol in gospel, eventually moving into pop and soul music, following the move of many of the black vocal groups who wanted to cash in on the r&r audience. From initial religious subjects, these groups changed to sing songs with lyrics about idealized romance and teenage love, wearing suits and performing snappy dance numbers for audiences, and changing their names – for instance, the Royal Sons to the "5" Royales in 1952, and the Gospel Starlighters to the Famous Flames, featuring James Brown.[17] A few groups featured lyrics more characteristic of blues, such as the Royals (later Midnighters) with their "Annie" series from 1954 and the Dominoes' crossover hit, "Sixty Minute Man" of 1951. Eventually, however, most of these vocal groups, which evolved into the "doo-wop" vocal groups of the 1950s (many of which were recorded by Bobby Robinson of Harlem including the Orioles, the Ravens, Mellow Moods, and myriad other names grouped into birds, insects, flowers, and cars) projected an innocence that represented an appropriation of the vocal style of gospel but with a loss of its passion or meaning. The simplified musical form, using the progression I–VI–IV–V–I became as ubiquitous as the twelve-bar blues form.

In a seminal doo-wop recording, the black vocal group the Chords, singing in harmony over a standard combo of saxophone, guitar, bass, piano, and drums, recorded "Sh-Boom" in 1954 in New York City for the Atlantic "Cat" label. The song included "Sh-Boom" and "da-da-da" in the accompanying parts, influenced by jazz scatting and the nonsense lyrics of jump blues, a bass voice solo line along with offbeat guitar riffs, and a heavy sax solo. Appearing on the pop charts, it was covered in Chicago by a white Canadian vocal quartet called the Crew Cuts on the Mercury label. The new version added an orchestra and choir background, along with a walking bass section. The Chords were on to something new, the Crew Cuts were reminiscing on the swing era; typically, however, the Chords went to no. 5 on the pop charts, then were not able to re-create their success and faded, but the Crew Cuts made it to no. 1 and sold a million records and had a run of hits.[18]

Following "Sh-Boom," vocal group music dominated radio in the 1950s, becoming a crossover phenomenon. While the doo-wop groups had always been somewhat vacuous in their lyric content, the Coasters achieved chart success with straight parody recordings by Lieber and Stoller, who were part of the rising production teams for records, which led to Phil Spector and George Martin in the 1960s. Lieber and Stoller epitomize the Tin Pan Alley-like songsmith tradition that persisted in the development of r&r; like

Irving Berlin and George Gershwin before them, these writers were white and Jewish and felt an affinity for black music, writing new songs using black music elements, and working with record labels and producers to create hit songs "in the style of," such as "Hound Dog" written for Big Mama Thornton but a hit for Elvis. Their parody records had a fast shuffle beat, nonsense lyrics, and "yakety" sax chorus, in songs like "Yakety Yak" (1958) and "Charlie Brown" (1959). The Platters were another successful group, lasting from the 1950s to the late 1960s, one of the few black vocal groups with no. 1 hits on pop charts in the late 1950s. The Drifters, formed in 1953 with lead singer Clyde McPhatter, who had a gospel background, transformed in 1958 to a group name with changing personnel – forerunners of continuing phenomena in the 1960s – recording commercial r&b, with violins instead of guitars and influencing Motown. These groups used various strategies, from vocal purity, pop instrumentations and schlocky arrangements, suits and funny hair-dos, to humor, to cross over to the white audience. The level of vocal ability on many of the vocal group recordings is astounding, however, and shows a wide variety of influences.

The Ravens' recording of "Give me a Simple Prayer" is a fusion of gospel sentiments and stylings with a doo-wop setting, illustrating the religious origins of the vocal group sound also clear in the Moonglow's "Ten Commandments of Love." In style, The Ravens' song could be a love song, but with solace supplied by inspiration from above rather than a girl. The piano plays the standard eighth-note high chords over a slow bass and drums with cymbal also tapping out the eighths.[19] Following a group fanfare imitating a wordless church choir invocation and a solo piano arpeggio, the solo vocal part starts off muted, but grows in intensity over a "ba-do" vocal group setting that evolves into words to accompany the singer. The ending is marked by voices reaching into the stratosphere as the climax of the gradual ascent throughout.

With the rise of r&r in the mid-1950s, the male and emerging female vocal groups turned to up-tempo vocal r&r songs. The laid-back lyrics and emotion were replaced by a youthful urgency, evident in songs like "Why do Fools Fall in Love," by Frankie Lymon and the Teenagers in 1955. The fast rise and fall of many vocal groups is exemplified by Lymon's ascent into stardom at age thirteen, then descent into drugs and death at age twenty-five in 1968. As was customary at the time, many of the songs by the black groups were covered by white vocal groups, with some appropriation of styles, but the original groups were already so bland in their subject matter and pure vocal quality that the white groups often didn't have far to go in their versions.[20] As the decade progressed, following the example of Ray Charles, vocal groups began to add some urgency and meaning – soul elements – to their styles, culminating in the vocal groups of Motown and others, including the Staples

Singers, a Chicago family band of bluesy gospel with hit songs on gospel, r&b, and soul charts through the 1970s.

In the late 1950s and 1960s, "girl" groups joined the male doo-wop and r&r vocal groups. Singing songs written by production teams such as the Brill Building writers from New York (the Shirelles, Chiffons, Shangri-Las, Ronettes, Chantels, Marvelettes, Crystals, Ikettes) and the Holland-Dozier-Holland writing team of Motown (the Supremes, Martha and the Vandellas), these groups had huge hit records but mostly came and went quickly. The singing on these records is generally very pop-oriented, with the grain of the voice muted for a generic sound. As Ray Charles did with doo-wop male groups, Aretha Franklin reinfused the female groups with the gospel elements of soul in her Atlantic recordings in the mid-1960s.

Solo black singing at the beginning of the 1950s was dominated by the style of Nat King Cole, a singer with a beautiful tone and classical control of pitch and timbre that was sufficiently appealing to a mass audience that Cole had his own television show (1956–57). Times were, though, still so dangerous that he was dragged from the stage and beaten at a 1956 concert in Birmingham Alabama by the White Citizens Council in a backlash against r&r, since he represented "nigger" music.[21] In the mid-1950s, "Brother" Ray Charles, black, blind, a heroin addict during his greatest recordings, added gospel vocal and musical elements to an r&b style developed by working with Guitar Slim in New Orleans – gospel piano licks and a backing female chorus (the Raelettes) that responded to Charles in the manner of a church choir following the preacher – and so initiated soul music, linking the spiritual with the sexual. The new style, songs like "I Got a Woman" and "Hallelujah, I Love Her So," and the breakthrough hit, "What'd I Say," was controversial, and Charles was criticized for violating the sanctity of the church with the music of the devil, in a continuance of the confrontation between these two forces found throughout the history of blues and gospel.[22] In the early 1960s, Charles moved from Atlantic to R.C.A. Victor, and into an eclectic mix of styles that included c&w and pop, as well as gospel and r&b.

Ray Charles' "I Got a Woman" (1953), is a shuffle r&b tune with the usual elements, the Texas "lope" and Kansas City swing, but the vocals add the gospel element, with its wide range and embellishments, particularly toward the ending, with the "she's all right" repetitions imitating gospel endings. Charles reportedly improvised new lyrics to a gospel tune and developed the song from a combination of r&b and gospel elements. Charles' biggest hit, "What'd I Say" from 1959, came from an improvised interchange between the singer, backing group, band, and audience: the preacher with his congregation. The Wurlitzer electric piano dominates an opening outlining the blues form with solos over a Latin drum beat. The r&r feel of the opening is supplemented with answering choir and brass entries, but gives way to a gospel dialogue, "unnh-hunnh" patter, over Charles' moans, cries, and gospel feel, with "shake that thing" and "I feel alright" expressing his passion for the body instead of the Lord.

Charles, covered by Presley among others, incorporated gospel elements into r&b, while Sam Cooke began from gospel and added pop and r&b elements. Both these singers, and James Brown, followed the gospel vocal styles of the Reverends Julius Cheeks and Claude Jeter; these two sang in church and jubilee quartets (1940s) and Cheeks perfected a hard-shouting style in the Sensational Nightingales while Jeter featured his falsetto in the Swan Silvertones.[23] After singing gospel in the Soul Stirrers (1950), Cooke released a secular song, "Lovable," under the name of Dale Cook, then, "You Send Me," a no. 1 pop and r&b hit on Keen records in 1957. His success at crossing over to the white pop and black r&b audiences invoked condemnation by his gospel audience, but he continued, establishing a record and publishing company, Sar and Kags music, until his death in 1964. The female counterpart to both Charles and Cooke was "Lady Soul," Aretha Franklin, following in the footsteps of her father, Rev. C. L. Franklin, who had recorded over seventy albums of preaching and singing with Chess Records. In 1967, Franklin moved from an unsuccessful stint at Columbia singing pop and jazz to Atlantic, where her recording in the Fame Studios of Muscle Shoals ("I Never Loved a Man"), then New York – with the same white southern musicians – reasserted the female element from the gospel tradition in soul, recalling influences Clara Ward, Roberta Martin, and Mahalia Jackson, and crossing over to the pop charts in the process. Franklin's range and fluency is evident on "Do Right Woman, Do Right Man," where, over a gospel piano and organ, she builds her musical and lyric argument slowly, leading to powerful but understated climaxes with backing choir. She wrote many of her songs, yet many hits were written by whites – "(You Make Me Feel Like) A Natural Woman" by Brill Building writers Carole King and Gerry Goffin, and "Chain of Fools" by Don Covay, for instance, continuing the legacy of Lieber and Stoller. However, her recording of Otis Redding's "Respect" – no. 1 on both the pop and r&b charts – created an anthem for the black movement and set the tone for the age in terms of feminism and the musical style of mixed-race southern soul topped by a distinctive black voice: the blues and gospel reconciled. In 1972, her double LP of gospel, *Amazing Grace*, went to no. 7 on the pop chart in a remarkable crossover. Her mix of gospel, soul, and funk, backed by the Sweet Inspirations including Cissy Houston, inspired Whitney Houston, Patti LaBelle, Anita Baker, and the more recent Erykah Badu, among many others.

In the 1960s, soul music dropped its r&b basis in the blues form to take on a new harmonic and rhythmic vocabulary in manifestations from the Stax/Volt labels in Memphis and Fame label in Muscle Shoals, Alabama, the Vee-Jay label in Chicago, and the Motown/Tamla labels in Detroit. From Memphis and Muscle Shoals, both distributed by Atlantic Records, the passion of gospel and the jump blues/jazz band instrumentation of r&b combined with the southern white honky-tonk influences of many of the local session players in racially mixed house bands. The result was the records of Otis Redding, Wilson Pickett, Jackie Wilson, Aretha Franklin, and others, with their distinctive rhythmic drive, instrumental setting, and gospel-derived vocals. Stax, with multiracial house band "Booker T. and MGs," notably combined the talents of black and white musicians, backing almost exclusively black stars, to become a major force in the music of the 1960s. It was begun in 1959 by whites Jim Stewart and Estelle Axton in Memphis, adding black executive Al Bell in 1965. With Atlantic's distributorship and production from Jerry Wexler, hits from William Bell, Otis Redding, Sam and Dave, Wilson Pickett, Isaac Hayes, and even instrumental records like "Green Onions" followed. Redding was the star, from Macon, Georgia, and he was ambitious composing, arranging, and (in one of the rising number of examples of black musicians influenced by the white music of the 1960s) listening to the Beatles and Bob Dylan. With his success at Monterey he was poised for the mass white market, but he died in a plane crash in 1967, his posthumous folk-like no. 1 hit, "Sitting on the Dock of the Bay" hinting at a new fusion of soul and c&w.

Fame Studios in Muscle Shoals was started in 1958 by Tom Stafford, Rick Hall, and Billy Sherrill. They added writers and players Dan Penn and Spooner Oldham, and singers Etta James, Arthur Alexander, Jimmy Hughes, Percy Sledge – whose hit "When a Man Loves a Woman" defined the sexual tension characteristic of soul music – Wilson Pickett, Arthur Conley, and, most famously, Aretha Franklin. As with r&r and r&b, British fans took on soul music, with tours by the big singers, magazines, clubs, and, of course, appropriations, as in the Beatles album *Rubber Soul*. While the British took over r&r, however, they fell short imitating soul; the Beatles, among others, could not reproduce the soul sound.

The rise of soul alongside rock music is seen in the history of Atlantic records, the distributor for the Stax and Fame labels. Like many labels, such as Chess from the Polish Chess Brothers and Modern Records from the Lebanese Bihari Brothers, Atlantic Records was started by first generation Americans of immigrant parents. Formed in 1947 by Ahmet and Nesuhi Ertegun, sons of a Turkish Ambassador, and including Herb Abramson and later Jerry Wexler (1953), Atlantic used the talents of music director Jesse Stone, engineer Tom Dowd, and top studio musicians to record black jazz, r&b, and r&r, appealing to the r&b audience with slick production and effective distribution. Atlantic's production, all-white owners, producers, arrangers, mixed race writers and studio musicians, and black stars, represents the recording industry set-up for the chart-topping r&b songs in the 1950s. In the 1960s, Atlantic became the distributor for Stax/Volt and Fame and so aided and profited from the enormous success and influence of soul music. Atlantic's r&b and soul recordings included Joe Turner, Sticks McGee, Clovers, Ruth Brown, Ray Charles, LaVern Baker, the Drifters, the Coasters, Clyde McPhatter, Solomon Burke, Wilson Pickett, Aretha Franklin, Rufus Thomas, Albert King, Otis Redding, and others. With the changing climate in the 1960s, however, when racial boundaries were re-established in the recording world, Atlantic moved more to white imitation models, like Bobby Darin and Sonny and Cher, then to the white rock groups, like Cream, Led Zeppelin, the Rolling Stones, and even the Bee Gees, whose music was based on the styles of the black musicians that the label had previously recorded.

In Chicago, the labels on "Record Row," including Chess and Vee-Jay, moved into soul recordings in the 1960s, featuring Etta James, Fontella Bass, Curtis Mayfield and Jerry Butler of the Impressions, and producer Carl Davis. The smooth soul sounds played on the black radio station W.V.O.N, continuing into the mid-1970s with groups like the Chi-Lites. Mayfield, along with Isaac Hayes, were instrumental in the evolution of the 1970s "blaxploitation" movie soundtracks like *Superfly* and *Shaft* that provided a brief moment of mass interest in black film. This music, along with James Brown's funk, has been the most influential and the source for most of the digital samples in rap music.

Motown from Detroit and later Los Angeles was an evolution of 1950s vocal groups tailored to appeal to the mass white audience, with an urban, sophisticated, show-business atmosphere. Impressed by the songwriting from the "Brill Building" writers in the early 1960s – Bobby Darin, Neil Sedaka, Neil Diamond, Carole King and Gerry Goffin, and others – and in the spirit of "professionalism" in pop music, Motown founder Berry Gordy worked initially with Jackie Wilson to create a hybrid black pop style. By careful sculpting of the grain in the sound and balancing of elements drawn from black sources with pop appeal to the white audience, Gordy then founded Motown (1959), which came to be known as "Hitsville, U.S.A." Gordy and others were so successful in integrating black music into pop that for two years in 1963–65, the Billboard charts did not list a separate national r&b chart.[24] The Motown lineup included groups such as the Marvellettes, Miracles, Temptations, Diana Ross and The Supremes, Gladys Knight and the Pips, the Jackson 5, Marvin Gaye, Mary Wells, Martha Reeves and Vandellas, Velvettes, Four Tops, Smokey Robinson, and writers Holland/Dozier/Holland among others, while Gordy's methods included creating a finishing school for his performers with instructions on deportment and control of media exposure. Critics of Motown accused Gordy of bleaching out the "blackness" of his performers, but Motown produced hit music, slickly produced, varied in instrumentation, celebrating love, dancing, soul, funk, pop, memorable tunes, and celebration. There was even a little protest thrown in to reflect the times, for instance, in "What's Going On," Marvin Gaye's protest song with the memorable James Jamerson bass line and "War" by Edwin Starr in a quintessential protest statement.[25] Into the 1970s, Motown artists were part of the move to electronic and psychedelic soul, funk and disco, anticipated by the Chambers Brothers (a black hippie group with a white drummer and their 1967 hit "Time Has Come Today"), in tunes like "Papa was a Rollin' Stone" from the Temptations which incorporated the Isaac Hayes "Shaft" wah-wah guitar and echo effects. Michael Jackson, the most famous of Gordy's protégés, came to symbolize the combination of white and black, pop and soul, elements, and is perhaps the extreme consequence of Gordy's attitude. Jackson, the "King of Pop," left Motown for Epic records in 1976, and with his surgically created white features superimposed on music with gospel and blues elements carefully muted, created a massive crossover appeal, highlighted by his dancing style and videos and adorned by his marriage (then divorce) to Elvis Presley's daughter and his purchase of the Lennon–McCartney songbook.

The vocal urgency and syncopated dance rhythms of gospel along with top-notch r&b house bands came together most clearly in the music of James Brown. Combining a Little Richard-style act with other theatrics from Joe Tex and a pleading version of Ray Charles gospel/soul, Brown started as a singer with the Gospel Starlighters then the Fabulous Flames, and recorded the hit "Please, Please, Please" in 1956 for King records. With his *Live at the Apollo* in 1962 which reached no. 2 on the pop charts, Brown became "Soul Brother Number One."[26] Building on his traveling road show and hot bands, and following Bo Diddley's rhythmic focus and recasting of African rhythms, with "Papa's Got a Brand New Bag" of 1965, Brown moved to a rhythmically charged vamp as the basis for the whole song, minimizing elements of melody and harmony: soul changed to funk. A new guitar style emerged, influenced by Stax's Steve Cropper, aping the "hit" of a brass section, and the bass and drummer, players like Bootsie Collins and Clyde Stubblefield, became the lead players. A succession of hits, "Cold Sweat," "I Got The Feeling," "Sex Machine" and others followed, influencing all forms of black music. Examples include Stevie Wonder and Marvin Gaye at Motown (notably with Gaye's *What's Going On* of 1971 and Wonder's *Inner Visions* of 1973, with the funky, inspirational "Higher Ground," subsequently covered by the Red Hot Chili Peppers), and leading to Sly and The Family Stone, George Clinton's Parliament-Funkadelic, and Curtis Mayfield's and Isaac Hayes' versions of 1970s funk.

Building on Hendrix and Brown, Clinton's "extreme funk," combined with hippie culture, appealed to whites and blacks in the 1970s, as an "alternative nation" with an "Afrodelic" image crossing the boundaries on the shared experiences of drugs and funky music. It was accompanied by a move in the opposite direction, in the Philadelphia sweet soul sounds of male black groups, such as the Delfonics, Billy Paul, and the O'Jays, who revived the doo-wop spirit soaked with the beautiful side of soul. Popular bands such as Earth, Wind, and Fire and Kool and the Gang ("Celebration" in 1980) found niches in between hard funk and soft soul, and dance records that defined disco – the watered-down version of soul and funk that celebrated black then white urban and gay cultures – became hugely popular, appropriated egregiously by white band the Bee Gees and in the movie *Saturday Night Fever.*

Blues and gospel beyond the 1960s

The legacy of classic rock music and its format borne of r&b dominated until the 1990s, but has given way to a multitude of new styles, rap and techno-pop in particular. Blues-based guitarists and bands nonetheless persist: Stevie Ray Vaughan's *Texas Flood* of 1985, Robert Cray's *Strong Persuader* in 1986, John Lee Hooker's revival in *The Healer* in 1989, and the continuing Johnny Winter, ZZ Top, and Steve Miller Band, along with the Allman Brothers and Lynyrd Skynyrd in the legacy of the immensely successful southern U.S. Creedence Clearwater Revival.

Soul music returns every few years, powered by white appropriations such as the *Blues Brothers* movie of 1980, and the *Commitments* movie and soundtrack, which associated the Irish underclass with their black counterparts in the U.S. But the banner of soul and funk for black audiences has persisted in the T.V. show *Soul Train*, started in 1970 by Don Cornelius and continuing as the longest-running syndication show, providing "cultural common ground" for African Americans, with the "Soul Train Dancers," and the Soul Train Music Awards and Soul Train Lady of Soul Awards honoring r&b, rap/hip-hop, jazz and gospel artists. Judging by the online comments at the web site, many viewers want to see shows from the first decade revived, particularly those of James Brown, so that new fans can see the "classic" r&b artists, who continue their immense influence.

While whites have generally kept the blues past alive in re-creations, Prince, strangely from Nordic Minnesota, home of Garrison Keiler's white bread *Prairie Home Companion* and Jesse Ventura's white-trash wrestlers, has been one of the most adventurous musicians of the 1980s and 1990s. Along with Janet and Michael Jackson, he combined funk and dance music, but added white hard rock and r&r heavy guitar elements. Prince, like Jackson, is a crossover artist, combining many elements, and like Little

Richard, reveling in sexual ambiguity and excess. Prince's "slave" contract struggles and his loss of identity to an unpronounceable symbol can all be read as part of his struggle to find an identity in the white-controlled music business.

If the blues and gospel expressed the condition of blacks early in the twentieth century, and r&b, then soul were increasingly integrated forms of the blues reinfused with gospel as blacks gained in social and economic status, then rap is the expression of the problems – poverty, unemployment, drugs, gangs – that remain in the inner city. Fused from gospel's preacher style of speaking, the Jamaican tradition of rhyming over discs in clubs, the technology of the DJ and the house party, and the syncopated, dance beats and reduction of melody and harmony to rhythm of James Brown's funky music, rap adds stark lyrics revealing the conditions of lives led in the black community. Rap also emerged in response to white appropriations of black music. With every inventive new form taken and covered by whites for more money, fame, and influence, and with no interest in r&r or rock, particularly in its punk or grunge manifestations of the 1970s or 1980s, black musicians took to the streets in spoken poetry over the tools of the DJ's trade: the scratching turntable and heavy beat. Dating from Sugar Hill's "Rapper's Delight" of 1979, using an underlying disco track, and pioneers Afrika Bambaataa and Grandmaster Flash (Joseph Sadler), blacks created a music, like bebop, that whites had great difficulty in coming to terms with, since rap seemed to defy all musical standards. As with r&b, however, whites were involved in the production and record labels. Arthur Baker, for instance, is an influential and early hip-hop producer, crossing over to introduce the art of remixing into the pop mainstream, and working with Bambaataa. With the advent of digital sampling, rappers were themselves accused of stealing rock music samples and electronically recycling funk. Appropriation did come, starting in reverse with Run DMC's cover of Aerosmith's "Walk This Way" (1986) and subsequent video on M.T.V., and also in traditional form with the white Beastie Boys, Vanilla Ice, and Eminem. On M.T.V., which originally was slow to show black videos, rap had an equally difficult time breaking in, but rap shows like "M.T.V. Raps" quickly became popular and rap is currently a staple of M.T.V. and "the Box" Video channel (now M.T.V.2). Rap has become a music of fusion in the wake of its exposure and appropriation, with rap-funk – George Clinton crossed with Coolio and Ice Cube – and rap-metal, led by mostly white bands like Limp Bizkit, who build on the heavy black rock of Bad Brains and Living Color but add white-boy heavy metal rap on top. In a Motown celebratory release of 1998, Puff Daddy is acclaimed as the new Berry Gordy as rap becomes corporate, with families of groups coalescing around Def Jam records and producers like Dr. Dre. Some rap has kept its original edge, with "gangsta" wars that have resulted in the death of rappers Tupac Shakur, the Notorious B.I.G., and others.

Jamaicans in the 1950s listened to the latest r&b at public dances, evolving a system of DJs and sound systems. Hybrid forms started combining r&b elements with native music, producing ska (1961), rocksteady (1967) and reggae (1968), which were appropriated soon after in Britain and later the U.S. Clapton, for instance, covered a Bob Marley tune, "I Shot the Sheriff" (1974), to introduce white audiences to a white-washed reggae beat, and the Police introduced ska to white America. In Jamaica, reggae took on nationalist and religious connotations. First singer Jimmy Cliff was popular, then Bob Marley, the reggae superstar born of mixed-race parents, became their patron saint. Reggae thus became symbolic for Jamaicans as blues and gospel had for African Americans. Along with reggae musical forms, Jamaican dance hall culture became part of the rave dance scene in the U.S. and Britain.[27]

With the rise of rap, blues has become largely a historical form. On the Internet, sites like the "House of Blues" have sprung up, and the legacy of the blues is available for download and has been celebrated; journals like *Living Blues* and labels like Alligator promote young players but mostly revive memories of the past. The coalition of "white intellectuals, college students, liberals, cognoscenti [who] rediscovered the blues in their quest for 'truth,'" as well as the many European and world blues fans, lives on and promotes "authentic" blues online.[28] B. B. King, in particular, since his 1968 concert at the Fillmore West in San Francisco to a mostly white audience, has become a beloved American Ambassador of music. Taking over the role from Louis Armstrong and traveling through the world, King has established blues alongside jazz as the U.S.'s native music. His many honors include multiple Grammies, a Kennedy Center award, induction into the Rock and Roll Hall of Fame, three Blues Image awards from the N.A.A.C.P., and a National Endowment for the Arts Heritage Award, and his influence, among others, has prompted the Grammy Awards to include categories for Traditional Blues Album and Contemporary Blues Album. John Lee Hooker is also celebrated, with a 1989 Grammy for his CD, *The Healer*, which includes duets with many disciples. The awards these artists get are emblematic of the showering of "Hall of Fame" accolades given to the black forerunners of contemporary popular music. While the origins of the Grammies are steeped in racism and the white recording establishment wanting to stop r&r and r&b, admitting only jazz from black sources, these and other awards have come to recognize the sources of much American popular music.[29] With the aging and deaths of the original r&b performers like Joe Turner, who died broke and with debts in 1987, the level of rip-offs has come out to embarrass some of the companies, like Atlantic, who profited from their talents. Atlantic has "'recalculated' the royalties due on foreign sales and reissues of old records" and "contributed $2 million to establish a foundation that makes tax-free grants to the down-on-their-luck pioneers of rhythm and blues."[30]

In the gospel world, the title role in the 1960s was played by James Cleveland, the "Crown Prince of Gospel," who, following Joe May, the "King of Gospel Singers" in the 1950s, expanded on gospel's boundaries into popular styles, a "soul man, the first to really wed gospel and pop" creating the modern gospel sound. Cleveland started an annual Gospel Music Workshop of America in 1968 to spawn a revival of the gospel choir, and his death at age sixty from AIDS caused some soul-searching in the gospel community.[31] The gospel choir tradition championed by Cleveland continues, with groups like the Mississippi Mass Choir hitting the charts and winning Gospel, Traditional, and Spiritual awards for their recordings and videos, and accolades from *Billboard Magazine* and N.A.R.M. (National Association of Record Merchandisers). In the mid-1970s, the Edwin Hawkins Singers' "Oh Happy Day" was a no. 1 song, the biggest gospel hit of all time, and in its wake artists such as Andrae Crouch, the Winans Family, and Sweet Honey in the Rock made their way into the mainstream. The gospel vocal group has found a popular voice in Take 6, a highly successful crossover ensemble drawing from virtually all aspects of their heritage.

The piano remains the primary instrumental signifier of the gospel song. Gospel piano style, particularly in its boogie-related elements, originally influenced the rock'n'rollers Jerry Lee Lewis, Little Richard and Fats Domino, and formed an essential part of Ray Charles' soul innovations, Aretha Franklin's initial recordings, and Stevie Wonder's Motown songs. It has continued to wind its way through the solo piano tradition in rock music, from Carole King to Leon Russell, Stevie Winwood, Elton John, Billy Joel, and Bruce Hornsby, and songs like the Beatles' "Let It Be" and Paul Simon's "Bridge Over Troubled Water."

Like blues players, accolades have come to gospel singers. Marion Williams received a MacArthur genius award and the Kennedy Center Honors in 1993 as part of the mass recognition by the media of the wellsprings of American music. The Grammy Awards include categories Rock Gospel, Southern, Country, or Bluegrass Gospel, Pop/Contemporary Gospel, Traditional Soul Gospel, Contemporary Soul Gospel, and Gospel Choir or Chorus. Gospel elements have continued in the parallel white and black streams, with "Contemporary Christian" the trade name for white gospel; ironically, Pat Boone switched from his successful role as an r&r cover artist to his equally successful Christian white-gospel albums in the 1970s. The breadth of fusion and crossover in Christian–gospel music is indicated by the Gospel Music Association's Dove awards, with categories for Rap/Hip Hop/Dance, Modern Rock/Alternative, Hard Music, Rock, Pop/Contemporary, Inspirational, Southern Gospel, Bluegrass, Country, Urban, Traditional and Contemporary Gospel, Instrumental, and Praise & Worship.

The Philadelphia "beautiful" sound of the Delfonics and other groups in the 1970s persists in "contemporary r&b" styles with Luther VanDross and many others, continuing a tradition of romance-soaked slightly funky tunes with strings (real or synthesized) setting the generally overblown mood. Motown continues in L.A., with Boyz II Men, reviving the *a cappella* group love style, and Babyface Edmonds, a writer, performer in Sam Cooke mold, re-creating a sugary, love-filled style. The vocal inflections and timbres of gospel, after working through soul, continue to influence female vocal styles – Whitney Houston, Patti LaBelle, Anita Baker, but also the white Michael Bolton, Mariah Carey and Christina Aguillera, who mechanically ornament every note and appear in videos with black rappers and dancers in excessive attempts at "authenticity" – and in a diluted pop fashion in the resurgence of the male vocal group ('N'sync, Backstreet Boys, Westlife).

Following jazz, which was a music fusing different styles from its inception, blues and gospel-influenced forms have been fused with music from around the world in the last decades of the twentieth century. Robert Palmer has noted the global influences in U.S. popular music from the 1960s, citing music from Africa, Europe, and India in the rhythms, harmony, and melody of blues-based forms.[32] The rise of "world music" – a term which reflects a Western focus on music from all different countries – has set the tone for new definitions of appropriation, crossover, and fusion of and between styles from around the world. The white face of this music has been presented by David Byrne, Peter Gabriel, Paul Simon, and others who variously promote and appropriate its elements. As with blues and gospel, the many styles represent the hopes, aspirations, fears, and humanity of people from all racial and geographical groups, and the continuing cry for individual and collective freedom.[33]

Themes

Throughout this chapter, and to an extent throughout the Companion, several themes have recurred in the story of blues and gospel appropriations. The first is the essential racial and economic point: the white entertainment industry cashes in on appropriated versions of largely black musical styles by appealing to the mass audience, altering the context and leaving the original performers and writers with little or no compensation and/or acknowledgment. The practice, excoriated in Sonny Boy Williamson

II's song "(I Ain't) Fattenin' (No More) Frogs For Snakes," is part of the exploitation of blacks by whites throughout American history, where blacks are excluded from positions of ownership or authority.[34] This theme includes four related components. First, in court cases in the 1940s and 1950s, copyright for musical arrangement was disallowed, in a ruling that only traditional song elements could be copyrighted. After this ruling, upholding the traditional elements of the notated song in the Tin Pan Alley tradition versus the stylistic elements of records, a performer's style could be copied, without compensation. In practice, however, there was constant litigation over cover versions, but the original black performers mostly lost out to white cover versions.[35] Second, in competition between major labels with national distribution and small independent, regional labels, the larger companies quickly covered regional hits or styles. The sales and distribution of promotional copies of covers hurt the original artists, who often had a royalty based only on their own recordings. The big labels also signed up the original artists and, inevitably, diluted the original style in the rush for higher sales and put the smaller labels out of business. Moves by Elvis Presley (1955) and Ray Charles (1960) to RCA Victor from the Sun and Atlantic labels are often cited as examples.[36] Third, when songs were recorded, publishing and songwriting copyrights were often given to producers, record-label owners, and even DJs, who were assured of continuing income with sales, especially if the song went into multiple versions, while the original artists were paid on a once only "for hire" basis or given minimal royalties. Thus, Chuck Berry's first song "Maybellene" has DJ Alan Freed added as a "writer" as payola for his services. Little Richard was paid $50 for "Tutti Frutti" by Art Rupe of Specialty Records, with a royalty of 1/2 cent per record (instead of the standard 2 cents), then sold all his rights for $10,000 when he turned to religion, and later settled in a suit for $40,000, for songs that made millions.[37] Frankie Lymon and the Teenagers received a 1 cent per record royalty for "Why Do Fools Fall in Love," only after recording session costs were paid off, with publishing and writer credits assigned to the record label.[38] Record labels also owned the master tapes, so that performers had no access to their own recordings. This form of economic appropriation applied to white and black musicians, but blacks suffered disproportionately as their styles were the ones that set the trends. Finally, the fourth consideration is that the music industry is a business, designed to make money; any time big money became involved, the usual criminal-type elements emerged: shake-downs, rip-offs, bribes, beatings, intimidation, and the mob. In such a climate, with profit as the sole motivator, all involved parties were subject to abuse, but particularly the artists, who were regarded as expendable cash cows, and black artists, in particular, who had few rights or recourse.[39]

The second theme is the connection between the metaphor of the "grain" in the sound and distinctions between blues and gospel-related music and "pop" versions of these styles.[40] Both blues and gospel are essentially vocal musics, with string bending and the bottleneck slide on the guitar and the inflections of the harmonica as surrogates for the sliding, bending, expression found in vocal blues, and the vocal virtuosity in choirs and in small groups – sometimes with voices imitating instruments – in gospel. Pop music versions are those in which appropriated elements – particularly vocal – are transformed by reducing or eliminating the grain in the sound:

(1) vocal quality is made purer, with less "noise" in the sound from articulation, and the continuity of pitch and timbre is closer to classical music;
(2) the vocal line is smoothed out, removing many of the nuances and ornamental figures used in blues and gospel expression;
(3) lyrics are altered from real-life experiences to idealized states, generally of love and loss in an abstract sense;
(4) instrumentation and timbre are also made more pure, with less articulation and noise in the sound, and instruments characteristic of other musical styles are added (strings, harpsichords etc.), and;
(5) rhythm and phrase length is evened out and squared off, with ambiguities and fluidity curtailed.

These pop alterations have the effect of making the sound less personal and more objectified and predictable, and so more available to a wide audience. A related metaphor is the presence or feel of the "body" in the sound: the physical elements of exertion in the voice, and dance elements in the body, often linked back to African musical and dance forms, are a physicality that is removed in pop appropriations, with their flattening of texture, emotion, and expression.

The third theme in the appropriation of blues and gospel is a political and social one: the role of blues and gospel appropriations in the history of black Civil Rights. The rise of r&r from r&b in the 1950s and 1960s, the transformation of blues in British rock music and subsequent popularity of British musicians in the U.S., the blues revival lead by the folk-rock movement in the U.S.A., and the rise and crossover success of Motown and soul music, coincided with a series of social and legal events that led to the Civil Rights legislation of 1960s. The entry of black music into white society mirrored gains in rights of blacks themselves. Along with gospel music and its most successful proponent Mahalia Jackson, soul music, with its mixed-race house bands backing black singing stars was, in particular, associated with Martin Luther King. Setbacks occurred in this continuing struggle. King died in April 1968 in Memphis, following the riots in the previous year in Detroit and elsewhere, which heightened tensions between the white establishment and the new advocates of "Black Power." A backlash followed the militant outcries against white ownership of radio and recording companies by the "Fairplay Committee" at the 1968 N.A.T.R.A. (National Association of Television and Radio Announcers) convention and subsequent resegregated black music forms. Yet soul and funk music retained its influence in the black community. Thus the "crossover" associated with blues and gospel music-derived styles was a political as well as musical process.[41]

The fourth theme involves the problems inherent in the writing of a history for blues and gospel music and the appropriation of these elements. These problems are analogous to those of transcribing the oral and recorded forms of blues and gospel music in written notation: important elements are missed, and the choices made often force the music into contexts based more on the notation than the expression. Any history is a story of historical fiction, with "facts" presented from viewpoints that bias their interpretation. For instance, Robert Palmer dramatizes the problems of interpretation by comparing the story of the blues through the eyes of writers either fascinated or horrified by its influence on rock music, a "great man" theory of the blues, to a living history of day-to-day life in Mississippi or elsewhere, an "everyman" story where performers lived and played and recorded and died amid impoverished conditions, with none of their posthumous fame or influence in evidence.[42]

Many histories written from the former point of view – blues and gospel as precursor to rock – add a disapproving tone and tendency to find that black performers are authentic, original, and generally virtuous in their honest expression, while white performers and music industry types are inauthentic, rip-off artists, representative of the homogenizing marketplace and generally despicable in their appropriations. Such a view, while true in many cases, can also distort the musical situation. The view that awards Robert Johnson the mantle of the original master of country blues and Eric Clapton a condemnation as a shallow imitator, for instance, ignores the traditional evolution of blues songs, where continual reworking of lyrics, melodies, and instrumentation into ever new styles is fundamental. In this context, Johnson and Clapton are similar, in that they took from many existing sources and reworked songs, in either close covers or more dramatic reconstructions, to create their own styles.

Another effect of written histories of the blues with a view to the future has been attempts to define black styles as "authentic" by some precondition frozen in time: the case of Leadbelly is an example. Huddie Ledbetter, or Leadbelly, a folk-blues singer using an unusual twelve-string guitar, had a legendary life story: gaoled for murder in 1917, pardoned through his music in 1925, then gaoled and pardoned again by his music in 1934. "Discovered" by folklorist Alan Lomax in 1933, who was attempting to find a "pure" source for black blues and folksongs recordings for the Library of Congress, and who reasoned that gaol might be a place to find such an unaffected black source, Leadbelly was initially set in a frame of authenticity from this scholarly/museum keeper point of view: a primitive hayseed strumming his authentic songs – blues, lullabies, cowboy songs – on an old beaten-up guitar. Leadbelly eventually freed himself from this caricature and traveled in style (as far as France in 1949), singing a wide variety of music. Ironically, it was his signature song, "Goodnight Irene," with none of the blues elements he supposedly exemplified, which was covered by the Weavers and Pete Seeger in 1950 to become a big hit. Leadbelly was also unusual in that he had a white following, and he was later invoked as a forerunner of the folk movement of the 1960s, and of the skiffle craze in Britain, following the recording of his "Rock Island Line" by Lonnie Donegan (1956), that influenced the Beatles.[43]

Performers like Leadbelly, as well as Robert Johnson and others, are often defined as "folk" or "blues" performers in light of their influences and recordings, but at the time they sang songs in all different styles and their talents defy easy categorization. In Johnson's case, the preponderance of blues songs in his recordings may reflect only the recording date and interests of the recording label, not necessarily the sum total of the musician; like many blues singers, he was fluent in many styles, listened to the radio and recordings, traveled widely, and even admired Bing Crosby.[44] It is impossible in such cases to speak of "pure" forms of blues or gospel; they are both hybrid forms reflecting the interaction of races and classes and the effects of society, traveling, records, and radio. The expression is, however, individual, and while the story of blues and gospel developments and appropriations has not been kind to the original practitioners, their lives and art continue to speak to us.

Notes

1 Surveying the field: our knowledge of blues and gospel music

1 Oliver (1984) explores some of this other material.

2 Useful outlines of the social history of black Americans can be found in Carroll and Noble (1977), Marable (1984), and Zinn (1980).

3 The term was already common currency in jazz discourse. See Ulanov (1947).

4 For a fuller discussion of this issue, see Peter Narvaez (1993). Charters' later writings, e.g., *The Bluesmen*, are more considered in this respect: indeed, performance details are given at least as much coverage as lyrics, while the focus is on the individual artistry of particular singers.

5 The concept is crucial to much of the study of folksong in a variety of different cultures, while the practice of lines wandering from one blues to another had been noticed as early as 1911 by Howard Odum (see Oliver 1969: 27).

6 The concept was first introduced by Gates (1988).

6 "Black twice": performance conditions for blues and gospel artists

1 A Jim Crow car is a railroad car on which African Americans were "Jim Crowed" or discriminated against – segregated, overcrowded, given inferior facilities, etc.

7 Vocal expression in the blues and gospel

1 Paul Oliver discusses the relevance and difficulties of piecing the history of the blues together from recordings, in Oliver (1968). A similar argument can be made for the history of gospel singing, which had a parallel growth during the last century.

2 From Chris Albertson's notes to Bessie Smith, *The Complete Recordings Vol.1*, 1991, Columbia Roots and Blues Series.

3 Lomax's "Cantometrics" proposed a causal connection between sociological factors and songstyle, in a number of papers (1962, 1967) and subsequently the 1968 book which expanded all these earlier ideas more fully and which included dance style.

4 Register definitions are taken from Thurman and Welch (1997) in which (p. 239) they identify four registers with associated muscular activity. These are pulse register or vocal fry, lower register or modal register (commonly known as "chest" register), upper register (known as "head" register) and falsetto (male) or flute (female) register.

5 Estill's work is scientifically based and published but is also used practically and described as a teaching tool by Estill trainer Gillyanne Kayes (2000).

6 The development of the concept of a "classically" trained or "schooled" voice is discussed in detail in the definitive study: Potter (1998).

7 For a fuller history of the influence of conservatoire and Western classical traditions on African American musical history see Southern (1997: 265–96).

8 Alfred Wolfsohn developed a psychotherapeutic methodology of working with vocal timbres which developed the capacity for women to speak and sing in bass and men in soprano ranges, and developed extraordinary individual vocal flexibility. Roy Hart took this work into theatre practice after Wolfsohn's death eventually founding the Roy Hart Theatre based in France and demonstrated this vocal flexibility in Peter Maxwell Davies' *Eight Songs For A Mad King* which was written for the Roy Hart Theatre to perform. Paul Newham developed the work along more psychotherapeutic lines in Britain training vocalists to identify what is happening to a client by making identical vocal sounds and experiencing the laryngeal mechanisms at play.

9 Discussed in Kemp (1996: 173–82).

10 "Reach and collapse" is a common technique – singers reach upwards in pitch, or by increasing intensity through volumes, growls or wails, then release physically on the breath and with the body.

11 In "I asked for water, you gave me gasoline."

12 Gilbert Rouget has written and researched extensively into the complex relationship between music and trance behavior, many of his examples are from sub-Saharan communities and their diaspora. Some gospel churches embraced "speaking in tongues" and "being taken over by the spirit" as a central part of their practice.

13 In discussion with Dr. Maraire in Malawi at a Choral Conference I learned that the practice of high-registered male singers singing soprano was commonplace in his experience, and only discouraged, interestingly, by Western classical choral directors who found the timbres inconsistent with the requirements of the soprano parts.
14 Referring to Barthes' seminal essay on "The Grain of the Voice" (1988). He uses this terminology specifically to refer to two Western classical singers. I appropriate the sense because the concept is pertinent when here applied to blues and gospel singers.
15 His quotation begins Oliver's (1968) exploration describing the nature of "the spiritual" as elusive against other factors which may be more easily analyzed.

9 Keyboard techniques
1 A walking bass line was first used in a published composition by the late nineteenth- and early twentieth-century classical virtuoso and ragtime pianist "Blind" Boone in his "Rag Medley no. 11" of 1909. It was also a feature of early Harlem Stride pianist Eubie Blake's 1899 composition "Charleston Rag" where a left-hand walking bass in octaves supports the ragtime-influenced right hand.
2 I.e., the major scale with a flattened-seventh note.
3 The distinction straight/swing is that between metronomically even eighth notes and those where the first of a pair of eighth notes is lengthened at the expense of the second.
4 The "lick" became a signature element of Charles' right-hand playing. Starting with an ascending octave leap on the dominant it cascades down the tonic major arpeggio crushing major and minor thirds together, passes through chords IV and I dim coming to rest on I^7.
5 The "Hucklebuck" was a popular 1940s dance and Ammons' left-hand pattern was used as the basis for an r&b no. 1 hit of the same by Paul "Hucklebuck" Williams in 1949.

10 Imagery in the lyrics: an initial approach
1 Discussion in these areas can be found, for example, in Courlander (1963) or Oster (1969).
2 Spurgeon (1975: 5).
3 Katherine Baker. "Mistreated Blues." Chicago or Richmond, Ind., May 18, 1927. Issued on Gennett 6321. Reissued on Document DOCD 5182. (lyric transcription in MacLeod 5: 193)

4 Luella Miller. "Dreaming of You Blues." New York City, January 28, 1927. Issued on Vocalion 1081. Reissued on Document DOCD 5183. (lyric transcription in MacLeod 5: 203)
5 Charley Jordan. "Starvation Blues." Chicago, January 6, 1931. Issued on Vocalion 1627. Reissued on Document DOCD 5097. (lyric transcription in *R'sB*: 25)
6 Alice Moore. "Grass Cutter Blues." Chicago, May 22, 1936. Issued on Decca 7190. Reissued on Document DOCD 5039. (lyric transcription in sleeve notes to Agram Blues ABLP 2013)
7 Alice Moore. "Telephone Blues." Chicago, May 22, 1936. Issued on Decca 7190. Reissued on Document DOCD 5039. (lyric transcription in sleeve notes to Agram Blues ABLP 2013)
8 Luella Miller. "Smiling Rose Blues." Chicago or St. Louis, Mo., April 26, 1927. Issued on Vocalion 1104. Reissued on Document DOCD 5183. (lyric transcription in MacLeod 5: 205)
9 Rev. J. M. Gates. "Hitler and Hell." Atlanta, Ga., October 2, 1941. Issued on Bluebird B8851. Reissued on Document DOCD 5484. (*R'sB*: 172)
10 Lizzie Washington. "Mexico Blues." Chicago or Richmond, Ind., May 19, 1927. Issued on Black Patti 8054. Reissued on Document DOCD 5182. (lyric transcription in MacLeod 5: 196)
11 Tampa Red. "Stormy Sea Blues." Chicago, April 3, 1936. Issued on BlueBird B6425. Reissued on Document DOCD 5207. (lyric transcription in MacLeod 6: 23)
12 Edgewater Crows. "No Bonus Blues." Hattiesburg, Miss., July 15, 1936. Issued on Melotone 7-01-62. Reissued on Document DOCD 5611. (lyric transcription in *R'sB*: 126)
13 Francis "Scrapper" Blackwell. "Springtime Blues." Richmond, Ind., February 4, 1930. Issued on Gennett 7158. Reissued on Blues Documents BDCD 6029. (lyric transcription in sleeve notes to Agram Blues ABLP 2008)
14 Josh White. "Low Cotton." New York City, August 15, 1933. Issued on Banner 32858. Reissued on Document DOCD 5194. (lyric transcription in *R'sB*: 68)
15 Katherine Baker. "Wild Women Blues." Chicago or Richmond, Ind., May 18, 1927. Issued on Gennett 6194. Reissued on Document DOCD 5182. (lyric transcription in MacLeod 5: 192)
16 Walter Davis. "Moonlight Is My Spread." Chicago, 31 October, 1935. Issued on BlueBird B6167. Reissued on Document DOCD 5282. (lyric transcription in MacLeod 8: x)

17 Charlie Spand. "Hard Time Blues." Grafton, Wis., September 1931. Issued on Paramount 13112. Reissued on Document DOCD 5108. (lyric transcription in *R'sB*: 26)

18 *Ibid.*

19 "Big" Joe Williams. "Providence Help the Poor People." Chicago, February 25, 1935. Issued on Bluebird B5930. Reissued on Blues Documents BDCD 6003. (lyric transcription in *R'sB*: 74)

20 "Big" Joe Williams. "His Spirit Lives On." Chicago, 1945. Issued on Chicago 103. Reissued on Agram Blues ABCD 2017. (lyric transcription in *R'sB*: 74)

21 Huddie "Leadbelly" Ledbetter. "Red Cross Sto'." Washington, D.C., August 23, 1940. Unissued Library of Congress. Issued on Document DLP 610. (lyric transcription in *R'sB*: 58)

22 *Ibid.*

23 Peter "Doctor" Clayton. "Pearl Harbor Blues." Chicago, March 27, 1942. Issued on Bluebird B9003. Reissued on Document DOCD 5179. (lyric transcription in *R'sB*: 151)

24 Soul Stirrers. "Pearl Harbor – Part 1." Chicago, July 2, 1947. Issued on Aladdin 2025. Reissued on Imperial LMLP 94007. (lyric transcription in *R'sB*: 157)

25 Robert "Barbecue Bob" Hicks. "We Sure Got Hard Times." Atlanta, Ga., April 18, 1930. Issued on Columbia 14558-D. Reissued on Document DOCD 5048. (lyric transcription in *R'sB*: 20)

26 Rev. R. H. Taylor. "The Bonus Have Found the Stingy Mens Out." Hattiesburg, Miss., July 21, 1936. Issued on Melotone 6-11-64. Reissued on Agram Blues ABCD 2017. (lyric transcription in *R'sB*: 127)

27 Huddie "Leadbelly" Ledbetter. "Mr. Hitler." New York City, January 20, 1942. Unissued Library of Congress. Issued on Rounder CD 1046. (lyric transcription in *R'sB*: 173)

28 Sonny Boy Williamson. "Check up on My Baby." Chicago, December 14, 1944. Issued on Bluebird 34-0722. Reissued on Document DOCD 5058. (lyric transcription in *R'sB*: 179)

29 Edith North Johnson. "You Know That Ain't Right." Long Island City, N.Y.C., c. December 1928. Issued on QRS R7048. Reissued on Agram Blues ABCD 2016. (lyric transcription in the sleeve notes)

30 Alice Moore. "Telephone Blues." Chicago, May 22, 1936. Issued on Decca 7190. Reissued on Document DOCD 5039. (lyric transcription in sleeve notes to Agram Blues ABLP 2013)

31 Alice Moore. "Doggin' Man Blues." Chicago, March 25, 1937. Issued on Decca 7380. Reissued on Document DOCD 5291. (lyric transcription in sleeve notes to Agram Blues ABLP 2013)

32 Mary Johnson. "Muddy Creek Blues." Brunswick 7093. Reissued on Document DOCD 5305. (lyric transcription in sleeve notes to Agram Blues ABLP 2014)

33 *Ibid.*

34 *Ibid.*

35 Mary Johnson. "Rattlesnake Blues." Richmond, Ind., September 22, 1932. Issued on Champion 16570. Reissued on Document DOCD 5305. (lyric transcription in sleeve notes to Agram Blues ABLP 2014)

36 Luella Miller. "Rattle Snake Groan." New York City, January 28, 1927. Issued on Vocalion 1081. Reissued on Document DOCD 5183. (lyric transcription in MacLeod 5: 203)

37 Will Weldon (Casey Bill). "Spider Blues." Chicago, October 20, 1937. Issued on Vocalion 04318. Reissued on Document DOCD 5219. (lyric transcription in MacLeod 6: 175)

38 Alice Moore. "I'm Going Fishing Too." Chicago, May 22, 1936. Issued on Decca 7253. Reissued on Document DOCD 5039. (lyric transcription in sleeve notes to Agram Blues ABLP 2013)

39 Huddie "Leadbelly" Ledbetter. "Red Cross Sto'." Washington, D.C., August 23, 1940. Unissued Library of Congress. Issued on Document DLP 610. (lyric transcription in *R'sB*: 58)

40 *Ibid.*

41 Louis Jordan. "Ration Blues." Los Angeles, October 4, 1942. Issued on Decca 8654. Reissued on Decca BM 03545. (lyric transcription in *R'sB*: 184)

42 Sonny Scott. "Red Cross Blues No. 2." New York City, July 20, 1933. Issued on Vocalion 02614. Reissued on Document DOCD 5450. (lyric transcription in *R'sB*: 53)

43 Earl Thomas. "Bonus Men." Chicago, July 7, 1936. Issued on Decca 7221. Reissued on Document DOCD 5645. (lyric transcription in *R'sB*: 126)

44 Edith North Johnson. "Nickles Worth of Liver Blues." Richmond, Ind., September 7, 1929. Issued on Paramount 12823. Reissued on Agram Blues ABCD 2016. (lyric transcription in the sleeve notes)

45 Edith North Johnson. "Honey Dripper Blues." Richmond, Ind.; September 7, 1929. Issued on Paramount 12823. Reissued on Agram Blues ABCD 2016. (lyric transcription in the sleeve notes)

46 Edith North Johnson. "Soothing Syrup Blues." St. Louis, May 15, 1961. Issued on Folkways LP 3815. (lyric transcription in sleeve notes to Agram Blues ABCD 2017)

47 Edith North Johnson. "Ain't No More To Be Said." Chicago, November 16, 1929. Issued on OKeh 8748. Reissued on Agram Blues ABCD 2016. (lyric transcription in the sleeve notes)

48 Lizzie Washington. "Skeleton Key Blues." Chicago or Richmond, Ind., April 19, 1927. Issued on Gennett 6134. Reissued on Document DOCD 5182. (lyric transcription in MacLeod 5: 194)

49 Luella Miller. "Wee Wee Daddy Blues." Chicago, August 1, 1928. Issued on Vocalion 1234. Reissued on Document DOCD 5183. (lyric transcription in MacLeod 5: 210)

50 Jack Kelly. "President Blues." New York City, August 2, 1933. Issued on Banner 32857. Reissued on Agram Blues ABCD 2017. (lyric transcription in *R'sB*: 66)

51 Luella Miller. "Tombstone Blues." Chicago, January 24, 1928. Issued on Vocalion 1151. Reissued on Document DOCD 5183. (lyric transcription in MacLeod 5: 208)

52 George Noble. "T. B. Blues." Chicago, March 20, 1935. Issued on Vocalion 02954. Reissued on Document DOCD 5191. (lyric transcription in MacLeod 5: 315)

53 Alice Moore. "Blue Black and Evil Blues." Chicago, July 19, 1935. Issued on Decca 7132. Reissued on Document DOCD 5291. (lyric transcription in sleeve notes to Agram Blues ABLP 2013)

54 Elizabeth Washington. "Riot Call Blues." Chicago, August 2, 1933. Issued on BlueBird B5229. Reissued on Document DOCD 5182 and 5315. (lyric transcription in MacLeod 5: 198)

55 Alice Moore. "Push Cart Pusher." Chicago, October 26, 1937. Issued on Decca 7393. Reissued on Document DOCD 5291. (lyric transcription in sleeve notes to Agram Blues ABLP 2013)

56 Jack Kelly. "President Blues." New York City, August 2, 1933. Issued on Banner 32857. Reissued on Agram Blues ABCD 2017. (lyric transcription in *R'sB*: 66)

57 *Ibid.*

58 Edith North Johnson. "Ain't No More To Be Said." Chicago, November 16, 1929. Issued on OKeh 8748. Reissued on Agram Blues ABCD 2016. (lyric transcription in the sleeve notes)

59 Lizzie Washington. "Sport Model Mamma Blues." Chicago or Richmond, Ind., May 19,

1927. Issued on Gennett 6195. Reissued on Document DOCD 5182. (lyric transcription in MacLeod 5: 196)

60 Rev. J. M. Gates. "Hitler and Hell." Atlanta, Ga., October 2, 1941. Issued on Bluebird B8851. Reissued on Document DOCD 5484. (lyric transcription in *R'sB*: 172)

61 Lizzie Washington. "My Low Down Brown." Chicago or Richmond, Ind., April 19, 1927. Issued on Gennett 6126. Reissued on Document DOCD 5182. (lyric transcription in MacLeod 5: 194)

62 Edith North Johnson. "You Ain't No Good Blues." Long Island City, N.Y.C., *c.* December 1928. Issued on QRS R7048. Reissued on Agram Blues ABCD 2016. (lyric transcription in the sleeve notes)

63 Beckson and Ganz (1972: 162).

64 Rev. J. M. Gates. "Hitler and Hell." Atlanta, Ga., October 2, 1941. Issued on Bluebird B8851. Reissued on Document DOCD 5484. (lyric transcription in *R'sB*: 172)

65 Joe Pullum. "C.W.A. Blues." San Antonio, Tx., April 3, 1934. Issued on Bluebird B5534. Reissued on Document DOCD 5393. (lyric transcription in *R'sB*: 69)

66 Jimmy Gordon. "Don't Take Away My P.W.A." Chicago, October 2, 1936. Issued on Decca 7230. Reissued on Agram Blues ABCD 2017. (lyric transcription in *R'sB*: 107)

67 Charlie McCoy. "Charity Blues." Chicago, August 13, 1934. Issued on Decca 7046. Reissued on Blues Documents BDCD 6019. (lyric transcription in *R'sB*: 106)

68 Charley Jordan. "Look What a Shape I'm In (Bonus Blues)." Chicago, November 2, 1937. Issued on Decca 7455. Reissued on Document DOCD 5099. (lyric transcription in *R'sB*: 129)

69 Katherine Baker. "Wild Women Blues." Chicago or Richmond, Ind., May 18, 1927. Issued on Gennett 6194. Reissued on Document DOCD 5182. (lyric transcription in MacLeod 5: 192)

70 Zion Travelers. "Movin' up the King's Highway." Los Angeles, March 18, 1954. Issued on Score 5054. Reissued on Imperial LP 9240. (untranscribed)

71 Biddleville Quintette. "This Train Is Bound for Glory." Chicago, *c.* January 1927. Issued on Paramount 12448. Reissued on Document DOCD 5361. (lyric transcription in MacLeod 10: x)

72 Mother McCollum. "Jesus Is My Air-O-Plane." Chicago, *c.* mid-June 1930. Issued on Vocalion 1616. Reissued on Document DOCD 5101. (lyric transcription in MacLeod 3: 184)

73 Jaybird Coleman. "I'm Gonna Cross the River of Jordan – Some O' These Days." Birmingham, Al., August 5, 1927. Issued on Silvertone 5172. Reissued on Document DOCD 5140. (lyric transcription in MacLeod *Yazoo 21–81*: 28)

74 Selah Jubilee Singers. "I'll Fly Away." New York City, February 21, 1941. Issued on Decca 7831. Reissued on Document DOCD 5499. (lyric transcription in MacLeod 13: x)

75 Rev. McGhee. "I'm a Soldier in the Army of the Lord." Clarksdale, Miss., *c.* 19 or 26 July, 1942. Issued on Library of Congress AFS LP 59. Reissued on Document DOCD 5312. (lyric transcription in MacLeod 8: x)

76 Rev. Sister Mary Nelson. "The Royal Telephone." Chicago, April 21, 1927. Issued on Vocalion 1109. Reissued on Document DOCD 5072. (lyric transcription in MacLeod 2: 298)

77 Alphabetical Four. "I Want Two Wings to Veil My Face." New York City, August 16, 1938. Issued on Decca 7507. Reissued on Document DOCD 5374. (lyric transcription in MacLeod 10: x)

11 Appropriations of blues and gospel in popular music

1 Liner notes for Chuck Berry: *The Chess Box*, MCA Records 1998.

2 Barthes (1988).

3 Freed and other DJs themselves appropriated black DJ styles. See George (1988).

4 Los Angeles was also somewhat prominent with Roy Milton, Joe Liggins, T-Bone Walker, Johnny Otis, Charles Brown, and many record labels.

5 Booklet from Bo Diddley, *The Chess Box*, MCA Records, 1990, and Diddley's interview in *The Rolling Stone Interviews: The 1980s*, pp. 181–90.

6 That Elvis did not continue in r&r, but aside from the introduction concert to his 1968 comeback fell back into the crooning ballads and pop mannerisms of predecessors such as Dean Martin, a succession of bad movies contracted by his prototypical evil manager, Colonel Tom Parker, and eventual Las Vegas show hell, is one of the ironic, but truly American, aspects of the story.

7 Dawson and Propes (1992).

8 Haley's "Rock Around the Clock" has come to represent the 1950s by its use in movies of the time like *Blackboard Jungle*, and the later George Lucas movie *American Graffiti* and associations with the TV show *Happy Days*. As with the white Original Dixieland Jazz Band, however, most listeners had no idea of the appropriations involved. Belz

(1972: 33–8) and Clarke (1995: 382) note Haley's sixty U.S. chart hits in seven years. Friedlander (1996: 39) adds that "approximately twenty-five major movies were devoted to the subject of rock and roll," including Chuck Berry in *Rock, Rock, Rock, Mr. Rock and Roll*, and *Go Johnny Go* and Little Richard in *Don't Knock the Rock* and *The Girl Can't Help it*.

9 Marcus (1975).

10 Szatmary (1991: 29–30), notes in 1968 Dick Waterman, a manager for many of the older blues players, tried to help Crudup get royalties, $60,000 from Hill and Range Songs, which owned Crudup's songs, but owner, Julian Aberbach, wouldn't sign the deal.

11 The list could include Jimmy Page (Led Zeppelin), Peter Green (Fleetwood Mac), Jeff Beck (Jeff Beck Group), Alvin Lee (Ten Years After), and many others.

12 Headlam (1997).

13 See Hatch and Millward (1987) on families of blues songs. Storm Roberts (1972: 197) traces such songs like "Spoonful Blues" back to African music: not harmonically structured, just shifting chords in an overall repetitive form with one-chord accompaniment.

14 See Murray (1989: Ch. 3).

15 See Headlam (1995 and 1997).

16 Young (1997: 235).

17 Oliver (1986) and Heilbut (1997); Malone (1974: 226) notes the c&w influence on gospel, as in the 1948 song "Gospel Boogie," by white group, the Homeland Harmony Quartet.

18 Miller (1999: 67–78); Clarke (1995: 370–1), and Belz (1972: 26–7).

19 i.e., quavers [ed.].

20 See Guralnick (1986: Ch. 1); Miller (1999: 76–7) calls vocal covers a "switch."

21 Clarke (1995: 414).

22 The father of gospel, Dorsey, set the standard for this confrontation: he started as blues singer Georgia Tom, singing sexually charged blues of the twenties, but became the Rev. Thomas A. Dorsey, writing gospel standards "Peace in the Valley" and "Take my Hand, Precious Lord" and becoming a leading publisher of religious songs. See Heilbut (1997: Ch. 2). Broughton, Ellingham, Muddyman, and Trillo (1994: 632) note the gospel saying "The Devil Stole the Beat" for this phenomenon.

23 Heilbut (1997: Ch. 7).

24 Belz (1972: 180).

25 George (1987).

26 And the "Godfather of Soul," and "The Hardest Workin' Man in Show Business."

27 Miller (1999: 304–11).

28 Keil (1966: 100–101).

29 Schipper (1992).

30 Wade and Picardie (1990: 20–1).

31 Heilbut (1997: 218, 350).

32 Palmer (1995: 75–7); Palmer notes James Jamerson, the bass player for Motown, citing African, Cuban, and Indian scales in his work (p. 88).

33 Broughton, Ellingham, Muddyman, and Trillo (1994).

34 Perry (1988: 58) details the N.A.A.C.P's 1987 report on racism in the music industry, called *The Discordant Sound of Music*. Among other facts, of 9,000 radio stations, fewer than 400 were for black listeners, and in general, blacks were underrepresented in positions of authority, ownership, had less pay, were bypassed for promotion, and too little money was spent promoting black artists and with minority businesses. This situation represents the state of the music industry throughout the twentieth century.

35 Clarke (1995: 368), referring to the 1940s developments in r&b and pop: "Along the way an historic court case settled the question of whether music arrangements could be copyrighted, and the answer was that they could not. 'A Little Bird Told Me,' a song by Harvey O. Brooks, was recorded by Paula Watson on a Supreme label. Decca copied not only the arrangement but also the vocal style to the last inflection, and had a big hit in 1948 by Evelyn Knight . . . Supreme sued, and lost." Stokes, Tucker, and Ward (1986: 75), notes that Don Robey of Duke-Peacock Records successfully sued Sam Phillips of Sun Records for "Bear Cat" infringing on "Hound Dog," and that LaVern Baker found no legal recourse in trying to stop cover girl Georgia Gibbs from stealing her style and arrangements (p. 93).

36 Booklet to Ray Charles: *The Birth of Soul, The Complete Atlantic Rhythm and Blues Recordings 1952–59*, Atlantic/Atco Remasters, 1991.

37 Wade and Picardie (1990: 74).

38 Stokes, Tucker, and Ward (1986: 127–8). Clarke (1995: 113–20) chronicles the rip-off by George Goldner and Morris Levy on the "Gee" label, where the song was "sold" for $50, but in continuing litigation was awarded to the two remaining members of the Teenagers, Herman Santiago and Jimmy Merchant, for their original version, "Why do Birds Sing so Gay?" in 1991 – thirty-six years later.

39 Wade and Picardie (1990: Chs. 2–4).

40 "Pop" music is often defined just as music that is "popular" in terms of sales, as in Palmer (1995: 9). In this view, any kind of music can be pop music, from Robert Johnson to Lawrence Welk. Another view places pop in the tradition of Tin Pan Alley songsters, whose songs were published as sheet music and were intentionally simple enough to be easily remembered. A history of popular music that follows the Billboard charts exclusively misses much influential music, but documents record company roles and public interest. See Belz (1972: Introduction). See Clarke (1995) for the balance of the popular and the "real," or lasting and influential.

41 Perry (1988); George (1988); Jones (Bakara) (1963).

42 Palmer (1982: 1–20).

43 Miller (1999: 186–8); Davis (1995: 164–72), who asserts that "Irene" was originally a Tin Pan Alley waltz by an Irish composer, and Hatch and Millward (1987: 12) on Leadbelly's cover versions.

44 Booklet to Robert Johnson: *The Complete Recordings*, Columbia, 1990.

Bibliography

Baker, Paul. 1985. *Contemporary Christian Music*. Westchester, Ill.: Crossways.

Bane, Michael. 1982. *White Boy Singin' the Blues*. New York: Penguin Books.

Baraka, Amiri (LeRoi Jones). 1995. *Blues People*. New York: Morrow Quill, 1963. Reprint: New York: Payback.

Barthes, Roland. 1988. "Le grain de la voix," *Musique en jeu*, 9 (1972); translated in *Image, Music, Text*. Essays selected and translated by Stephen Heath. New York: The Noonday Press, pp. 179–89.

Beckson, Karl and Arthur Ganz. 1972. *A Reader's Guide to Literary Terms*. London: Thames and Hudson (originally 1961).

Belz, Carl. 1972. *The Story of Rock*. New York: Oxford University Press.

Bennett, Lonnie. 1988. Unpublished interview with Steve Tracy. October 18.

Blackwell, Lois S. 1978. *The Wings of the Dove*. Norfolk, VA: The Donning Co.

Blesh, Rudi and H. Janis. 1960. *They All Played Ragtime*. London: Sidgwick & Jackson.

Boyd, Eddie. 1977. "Living Blues Interview: Eddie Boyd." *Living Blues* 35, pp. 11–15.

Boyd, Horace Clarence. 2000. *The Golden Age of Gospel*. Urbana: University Of Illinois Press.

Boyer, Horace Clarence (text) with Lloyd Yearwood (photography). 1995. *How Sweet the Sound: The Golden Age of Gospel*. Washington, D.C.: Elliott & Clark Publishing.

Brogger, Arne. 1995. "The Blues Comes to the BBC" on http://www.thebluehighway.com/

Brooks, Lonnie, Cub Koda, and Wayne Baker Brooks. 1988. *Blues for Dummies*. Forest City, CA: IDG Books Worldwide.

Broughton, Simon, Mark Ellingham, David Muddyman, and Richard Trillo. 1994. *World Music: The Rough Guide*. London: Rough Guides Ltd.

Broughton, Viv. 1985. *Black Gospel*. Poole: Blandford.
1996. *Too Close to Heaven: The Illustrated History of Gospel Music*. London: Midnight.

Brunning, Bob. 1986. *Blues: The British Connection*. Poole: Blandford Press.

Carroll, P. N. and D. W. Noble. 1977. *The Free and the Unfree*. Harmondsworth: Penguin.

Caston, Leonard 'Baby doo'. 1974. *From Blues to Pop: Autobiography*. J.E.M.F. Folklore Centre, University of California, Los Angeles, Pamphlet.

Chapple, Steven and Reebee Garofolo. 1977. *Rock 'n' Roll is Here to Pay: The History and Politics of the Music Industry*. Chicago: Nelson Hall.

Charles, Ray, and D. Ritz. 1992. *Brother Ray: Ray Charles; Own Story*. New York: Da Capo.

Charters, Samuel. *The Blues Makers.* 1977. New York: Da Capo Reprint of *The Bluesmen.* Oak Publications; and *Sweet as Showers of Rain.* Oak Publications.
    1975a. *The Country Blues.* New York: Da Capo (originally 1965).
    1975b. *The Legacy of the Blues.* London: Calder & Boyars.
    1970. *The Poetry of the Blues.* New York: Avon Books (originally 1963).
Chilton, John. 1992. *Let the Good Times Roll: The Story of Louis Jordan and His Music.* London: Quartet Books.
Clapton, Eric. 1990. "Discovering Robert Johnson," Booklet to *Robert Johnson: The Complete Recordings.* Columbia, pp. 22–23.
Clarke, Donald. 1995. *The Rise and Fall of Popular Music.* New York: St. Martin's Press.
Clemen, Wolfgang. 1977. *The Development of Shakespeare's Imagery.* London: Methuen, 2nd ed. (original 1951).
Coghlan, B. and members of the Roy Hart Theatre. 1985. *The Human Voice and the Aural Vision Of The Soul.* Totnes: Dartington Theatre Press.
Cohn, Nik. 1970. *Rock from the Beginning.* New York: Pocket Books; reprint of Stein and Day, Inc., 1969 (formerly *Awopbopaloobop, alopbamboom: Pop from the Beginning,* Paladin, London, 1970).
Coker, Jerry. 1964. *Improvising Jazz.* Englewood Cliffs: Prentice Hall.
Considine, J. D. 1990. "Led Zeppelin." *Rolling Stone* 587, September 20.
Cook, Bruce. 1973. *Listen to the Blues.* New York: Charles Scribner.
Courlander, Harold. 1963. *Negro Folk Music, U.S.A.* Columbia University Press.
Cross, Charles R. and Erik Flannigan (eds.). 1991. *Led Zeppelin: Heaven and Hell.* New York: Harmony Books.
Cusic, Don. 1990. *The Sound of Light: A History of Gospel Music.* Bowling Green, OH: Bowling Green State University Press.
Davis, Francis. 1995. *The History of the Blues.* New York: Hyperion.
Dawson, Jim and Steve Propes. 1992. *What Was the First Rock 'n' Roll Record?*
Dixon, Robert M. W., John Godrich and Howard W. Rye. 1997. *Blues and Gospel Records 1890–1943.* 4th ed. Oxford: Oxford University Press.
Dixon, Willie with Don Snowden. 1989. *I Am the Blues.* London: Quartet Books.
Dunn, Leslie C. and Nancy A. Jones. 1994. *Embodied Voices: Representing Female Vocality in Western Culture.* Cambridge: Cambridge University Press.
Eisen, Jonathan (ed). 1969. *The Age of Rock: Sounds of the American Cultural Revolution.* New York: Vintage.
    1970. *The Age of Rock 2: Sounds of the American Cultural Revolution.* New York: Vintage.
Ellis, Tom. 1996–7. "Paul Butterfield." Multi-part article in *Blues Access* 27–29.
Ellison, Mary. 1989. *Extensions of the Blues.* London: John Calder.
Erlewine, Michael, Vladimir Bogdanov, Chris Woodstra, and Cub Koda (eds.).
    1999. *All Music Guide to the Blues.* San Francisco: Miller Freeman Books.
Estill, J. 1980. "Observations About Quality Called 'Belting.'" *Transcripts of the 10th Symposium, Care Of the Professional Voice,* pp. 30–9.
    1988. "Belting and Classic Voice Quality: Some Physiological Differences." *Medical Problems of Performing Artists,* pp. 37–43.

Felder, Ray. 1988. Unpublished interview with Steve Tracy. November 10.

Ferguson, H-Bomb. 1984. Unpublished interview with Steve Tracy. February 8.

Ferris, William. 1978. *Blues From the Delta.* Garden City, N.Y.: Anchor Press Co. (originally 1970).

Floyd, Samuel. 1995. *The Power of Black Music.* New York: Oxford University Press.

Fox, Jon Hartley. 1987. Transcript of "King of the Queen City: The Story of King Records," program 4 (first aired on WYSO-FM).

Friedlander, Paul. 1996. *Rock and Roll: A Social History.* New York: Westview Press.

Frith, Simon (ed.). 1981. *Sound Effects: Youth, Leisure, and the Politics of Rock 'n' Roll.* New York: Pantheon Books.

  1988. *Facing the Music.* New York: Pantheon Books.

  1998. *Performing Rites.* Oxford: Oxford University Press.

Frith, Simon and Andrew Goodwin (eds.). 1990. *On Record.* New York: Pantheon Books.

Frith, Simon and Howard Horne. 1987. *Art into Pop.* London: Methuen.

Garon, Paul. *Blues and the Poetic Spirit.* 1975. London: Eddison Bluesbooks.

Gates, Henry Louis Jr. 1988. *The Signifying Monkey: A Theory of Afro-American Literary Criticism.* New York: Oxford University Press.

George, Nelson. 1987 *Where Did Our Love Go? The Rise & Fall of the Motown Sound.* New York: St. Martins Press.

  1988. *The Death of Rhythm and Blues.* New York: Plume.

Gert zur Heide, K. 1970. *Deep South Piano: The Story of Little Brother Montgomery.* London: November Books.

Gioia, Ted. 1997. *The History of Jazz.* New York: Oxford University Press.

Gillett, Charlie. 1971. *The Sound of the City: The Rise of Rock 'n' Roll.* London: Souvenir Press.

  1975. *Making Tracks: The History of Atlantic Records.* London: W. H. Allen.

Gleason, Ralph J. 1969. "Perspectives: Lets Spread the Goodies Around." *Rolling Stone*, May 3.

Goode, Mort. 1969. Sleeve notes to *black is brown and brown is beautiful.* Skye LP SK-13.

Goodwin, Andrew. 1990. "Sample and Hold: Pop Music in the Digital Age of Reproduction," in Frith & Goodwin 1990.

Groom, Bob. 1971. *The Blues Revival.* London: Studio Vista Limited.

Guralnick, Peter. 1986. *Sweet Soul Music: Rhythm and Blues and the Southern Dream of Freedom.* Boston: Little, Brown, and Co.

  1989. *Searching for Robert Johnson.*

  1999. *Feel Like Going Home: Portraits in Blues and Rock 'n' Roll.* Boston: Little, Brown and Co. (Back Bay Books) (originally 1971).

Haralambos, Michael. 1970. "Soul Music and Blues: Their Meaning and Relevance in Northern United States Black Ghettoes," in Norman E. Whitten, Jr. and John F. Szwed (eds.), *Afro-American Anthropology.* New York: Free Press, pp. 367–83.

  1974. *Right On! From Blues to Soul in Black America.* London: Eddison Press Ltd.

Harris, Michael W. 1992. *The Rise of Gospel Blues: The Music of Thomas Andrew Dorsey in the Urban Church.* New York: Oxford University Press.

Harris, Sheldon. 1979. *Blues Who's Who: A Biographical Dictionary of Blues Singers.* Da Capo Press reprint, New Rochelle, N.Y.: Arlington House.

Hasse, J. E. (ed.). 1985. *Ragtime: Its History, Composers and Music.* London: Macmillan.

Hatch, David Hatch and Stephen Millward. 1987. *From Blues to Rock: An Analytical History of Pop Music.* Manchester: Manchester University Press.

Headlam, Dave. 1995. "Does the Song Remain the Same? Questions of Authorship and Identification in the Music of Led Zeppelin," in *Concert Music, Rock, and Jazz Since 1945: Essays and Analytical Studies.* University of Rochester Press, pp. 313–63.

1997. "Blues Transformations in the Music of Cream," in *Understanding Rock: Essays in Musical Analysis.* New York: Oxford University Press, pp. 59–92.

Heilbut, Anthony. 1997. *The Gospel Sound: Good News and Bad Times.* Revised ed. New York: Simon and Schuster (originally 1971).

Heylin, Clinton (ed.). 1992. *The Penguin Book of Rock & Roll Writing.* London: Penguin.

Hirshey, Gerri. 1984. *Nowhere to Run: The Story of Soul Music.* London: Macmillan.

Hopkins, Jerry. 1970. *The Rock Story.* New York: Signet.

Howard, Jay R. and John M. Streck. 1999. *Apostles of Rock: The Splintered World of Contemporary Christian Music.* Lexington, KY: The University Press of Kentucky.

Hughes, Langston. 1968. "Tambourines to Glory," in *Five Plays by Langston Hughes.* Bloomington: Indiana University Press, pp. 183–258.

Jahn, Mike. 1973. *Rock from Elvis Presley to the Rolling Stones.* New York: Quadrangle.

James, Elmore. 1969. Sleeve notes to *Los Blues de Elmore James.* Caracas: Disco Es Cultura.

Kaye, Lenny. 1970. "The Best of Acappella," in Eisen 1970, pp. 287–301.

Kayes, Gillyanne. 2000. *Singing and The Actor.* London: A & C Black.

Keil, Charles. 1991. *Urban Blues.* Chicago: University of Chicago Press (originally 1966).

Kemp, Anthony E. 1996. *The Musical Temperament: Psychology and Personality of Musicians.* Oxford: Oxford University Press.

King, B. B., with David Ritz. 1996. *Blues All Around Me: The Autobiography of B. B. King.* New York: Avon.

King, Freddie. 1976. Interview in *Guitar Player*, September.

Kofsky, Frank. 1967. "The Cream: An Interview with Eric Clapton," in Pauline Rivelli and Robert Levin (eds.), *Rock Giants.* New York: The World Publishing Company.

1978. *Black Nationalism and the Revolution in Music.* New York: Pathfinder.

Kostelanetz, Richard (ed.). 1997. *The B. B. King Companion.* New York: Schirmer.

Kriss, E. 1973. *Barrelhouse and Boogie.* New York: Oak Publications.

Laver, J. 1980. *The Phonetic Description of Voice Quality.* Cambridge: Cambridge University Press.

LaVere, Stephen C. Robert Johnson. 1990. Booklet to *The Complete Recordings of Robert Johnson*, in series Roots 'n Blues. Columbia Records.

Loder, Kurt. 1990. "The Roots of Heaven." Booklet, *Led Zeppelin Box Set Re-release*. New York: Atlantic Recording Corporation.

Lomax, Alan. 1952. *Mister JellyRoll: The Fortunes of Jelly Roll Morton, New Orleans Creole and "Inventor of Jazz."* London: Cassell.

1962. "Song Structure and Social Structure." *Ethnology* 4, pp. 425–51.

1967. "The Good and the Beautiful in Folk Song." *Journal of American Folklore*, pp. 231–5.

1968. *Folk Song Style and Culture*. Brunswick, NJ: Transaction Books.

1993. *The Land Where the Blues Began*. London: Methuen.

Lornell, Kip. 1995. *Happy in the Service of the Lord: African-American Sacred Vocal Harmony Quartets in Memphis*. 2nd ed. Knoxville: University of Tennessee Press.

Macleod, R. R. 1988. *Yazoo 1v20*. Edinburgh, Scotland: Pat.

1992. *Yazoo 21v83*. Edinburgh: Pat.

1994. *Document Blues v1*. Edinburgh: Pat.

1995. *Document Blues v2*. Edinburgh: Pat.

1996a. *Document Blues v3*. Edinburgh: Pat.

1996b. *Document Blues v4*. Edinburgh: Pat.

1997. *Blues Document*. Edinburgh: Pat.

1998. *Document Blues v5*. Edinburgh: Pat.

1999. *Document Blues v6*. Edinburgh: Pat.

2000. *Document Blues v7*. Edinburgh: Pat.

Malone, Bill C. 1974. *Country Music, USA*. Austin: Texas University Press.

Marable, M. 1984. *The Race, Reform and Rebellion*. London: Macmillan.

Marcus, Greil. 1975. *Mystery Train: Images of American Rock 'n' Roll Music*. New York: E. P. Dutton.

Marsh, J. B. T. 1981. *The Story of the Jubilee Singers: With Their Songs*. Boston: Houghton, Mifflin and Company.

McKee, Margaret and Fred Chisenhall. 1981. *Beale Street Black and Blue: Life and Music on Black America's Main Street*. Baton Rouge: Louisiana State University Press.

Middleton, Richard. 1972. *Pop Music and the Blues*. London: Victor Gollancz.

Millar, Bill. 1974. *The Coasters*. London: W. H. Allen.

Miller, James. 1999. *Flowers in the Dustbin: The Rise of Rock and Roll, 1947–1977*. New York: Simon and Schuster.

Morse, David. 1971. *Motown and the Arrival of Black Music*. London: Studio Vista.

Murray, Albert. 1976. *Stomping the Blues*. New York: McGraw-Hill.

Narvaez, Peter. 1993. "*Living Blues* Journal: The Paradoxical Aesthetics of the Blues Revival," in Neil V. Rosenberg (ed.), *Transforming Tradition*. Urbana: Illinois University Press, pp. 241–57.

Newham, Paul. 1988. *Therapeutic Voicework: Principles and Practice for the Use of Singing as a Therapy*. London and Philadelphia: Jessica Kingsley.

Oakley, Giles. 1976. *The Devil's Music*. London: BBC Books.

Obrecht, Jas. 1990. "Muddy Waters," in *Blues Guitar: The Men Who Made the Music*. San Francisco: GPI Books.

1997. "The Blues Before Robert Johnson." *Guitar Player*, October.

Oliver, Paul. 1960. *Blues Fell This Morning: Meaning in the Blues*. London: Cassell.

1968. *Screening the Blues: Aspects of the Blues Tradition*. London: Cassell.

1969. *The Story of the Blues*. London: Penguin.

1984. *Songsters and Saints*. Cambridge: Cambridge University Press.

1986. "Blues," in the *New Grove Gospel, Blues, and Jazz*. New York: Norton.

Oliver, Paul (ed.). 1991. *The Blackwell Guide to Recorded Blues*. 2nd ed. Oxford: Blackwell.

Oliver, Paul, M. Harrison and William Bolcom. 1980. *The New Grove Gospel, Blues and Jazz*. London: Macmillan.

Oster, Harry. 1969. *Living Country Blues*. Detroit: Folklore Associates.

Palmer, Robert. 1982. *Deep Blues*. New York: Penguin.

1990. "Led Zeppelin: The Music." Booklet, *Led Zeppelin Box Set Re-release*. New York: Atlantic Recording Corporation.

1991. *Deep Blues, A Documentary*. Oil Factory/Channel 4 U.K.

1995. *Rock & Roll: An Unruly History*. New York: Harmony Books.

2001. "Delta Blues Cartel." *Mojo*, April.

Pareles, Jon and Patricia Romanowski (eds). 1983. *The Rolling Stone Encyclopedia of Rock and Roll*. New York: Rolling Stone Press.

Pearson, Barry Lee. 1990. *Virginia Piedmont Blues: The Lives and Art of Two Virginia Bluesmen*. Philadelphia: University of Pennsylvania Press.

Perry, Steve. 1988. "Ain't No Mountain High Enough: The Politics of Crossover," in Frith, 1998, pp. 51–87.

Potter, John. 1998. *Vocal Authority, Singing Style and Ideology*. Cambridge: Cambridge University Press.

Pratt, Roy. 1986. "The Politics of Authenticity in Popular Music: The Case of the Blues." *Popular Music and Society* 10/3, pp. 55–77.

Reagon, Beatrice (ed.). 1992. *We'll Understand It Better By and By*. Washington: Smithsonian Institute Press.

Regev, Motti. 1992. "Popular Music Studies: The Issue of Musical Value." *Tracking* 4/2, pp. 22 ff.

Reidel, Johannes. 1975. *Soul Music, Black & White: The Influence of Black Music on the Churches*. Minneapolis: Augsberg.

Rijn, Guido van. 1987. Sleeve notes to Alice Moore: *Lonesome Woman Blues*, Agram Blues ABLP 2013.

1988. Sleeve notes to Mary Johnson: *I Just Can't Take It*, Agram Blues AB 2014.

1991. Sleeve notes to Edith Johnson: *Honey Dripper Blues*, Agram Blues ABCD 2016.

1997. *Roosevelt's Blues: African-American Blues and Gospel Songs on FDR*. Jackson, Miss.: University Press of Mississippi.

Rolling Stone Editors (ed.). 1971. *The Rolling Stone Interviews*, 2 vols. New York: Warner.

Rooney, James. 1971. *Bossmen: Bill Monroe and Muddy Waters*. New York: Dial Press.

Rouget, Gilbert. 1995. *Music and Trance.* Chicago: University of Chicago Press.

Rowe, Michael. 1981. *Chicago Blues.* New York: Da Capo Press (originally 1973).

Russell, Tony. 1970. *Blacks, Whites, and Blues.* London: Studio Vista.

Sackheim, Eric. 1975. *The Blues Line: A Collection of Blues Lyrics from Leadbelly to Muddy Waters.* New York: Schirmer (originally 1969).

Sawyer, Charles. 1982. *The Arrival of B. B. King.* New York: Da Capo Press.

Schipper, Henry. 1992. *Broken Record: The Inside Story of the Grammy Awards.* New York: Carol Publishing.

Schwerin, J. 1992. *Mahalia Jackson, Queen of Gospel.* New York: Oxford University Press.

Shaar Murray, Charles. 1989. *Crosstown Traffic: Jimi Hendrix and the Rock 'n' Roll Revolution.* New York: St. Martin's Press.

  1999. *Boogie Man: The Adventures of John Lee Hooker in the Twentieth Century.* London: Penguin.

Shapiro, Anne Dhu. 1992. "Black Sacred Song and the Tune-Family Concept" in Josephine Wright (ed.), *New Perspective on Music: Essays in Honour of Eileen Southern.* Detroit: Harmonie Park Press.

Shaw, Arnold. 1970. *The World of Soul: Black America's Contribution to the Pop Music Scene.* New York: Cowles.

  1974. *The Rockin' '50s.* New York: Hawthorn Books, Inc.

Small, Christopher. 1987. *Music of the Common Tongue.* London: John Calder.

Smucker, Tom. 1970. "The Politics of Rock," in Eisen 1970, pp. 83–91.

Sokolow, Fred (transcr.). 1989. *Eric Clapton: Crossroads, Vol. 1.* Milwaukee: Hal Leonard Publishing Corporation.

Southern, Eileen. 1971. *The Music of Black Americans: A History.* New York: Norton (3rd ed. 1997).

Spotswood, Richard. 1991. Sleeve notes to *Bottles, Knives and Steel.* Columbia Records.

Spurgeon, Caroline. 1975. *Shakespeare's Imagery and What It Tells Us.* Cambridge: Cambridge University Press (originally 1935).

Storm Roberts, John. 1972. *Black Music of Two Worlds.* New York: Morrow by arrangement with Praeger Publishers.

Stuessy, Joe. 1994. *Rock and Roll: Its History and Stylistic Development.* 2nd ed. Englewood Cliffs: Prentice Hall (originally 1990).

Szatmary, David P. 1991. *Rockin' in Time: A Social History of Rock and Roll.* 2nd ed. Englewood Cliffs: Prentice Hall (originally 1987).

Taft, Michael. 1983. *Blues Lyric Poetry: A Concordance.* New York: Garland Publishing.

Thurman, Leon and Graham Welch (eds.). 1997. *Bodymind and Voice, Foundations of Voice Education.* Fairview Arts Medicine Center, Minneapolis: The VoiceCare Network, National Center For Speech and Voice.

Titon, Jeff Todd. 1977. *Early Downhome Blues: A Musical and Cultural Analysis.* Urbana: Illinois University Press (new ed. Chapel Hill: University of North Carolina Press, 1995).

  1990. *Downhome Blues Lyrics: An Anthology from the Post-World War II Era.* Urbana: University of Illinois Press (originally 1981).

Tobler, John and Stuart Grundy. 1983. *The Guitar Greats.* London: BBC Publications.

Tooze, Sandra B. 1997. *Muddy Waters: The Mojo Man.* Toronto: ECW Press.

Tracy, Steven C. 1993. *Going to Cincinnati: A History of the Blues in the Queen City.* Urbana: University of Illinois Press.

Tracy, Steven C. (ed.). 1999. *Write Me A Few Of Your Lines: A Blues Reader.* Amherst: University of Massachusetts Press, Amherst.

Traill, S. and Hon. Gerald Lascelles (eds.). 1957. *Just Jazz.* London: Peter Davies.

Ulanov, Barry. 1947. *Moldy Figs vs. Moderns.* New York: Metronome.

Van der Merwe, Peter. 1989. *Origins of the Popular Style: The Antecedents of Twentieth-Century Popular Music.* Oxford: Clarendon Press.

Van Vechten, Carl. 1926. "Negro 'Blues' Singers." *Vanity Fair* 26/1, pp. 67, 106, 108.

Wade, Dorothy and Justine Picardie. 1990. *Music Man: Ahmet Ertegun, Atlantic Records, and the Triumph of Rock 'n' Roll.* New York: Norton.

Walser, Robert. 1993. *Running with the Devil: Power, Gender, and Madness in Heavy Metal Music.* Hanover: Wesleyan University Press.

Ward, Ed., Geoffrey Stokes and Ken Tucker. 1986. *Rock of Ages: The Rolling Stone History of Rock and Roll.* New York: Rolling Stone Press.

Ward-Royster, Willa. 1997. *How I Got Over: Clara Ward and the World-Famous Ward Singers.* Philadelphia: Temple University Press.

Wells, John D. 1983. "Me and the Devil Blues: A Study of Robert Johnson and the Music of the Rolling Stones." *Popular Music and Society* 9/3, pp. 17–24.

Werner, Craig. 1999. *A Change is Gonna Come: Music, Race & the Soul of America.* New York: Plume.

Wicke, Peter. 1987. *Rock Music: Culture, Aesthetics, and Sociology.* Translated by Rachel Fogg. Cambridge: Cambridge University Press.

Williams, Paul. 1969. *Outlaw Blues: A Book of Rock Music.* New York: E. P. Dutton.

Winkler, Peter 1993. Review of *Running with the Devil* by Robert Walser, *Journal of Popular Music Studies* 5, p. 105.

Young, Alan. 1997. *Woke Me Up This Morning: Black Gospel Singers and the Gospel Life.* In *American Made Music Series*, General Editor David Evans. Jackson: University Press of Mississippi.

Zinn, Howard. 1980. *A People's History of the United States.* Longman: London.

Selected discography and videography

Berry, Chuck. *20th Century Masters*. MCAD 11944.

Blake, Blind. "Third Degree Blues." *Blind Blake: Complete Recorded Works in Chronological Order, Vol. 4*. Document CD 5027.

Broonzy, Big Bill. "Plow Hand Blues." *Big Bill Broonzy: Complete Recorded Works In Chronological Order, Vol. 10*. Document CD 5132.

Burnside, R. L. *I Wish I Was in Heaven Sitting Down*. Fat Possum 0332-2.

Carr, Leroy. *Sloppy Drunk*. Catfish KATCD 108.

Caston, Leonard "Baby Doo." "The Death of Walter Barnes." Decca 7763, 1940.

Cream. *Best of Cream*. ATCO SD 33-291.

Davenport, Cow Cow. "Jim Crow Blues." *Cow Cow Davenport: Complete Recorded Works in Chronological Order, Vol. 1*. Document CD 5141.

Diddley, Bo. *The Chess Masters Series*. Chess CXMD-4003.

Dorsey, Thomas. *Georgia Tom vol. 1 1928–1930*. Document BDCD-6021. *Georgia Tom vol. 2 1930–1934*. Document BDCD-6022.

Dranes, Arizona. *Arizona Dranes 1926–1929*. Document DOCD-5186.

Franklin, Aretha. *Aretha Gospel*. MCA Chess MCD 91521.

Golden Gate Jubilee Quartet. "Golden Gate Gospel Train." *Jubilation! Great Gospel Performances, Vol. 1: Black Gospel*. Rhino Records R2-70288.

Hawkins, Edwin. "Oh Happy Day." *Jubilation! Great Gospel Performances, Vol. 1: Black Gospel*. Rhino Records R2-70288.

Henderson, Rosa. "Back Woods Blues." *Rosa Henderson: Complete Recorded Works in Chronological Order, Vol. 2*. Document CD 5402.
"Chicago Policeman Blues." *Rosa Henderson: Complete Recorded Works in Chronological Order, Vol. 4*. Document CD 5404.

Hooker, John Lee. *The Real Folk Blues*. Chess, reissued MCA CHC 9271. *The Healer*. Silvertone ORE 508.

House, Eddie "Son." "County Farm Blues." *The Complete Library of Congress Sessions, 1941–1942*. Travelin' Man CD 02.

Howlin' Wolf. *The Collection*. Déjà vu DVLP 2032.

Jackson, Mahalia. "Precious Lord." *Mahalia Jackson: Gospels, Spirituals & Hymns*. Columbia Legacy CK-65596.
The Best of Mahalia Jackson. Columbia Legacy 480952 2.

James, Elmore. *One Way Out*. Charly TC-CRB 1008.

Johnson, Peter. *The Chronological Pete Johnson 1938–1939*. CLASSICS 656.

Johnson, Robert. *The Complete Recordings*. Columbia C2K-46222.

Jordan, Louis. *Choo-choo-ch'boogie*. MFP 50557.

King, Albert. *King of the Blues Guitar*. Atlantic ATL 40499.

King, B. B. *Greatest Hits*. ABC MCLC 1612.
"The Thrill is Gone." *Blues Masters: Vol. 7, Blues Revival*. Rhino Records R271128.

Lenoir, J. B. "Born Dead." *Vietnam Blues*. Evidence CD 26068.

Maceo, Big. *The Best of Big Maceo.* Arhoolie Folklyric CD 7009.

McCrackling, Jimmy. *The Walk.* Charly RED2 100.

McDowell, Fred. "Fred McDowell's Blues." *61 Highway Mississippi: Delta Country Blues, Spirituals, Work Songs & Dance Music.* Rounder Records CD-1703.

McTell, Blind Willie. "Monologue on Himself." *Blind Willie McTell (1940).* Document CD 6001.

Memphis Slim, Big Bill Broonzy, and Sonny Boy Williamson. *Blues in the Mississippi Night.* Rykodisc CD 90155.

Montgomery, Little Brother. *Little Brother Montgomery 1930–1936.* Document DOCD-5109.

Muddy Waters. "Hoochie Coochie Man." *Muddy Waters: The Chess Box.* Chess CHD3-80002.

  The Collection. Déjà vu DVLP 2034.

Preston, Jimmy. "Rock the Joint." *Jimmy Preston: Rock the Joint, Vol. 2.* Collectables Col-CD-5327.

Reed, Dock *et al.* "Jesus goin' make up my dyin' bed"; http://memory.loc.gov/afc/afcss39/268/2682b2.mp3

Smith, Bessie. "St. Louis Blues." *The Essential Bessie Smith.* Sony/Columbia C2K-64922.

Soul Stirrers. "Precious Lord." *Black Vocal Groups, Vol. 4, 1927–1939: Complete Recorded Works of Ernia Mae Cunningham, Davis Bible Singers, Diamond Four, Fa Sol La Singers, Fairview Jubilee Quartette, Famous Myers Jubilee Singers, Five Soul Stirrers.* Document Records DOCD-5552.

Sykes, Roosevelt. *Roosevelt Sykes vol. 4, 1934–1936.* Document DOCD-5119.

Vaughan, Stevie Ray. *Texas Flood.* Epic 463395/4.

Walker, T-Bone. *The Collection.* Déjà vu DVLP 2047.

Ward, Clara. "Precious Lord." *Gospel Warriors: 50 Years of Female Gospel Classics.* Spirit Feel SF-1003.

Williamson, Sonny Boy. "Stop Breaking Down." *Sonny Boy Williamson: Complete Recorded Works in Chronological Order, Vol. 5.* Document CD 5059.

Yancey, Jimmy. *Complete Recorded Works vol. 1, 1939–1940.* Document DOCD 5041.

Various. *Barrelhouse Blues & Boogie-woogie vol. 1.* Storyville STCD 8030.

  Boogie-woogie & Barrelhouse Piano vol. 1, 1928–1932. Document DOCD-5102.

  Boogie-woogie Blues. Biograph BCD 115 DDD.

  Chicago Guitar Killers. Blue Knight BN 073-1669.

  Chicago Piano 1929–1936. Document DOCD-5191.

  Down in Black Bottom: Lowdown Barrelhouse Piano. YAZOO 2043.

  Great Gospel Performers 1937–1950. Document DOCD5463.

  Harlem Hamfats – Hot Chicago Blues & Jive 1936–37. Arhoolie Folklyric 9009.

  Jubilation vol. 1: Black Gospel. Rhino R2 70288.

  Piano Blues and Boogie Classics. Arhoolie CD108.

  The Piano Blues Dallas 1927–1929. MAGPIE PYCD 15.

  St. Louis Barrelhouse Piano 1929–1934. Document DOCD-5104.

  The Slide Guitar. CBS CT 46218.

Sweet Heaven – The Sound of Gospel Music. Flapper LC1836.
Storefront & Streetcorner Gospel 1927–1929. DOCD-5054.
Texas Piano vol. 1, 1923–1935. DOCD-5224.
Texas Piano vol. 2, 1927–1938. DOCD-5225.
Say Amen Somebody. 1983. Directed by George T. Nierenberg. VHS, 100 min.,
    colour.

Index

Allen, Estelle 139
Allen, George N. 82, 83
Allison, Jesse 79
Ammons, Albert 136
Armstrong, Louis 69, 160
Atlantic Records 176–7

Baker, Arthur 180
Baker, Katherine 143, 145, 155
Baker, LaVern 105
ballad 22–3
Bambaataa, Africa 180
Baraka, Amiri 8, 9
Barbecue Bob (Robert Hicks) 147
barrelhouse 32, 130–1, 135
    characteristics of, 130–1
Barthes, Roland 161
Bass, Ralph 99
Beatles, The 169–70
Beck, Elder Charlie 105
Belafonte, Harry 166
Bennet, Lonnie 96
Berman, Bess 55
Berry, Chuck 108, 125, 158–60, 163, 184
Besman, Bernard 120
Black, Bill 165
Black Sabbath 127
Blackwell, Bumps 57
Blackwell, Scrapper 32, 136, 144
Blake, Blind 91
Blake, Eubie 131
Blakey, Rev. Johnny 113
Bland, Bobby 98
Bloomfield, Michael 127
blues
    African elements in 23–4
    animal imagery in 145–9
    boogie-woogie 32, 131–4, 136
    characteristics of 10, 21–2, 30–1
    city blues 7, 15–16
    classic blues 4, 5, 8
    country blues 3, 15–16
    downhome blues 3, 18
    education imagery in 153–4
    everyday imagery in 151–3
    food imagery in 149–51
    instrumental combinations in 24, 28, 31–3,
        38–40
    as type of jazz 26–7
    nature imagery in 143–5
    origins of 2, 20–1, 22–2
    personifications in 154–5
    regional variations of 14–16, 30–1, 38, 111–12
    rural blues 3, 15
    twelve-bar form 22–3
    urban blues 4, 15

Bolden, Alfred 139
Bond, Graham 140
Booker T & the MGs 126
Boone, Pat 161, 165, 182
Bostic, Earl 95
Boyd, Eddie 99
Boyer, Horace 92, 95, 110, 111, 112
Boyz II Men 183
Bradford, Perry 27
Bradley, Marie 103
Brenston, Jackie 164
Broonzy, Bill 4, 16, 32, 91, 96
Broughton, Viv 6
Brown, Clarence "Gatemouth" 123
Brown, Henry 135
Brown, James 175, 178, 179
Brown, Ruth 94, 105
Brown, Roy 162
Burleigh, Harry T. 106
Burnside, R. L. 9, 128–9
Butterfield, Paul 127
Byrd, Josephine 106

Campbell, Lucie E. 138
Canned Heat 127
Carr, Leroy 32, 136
Cephas, John 92, 101
Chambers Brothers, The 178
Charles, Ray 57, 135, 136, 140, 173–5
Charters, Samuel 8, 16, 141
Cheeks, Julius 110–11, 175
Chess Records 163
Chords, The 172
Christian, Charlie 122
Civil Rights movements 3, 4, 42, 56, 185
Clapton, Eric 17, 126, 127, 160, 167–8, 181, 186
Clash, The 125
Clayton, "Doctor" 36, 146, 148
Clemen, Wolfgang 142
Cleveland, James 58–9, 138, 182
Cliff, Jimmy 181
Clinton, George 178–9
Coasters, The 172–3
Cole, Nat King 174
Cooder, Ry 119–20, 128
Cooke, Sam 56–8, 98, 109, 172, 175
copyright 6
Courlander, Harold 10
Cream 168
Crew Cuts, The 172
Crosby, Fanny 13
cross-over 158–60, 185
    blues to pop 124, 169–70
    gospel to pop 56–7, 59–60, 139, 171–3
    pop to gospel 139–40
Crudup, Arthur "Big Boy" 36, 165–6

1 Mahalia Jackson

2 Fred McDowell

3 Bessie Smith, Late 1920s

4 Muddy Waters

5 Golden Gate Quartet

6 John Lee Hooker

7 Aretha Franklin

8 Rev. Gary Davis at Keele Folk Festival 1966

9 Thomas A. Dorsey as pianist with Ma Raviey